No  eem

PARTNERS FOR CHANGE
(PROGRAM GUIDE)

Partners for Change

(Program Guide)

A Peer Helping Guide for Training and Prevention

V. Alex Kehayan, Ed.D.

Jalmar Press
Rolling Hills Estates, California

Project Director: Janet Lovelady

Cover Design: Jeanne Duke
Artist: Kelly McMahon
Gameboard Designers: Rosette Khorenian, Talar Agasyan

Published by Jalmar Press
45 Hitching Post Drive, Bldg. 2
Rolling Hills Estates, CA 90274

ISBN 0-915190-69-9, paperback.   ISBN 0915190-87-7, spiral bound.

Kehayan. V. Alex
    Partners for change: A peer helping guide for training and prevention.
    V. Alex Kehayan
        p. cm.
    Includes bibliographical references.
    ISBN 0-915190-87-7
    1. Peer counseling of students— Handbooks, manuals, etc. 2. Peer—
group tutoring of students— Handbooks, manuals etc. I. Title.
LB1027.5.H43 1992
371.4'044— dc20   90-19735
                                                   CIP

First Edition

Printing 10   9   8   7   6   5   4   3   2   1

1010042

Partners for Change is dedicated to my wife Carolyn and son Cary, whose love and spirit inspired many of the ideas presented in these pages.

Acknowledgements

I am deeply grateful to the peer leaders of the Fort Lee Schools, without whose tireless support, patience, effort and contributions, *Partners for Change* could not have been written. To name a few, I would like to thank Behar Cami, Lisa Weissbart, Michelle Chachkes, Arye Sasson, Meredith Miller, Foffie Athanasenas, Rosette Khorenian, Talar Agasyan, Alyssa Kretecos, Peter Han, Emily Weiner, David Tully, Fran Di Costanzo, Jon Gosberg, and Ben Wexler. Special thanks are extended to Dr. Alan Sugarman, Superintendent of Schools, Fort Lee (NJ) Public Schools.

These people have offered their unselfish support and encouragement to make it possible to apply many of these approaches in the Fort Lee Public Schools.

Appreciation is also extended to the many creative professionals who offered consultation, time and effort, and expertise to make these programs work. Among the many are Carolyn Kehayan, Adele Garber, John Battaglia, Barbara Picocco, Ginny Huber, Leslie Appelbaum, James and Marie Warnke, Andrew Fineman, Dorothy Burland, and Carol Grappo. *Partners for Change* could not have been written without valuable feedback and thoughtfulness of the students who put life into the process.

Credits

Is a Lie Worth It, Section 2, Session 24-Metaphor Generator. Written by V. Alex Kehayan and Meredith Miller.

Better Late Than Never, Section 2, Session 24-Metaphor Generator. Written by V. Alex Kehayan and Jaimie Peters.

First Things First, Section 2, Session 24-Metaphor Generator. Written by John Battaglia and Matthew Goldberg.

Pathways to Solutions, Section 2, Session 34-Pathways to Solutions. Adapted from Garbo model by Joseph Yeager Found in Yeager, J. (1990). The Goal Strategy Book. Published by Comm-Tech Group, Inc. Newton, Pa.

String Maze, Section 8, Session 1, Part 2–String Maze. Written by Robert Ostermann.

National Peer Helping Association Code of Ethics, Section 2, Session 45-Ethics Code. Published by The National Peer Helpers Association (1989).

Farewell Feedback, Section 2, Session 46-Farewell Feedback. Adapted from an exercise written by Judy Williams, P.O. Box 186, Daleville, VA. 24083.

Facts and Myths about Chemical Dependency, Section 10, Session 1-Orientation. Based on information provided from documents published by U.S. Department of Health and Human Services (1983) and National Institute on Drug Abuse (1985).

The Zoo, Section 9, Session 2-Puppet Shows. Written by Angela Rokkos.

Planet 455, Section 11, Session 1-Planet 455. Written by Carolyn Kehayan.

IALAC, Section 11, Session 4-The IALAC Story. Adapted from a story concept written by Sidney Simon.

The Wrong Kind of Laughter, Section 11, Session 4-The IALAC Story. Written by Bill Sanders. To contact Bill concerning his youth talks or seminars, or his inservice teacher sessions, write to: Bill Sanders, 8495 Valleywood Lane, Kalamazoo, MI 49002 or call: (616) 323-8074.

All of Section 12 was developed with the assistance of PAIRS Program Committee, Fort Lee High School, Fort Lee, N.J.: Angela Rokkos, Lainie Aronheim, Joel Klasfeld, Jennifer Ornstein, Maria Jebejian, Lauren Meller, Alexis Rodriguez, Amos Schwartzfarb, Keith Jensen and Tara Tessaro.

All of Section 13 was developed with the assistance of the AIDS Peer Prevention Program Committee, Fort Lee High School, Fort Lee, N.J.: V. Alex Kehayan, Andrew Fineman, Carol Burghardt, Evan Lefkowitz, Kimberly Leitholf, Lara Gressle, Alyssa Kretecos, Andrew Hindman, and Radha Marharajh.

Factual content of Section 13 was based on information adapted from Fort Lee Board of Education AIDS Curriculum (1989), and U.S. Department of Health and Human Services (1983).

Index of Perception. Modified from Human Relations Development: A Manual for Educators by G. Gazda, F. Asbury, and F. Balzar. Boston: Allyn and Bacon, Inc. (1973).

Florida Key: Elementary Form. Written by Dr. William Purkey, Dr. Bob Cage, Dr. William Graves at the University of Florida. (1971).

TABLE OF CONTENTS

TABLE OF CONTENTS

P R O G R A M S

TABLE OF CONTENTS

P R O G R A M S

TABLE OF CONTENTS

P R O G R A M S

You give but little when you give of your possessions. It is when you give yourself that you truly give.

– Kahlil Gibran

INTRODUCTION

What Is Peer Helping?

Peer helping is the use of nonprofessionals of all ages in a variety of settings to provide learning and emotional support, personal growth, and guidance in a way that will enable clients to reach a greater potential. The concept of peer support originated as far back as the Greek Empire and has progressed throughout the years with many changes. Peer helping enlists the aid of fellow students, workers, and professionals to enhance students' lives and to help the students function competently.

Peers should not be used in place of licensed professionals or as mental health service providers. Peer leaders assume an auxiliary role — they are meant to serve as backups to professionals. They are often preventive agents who act as conduits or liaisons to identify problems and encourage others to obtain the necessary help from appropriate professionals.

Practitioners have coined a wide variety of terms for helping agents. These names include: peer facilitators, guides, listeners, counselors, helpers, and role models. *Partners for Change* uses the names peer leaders, guides, and partners to identify service providers. It designates clients as receiving students, receivers, and students. For the most part, the names are used interchangeably.

Who Should Use This Book?

Partners for Change is intended for educators, guidance counselors, psychologists, social workers, student assistance counselors, peer leaders, pastoral counselors, and substance abuse prevention agents in a variety of settings. Although intended primarily for educational settings, it can be adapted to other milieus such as: group homes, religious institutions, service organizations, police and probation facilities, and treatment centers.

For example, Smooth Transitions (Section 3), intended to facilitate adjustment for freshman students in their novel high school environments, may also be adapted to assist students entering middle schools or other schools. It may also be helpful to young people entering other settings such as camps, group homes, religious organizations, etc.

The training activities in this manual can help practitioners cultivate new skills for improved service delivery. The activities stress both traditional and innovative approaches which go beyond the usual counseling skills provided in practitioner training programs.

These include some of the transformative communication skills necessary to gain positive rapport and help clients access their positive resources and achieve desired outcomes. In addition, there are group building exercises and traditional communication techniques which involve nondirective counseling principles. For the educational setting, the activities also include valuable study skills, tutoring, test taking, and anxiety reduction.

Partners for Change also includes eleven program packages which focus on prevention and adjustment. Professionals and peers may use the initiatives to prevent substance abuse, self-destructive behavior, academic underachievement, negative peer pressure, and child abduction by strangers. The services assist others in developing their self-esteem, discrimination and problem-solving skills, school adjustment, productive leisure time activities, and positive peer support systems.

Research on these programs indicates that the receiving students have improved their grades, attendance, school involvement, and positive attitudes towards peer leaders. The peer leaders have improved their interpersonal communication skills and developed their creativity to initiate new services.

How Did This Book Originate?

Partners for Change evolved from my doctoral work on peer relations. I pioneered school based initiatives which have expanded through the years. The programs, which began in 1973, continue under the name Peer Outreach Service Team (POST). POST was developed through an extensive literature search. Its design was initially field tested and continues to operate in the Fort Lee Public Schools and other educational settings. The POST model is designed to dispatch trained peer leaders to reach out to others to prevent negative behavior. All of its eleven components have stood the test of formal assessments.

POST has extended its services to a variety of settings including religious organizations, private schools, and other public school districts throughout the country. It is currently endorsed by the National Association of School Psychologists Alternative Service Directory, and the National Mental Health Association. It is listed in ERIC and is recognized by the U. S. Office of Education as a model drug and alcohol prevention program. It has been awarded the A+ For Teachers Grant by WWOR-TV.

The POST model underscores the importance of identifying early warning signals and making necessary referrals to qualified professionals as needs arise. The peer leader selection procedure emphasizes carefully conceived criteria which include flexibility, commitment, ability to keep confidence, well-roundedness, empathy, and communication ability. Peer review, professional recommendations, and word-of-mouth are critical to recruitment and selection. Peer leaders make a pact to remain drug and alcohol free and must act responsibly in order to remain in their roles as peer leaders.

Supervision and professional backup are also essential features of The POST model. Each peer leader is assigned to a professional who serves as an advisor and consultant. Frequent supervisory sessions are held to monitor recipients' progress and to insure that proper referrals are made as needs arise.

Each program also has an evaluation component which enables peer leaders and program coordinators to assess the effectiveness of the services, make the necessary alterations, and continue to develop and modify the program procedures. Parents and participants are supplied with written safeguards and procedures. They authorize their children's participation through written consent.

What Are the Advantages of Peer Support?

There are many advantages of using trained peers as supportive agents to our nation's youth.

PREVENTION. It has become painfully obvious that some abhorrent behavior patterns are often initiated at the peer group level. Unfortunately, these negative patterns have proliferated throughout the past decade, including a myriad of self-destructive behaviors:

- scapegoating
- verbal abuse
- self-damaging behaviors
- substance abuse
- eating and sleeping disorders
- sexual abuse and violence
- teenage pregnancy
- high dropout rates
- general breakdown in stress related coping skills.

Since most of these issues are interrelated and emerge within the peer system, their warning signals are identified and recognized earlier within the peer group. A compelling case can be made for addressing these problems through goal oriented programs led by peers in groups or individually. Peer leaders are often the first to notice early warning signals. Thus, they are in a position to prevent self-destructive trends from becoming patterns. Programs that target early interventions using positive role models can often prevent long-term behavioral prolems.

Many professional groups are broadening their responsibilities to include early interventions conducted by trained peer leaders, who extend the range of professional services to a much greater population. Both group and individual peer programs serve as effective interventions.

ACCESS. Current research results validate the extensive impact of peer influence as a major force in behavioral change among adolescents. Multiservice peer initiatives dispatch positive peer role models who counterbalance negative influence.

Many programs using peers have been very successful in preventing negative, self-damaging behaviors such as substance abuse and delinquency. Students are a prime source of drug knowledge for most young people. Thus, trained high school peer leaders can sometimes communicate more effectively with their client populations than adult professionals.

COST EFFECTIVENESS. For a variety of reasons, peer interventions are much more cost effective to schools, agencies, and society than total reliance on professional involvement. First, since peers reach their contemporaries early, a drug problem may be recognized before it becomes an addiction. Without such intervention, a client would require the services of a rehabilitation center costing as much as $1000 per day.

It makes sense that early interventions, which are so easily provided by trained peers, can ultimately help save the general society millions of dollars of nonproductivity and medical costs. In the face of fiscal crises in institutions and schools, particularly in the area of special services, multiservice peer programs meet at-risk

students' increased needs expeditiously and economically.

BENEFITS TO RECEIVING STUDENTS. Many of our students passing through the schools succumb to the pressures of changing societal norms, alternate family structures, stresses generated from potential nuclear disaster, economic turmoil, and a massive information explosion. It is no wonder that lowered self-esteem and increased identity confusion have contributed to a number of self-defeating behaviors. One of the by-products of these pressures is social withdrawal and alienation witnessed by young people.

Peer outreach can reduce the sense of isolation by initiating one-to-one partnerships and promoting support networks to face mutual dilemmas and reach mutual goals. It is no secret that the expanding self-help network throughout the country has generated several peer support groups dealing with a number of disabilities including alcohol and substance abuse. AA has grown to be one of the most effective agencies in reducing relapse rates in recovering alcoholics. Thus, the benefits of peer support are widespread. It promotes a sense of cooperation, and makes people aware of mutual problems as well as mutually contrived resolutions.

BENEFITS TO PEER LEADERS. Some obvious benefits to trained leaders are the knowledge they receive and the ability they develop to transform their sensitivity into productive helping relationships. They seek high impact and positive behavior change in their client population. In addition, they get valuable information about careers in the human services by actually experiencing the activities and dynamics within that field.

They also learn about the dynamics of organizations, the burgeoning culture of networking and volunteerism, and the cooperative ethic which is developed through a comprehensive support system. Consequently, in addition to improving their communication and rapport skills, the peer leaders also improve their personal competency and self-esteem in their own interpersonal relationships. Finally, their experiences help them decide whether or not to pursue a career in the human service professions.

BENEFITS TO PROFESSIONALS. It is widely recognized that the greatest contribution professionals can make to the society is the perpetuation and extension of their skills to future generations. By teaching carefully selected peer leaders an abundance of helping skills, professionals extend support through concerned, ethical, humanistic young people. Thus, the professional sees fast results, receives positive feedback, and frequently becomes energized by sharing skills with enthusiastic young people.

How Should This Book Be Used?

Partners for Change is written with flexibility and diversity in mind. Users may follow the sequence or select individual sections. For example, The Metaphor Generator may become a centerpiece for a professional workshop on positive change. Or it can be incorporated into a training program for peers, practitioners, and paraprofessionals. The Preliminary Training Guide and eleven Program Packages are designed for hands-on application.

Partners for Change is conveniently divided into the following sections:

```
• Section 1:   Program Development
• Section 2:   Preliminary Training Guide
• Section 3:   Smooth Transitions
• Section 4:   Welcome
• Section 5:   One-to-One
• Section 6:   Peer Intervention Network
• Section 7:   Planning Leisure Activities Now
• Section 8:   Human Relations
• Section 9:   Kids 'R Safe
• Section 10:  Close Encounters
• Section 11:  Partners Against Scapegoating
• Section 12:  Peer Assistants To Interpersonal
               Relations
• Section 13:  HIV Awareness Program
```

Each section addresses different user needs. Section 1 deals with program set up, logistics, and process from an administrative overview. Section 2 enables the reader to train peer leaders in general helping skills, personal growth, and team building. Sections 3 through 13 are program guides for specific goals and populations.

SECTION 1: PROGRAM DEVELOPMENT. This section includes planning, preparation, implementation, and evaluation units to assist coordinators in the following ways:

- Developing program concepts.
- Formulating goals and objectives.
- Paving the way for acceptance.
- Meeting with gatekeepers and key individuals.
- Enlisting community support.

After the planning stage, coordinators assemble a staff, present the program to its constituents, recruit, and screen the peer leaders. Pretests may be given to peer leaders in order to assess baseline abilities in communication and interpersonal relationships.

An implementation unit focuses on the program process and enables coordinators to monitor and supervise their programs, gather data, analyze results, and provide ongoing evaluation. Steps for completing each program and generating new programs are also included. Thus, Section 1 is intended to be flexible, practical, and mindful of procedural safeguards throughout the operation of each component. Feel free to use any of its units as a guide as your needs dictate. It provides the general framework necessary to operate all of the individual programs in *Partners for Change*.

SECTION 2: PRELIMINARY TRAINING GUIDE. This section is written for professional practitioners and nonprofessionals. It includes the basic format for teaching the essential communication, group building, and tutorial approaches necessary to reach out to others effectively. It introduces innovative strategies such as transformative communication techniques and metaphor building as well as the traditional nondirective counseling skills for practitioners and peer leaders.

Section 2 includes a user friendly lesson plan format which enables the trainer to lead each activity with minimal preparation. Each session identifies the time limit, goals, objectives, materials, and process, including actual scripts for the trainer to illustrate the skills. Each session format also includes outcome indicators to assist the trainer in verifying the skills acquisition levels of the trainees. Convenient worksheets and practice exercises follow each session to provide reinforcement and peer rating opportunities.

Session formats, worksheets, and practice exercises are boxed to indicate that they may be reproduced for group members.

The Preliminary Training Guide is a sequential format which begins with icebreakers and warm-ups for trainees, establishes the structure of the program, and then teaches the basic elements of communicative helping skills. Following the basic communication skills is a more powerful nonverbal and transformative set of techniques designed to enhance the helping process.

Communication is then followed by study skills to assist students in streamlining the learning process. Personal support strategies are presented to protect the trainees from becoming overloaded and burning out. These strategies are designed to assist the helping agents in managing stress, solving problems, refusing to conform to negative peer pressure, and confronting others in constructive ways. Finally some group leadership skills, referral techniques, and personal evaluation exercises complete the training.

Appendix A has all the necessary forms and sample letters to enable the user to establish and implement the training sessions. These include such items as student nomination forms, evaluation instruments, student passes, feedback sheets, and questionnaires.

SECTIONS 3 - 13: PROGRAM PACKAGES.

The Program Packages present everything you need to plan, implement, and evaluate the intervention. They include a list of materials and the step-by-step procedures for implementation, as well as a paper trail of necessary worksheets and forms relevant to the program.

The packages encourage user input to promote a self-perpetuating process which encourages trained leaders to operate new program guides. The user is urged to be selective, flexible, and creative in using them as springboards to develop new initiatives. Each package includes four main components:

• Overview
• Paper Trail
• Trainer's Guide
• Leader's Guide

Overview

The Overview aids the coordinators in setting up the program, training leaders, implementing the program, and assessing its impact. As a supplement to the Trainer's and Leader's Guide, the Overview allows sufficient flexibility to enable users to modify any or all of its parts to meet the needs of the receiving population.

Paper Trail

Each Overview includes a Paper Trail. The Paper Trail lists the model forms, worksheets, and information sheets that enable the programs to unfold with optimum participation.

The model forms can be found in Appendix A and include written parent consent, student ID cards, and passes which authorize peer leaders to leave their classrooms and conduct sessions. These forms enable peer leaders to participate and be carefully monitored by professionals.

The worksheets and information sheets are located at the back of each section. The worksheets include action plans, task sheets, and checklists to reinforce the principles taught in the sessions. The information sheets provide response scenarios for reflection or reviews of vital information such as facts and myths about chemicals or HIV. All Program Packages include evaluation forms to gain participants' feedback.

All Paper Trail materials should be reproduced for classroom use by peers or professionals who lead the sessions to ensure each participant receives copies.

Trainer's Guide

The Trainer's Guide is a specially tailored experiential process designed to prepare the leader to implement the program. It includes observation, practice, and feedback and differs in format from program to program. For example, the Trainer's Guide for One-to-One, a program designed to assist younger students with social and academic adjustment, includes a simulated first session to practice helping skills. Most of the group-led programs enable the learner to observe the sessions conducted by advanced leaders and engage in structured feedback.

Leader's Guide

The Leader's Guide assists both peer and professional practitioners in their implementation of the program process. It is detailed and written in a way which is easily understood. **The Leader's Guide lesson plans for each session are boxed to indicate that they may be reproduced by peer leaders or professionals who lead the sessions.**

What Are the Eleven Programs?

The following descriptions represent a composite of the eleven Program Packages.

SMOOTH TRANSITIONS (SECTION 3).
Trained peers serve as guides to incoming high school students in order to facilitate academic and personal adjustment. The partnerships begin with a one-day structured experience at the middle school level where high school and graduating middle school students collaborate on a project. Then, the high school students continue the relationships by offering assistance to their younger, entering students.

WELCOME (SECTION 4). Juniors and seniors are trained to guide students who enter a school or community from another district. The focus of this program is on social, emotional, and academic adjustment to a novel educational setting. Particular attention is paid to the selection of cocurricular activities, social networking, and survival within the informal peer system.

ONE-TO-ONE (SECTION 5). This program trains peer leaders to offer social and academic support to young students. The students meet once a week during lunch (or other designated periods) to focus on one subject area and then follow up with a general discussion of social issues. This program is designed to prevent school failure, substance abuse, truancy, and potential dropouts.

PEER INTERVENTION NETWORK (SECTION 6). This program establishes an ongoing support group for middle school under-achievers. Students form partnerships to identify problems, generate goals, and develop action plans. Groups meet weekly before, during, and/or after school as necessary. When members improve their academic functioning, their group status is elevated as they assume roles as "experts."

PLANNING LEISURE ACTIVITIES NOW (SECTION 7). High school students who have coped well with independent time assist groups of younger students in grades six through eight. The high school peer leaders help them to overcome loneliness, time management problems, and anxiety. Typically, a trained high school junior or senior leads eleven sessions of structured experiences which begin with icebreakers and then move into supportive activities and development of alternative uses of open-time.

Coping strategies are also generated throughout the sessions. During Session 11, the group elects to continue or disband. All sessions are voluntary and held during lunch.

HUMAN RELATIONS (SECTION 8). Trained students provide structured experiences to middle school special education classes. These sessions are designed to promote self-awareness, self-esteem, positive social interaction, and coping skills. The students learn about the high school milieu from the high school students, who prepare them for their transitions to the new setting.

KIDS 'R SAFE (SECTION 9). Trained peer leaders conduct workshops on child safety and tactics which help young children learn to avoid contact with harmful strangers. High school students lead workshops with kindergarten, first, and second grade students to introduce discrimination skills necessary to distinguish friendly strangers from hostile strangers.

Mini-dramas and puppet shows presented by leaders illustrate safety strategies to avoid being kidnapped or abused. The students are also cautioned against accepting any food or other substance from strangers. The program is presented from a positive perspective.

CLOSE ENCOUNTERS (SECTION 10). This program enlists trained peer role models to lead four structured experiential and informational sessions with the younger students in order to prevent chemical dependency. Peer partners present some of the facts and myths of substance abuse and then assist younger students in developing and using refusal skills to avoid the temptations of chemical use and abuse. The sessions also elicit from the members some personal triumphs. Using symbols to represent earlier positive states, the peer leaders help receiving students to access these positive experiences in order to avoid the temptations of abusing drugs and alcohol.

PARTNERS AGAINST SCAPEGOATING (SECTION 11). In this program, two peer leaders enter middle school family life/health classes to lead four sessions of structured experiences designed to sensitize students to the adverse effects of verbal assaults, degradation, and stereotyping behavior.

High school partners begin the program with an intimidating posture and then shift the focus to assist the middle school students in developing ways to live in harmony. Coping skills to resist verbal abuse are also promoted. The PAS mission advocates cooperation as a pathway to the survival of humanity.

PEER ASSISTANTS TO INTERPERSONAL RELATIONSHIPS (SECTION 12). This program enlists the aid of four trained high school peer leaders (two boys and two girls) to hold six sessions on friendship and dating awareness for students in health or family life classes in grades eight and nine. The sessions are designed to be upbeat, active, and student-centered, using group exercises and role playing to illustrate the principles.

Participants are asked to define their existing relationships, explore how conflicts develop and can be avoided, and use refusal skills and conflict resolution techniques to develop more positive friendships. Assumptions and beliefs about the nature of friendship and cross-gender relationships are explored in impartial, nonthreatening formats.

HIV AWARENESS PROGRAM (SECTION 13). This program enables peer leaders to conduct four sessions for health or family life classes to reinforce the school's AIDS prevention curriculum. Recommended grade levels are eighth through tenth. Facts and myths about HIV and AIDS, potential risks and consequences, and reactions to infected individuals from their peers and family members are presented. Strategies to distinguish negative from positive responses to infected individuals and to provide support for others are also presented.

SECTION 1 —
PROGRAM DEVELOPMENT

SECTION 1 —
PROGRAM
DEVELOPMENT

Guiding Principles

The development and implementation of a peer support program requires time, energy, creativity, and some organizational skills. Dedication and effective leadership in its coordinators radiates to its participants and can make the difference between prolonged success or sudden failure.

Essential prerequisites of exemplary peer support programs include competent staff leadership, dedicated peer helpers, endorsement and support from the host institution, careful planning, and organization. A substantive focus which is accepted by all participants gives any program a sense of identity, importance, and energy.

If you are contemplating developing a peer program, you should ask yourself the following questions before going full speed ahead:

• What is the program's mission?
• With whom do I need to discuss my ideas: students, counselors, administrators, parents?
• Will they be likely to respond positively to this approach?
• What are the needs of the target population?
• How much time and energy do I need to expend?
• How extensive should the program be?
• Who will staff the program?

• What criteria do I want to establish for program participants?
• How will I recruit and screen the participants?
• What is my training orientation and what are the required activities, time commitment, and appropriate training resources?
• What are the space requirements and does the host setting have them?
• What strengths and professional skills do I offer the program?
• How much lead time do I need for planning?

Please use Appendix A to adapt any relevant forms and assessments to your program's needs.

Any new program initiated within a school or organizational setting tends to precipitate reactions which may permeate the entire system. Administrators are often concerned about the innovative programs which may threaten the existing norms and ways of operating within the setting. It is important to enlist their aid to overcome any logistical barriers which may derail the program's development or impede its functioning. Accordingly, your program should be entirely voluntary.

Appendix B gives you an overview of the relevant literature and research on peer helping. Such research documentation and program descriptions of various models may be worthy of inclusion in grant applications for funding or as justifications for the program's approval by local districts or agencies.

The following suggestions may be used to guide you, the coordinator, through any type of peer outreach service you intend to implement. They are based on extensive research and programming experience.

Human Resources

Potential peer leaders and receiving students or clients of the setting are essential to the development of any peer-assisted initiative. They are the key figures serving as agents or receiving the major impact. They are most intimately aware of the major issues to be addressed. You should first consult with selected peers and discuss your ideas about their needs, the program's mission, and their interest in becoming involved. The potential receivers should be consulted to determine how the program design might address their needs.

Guidance personnel are key figures in school systems who can make or break a peer support program. They are knowledgeable about students' strengths and weaknesses. However, peer programs often pose threats to their functional domains. Guidance personnel can be assets to a well-functioning program if approached with tact and consideration.

Teachers are also essential to the function of the program. They often make the most referrals and serve as gatekeepers who allow both peer leaders and recipients to engage in program activities. In addition, they have the most contact with the students and often can be allies in many of the group programs. But teachers are frequently inundated with enormous responsibilities to implement programs and added curricula. Constant interruptions of their work by innovative programs throughout the years often foster a sense of discontinuity of teachers' primary task.

You need to rally teacher support and invite their participation as supervisors, curriculum developers of group programs, or even coleaders. It is essential to enlist their involvement and form alliances to prevent any competition with peers around issues of academic turf and instructional competence. If a competitive relationship ensues, the ultimate victim becomes the student recipient whose academic progress may be undercut by rivalries.

Mission and Program Approach

Simplicity should be a guiding rule in developing any peer support program. Because impact radiates throughout a system, it is important to design a program which can be tightly controlled. You should set aside three months for planning and preparation which should include input from administration, teachers, and students on specific problems that might be addressed by peer assisted interventions.

Once the main problem is identified, then a mission statement can be developed and followed by an appropriate program design to address the major goals.

It is suggested that you start with one major goal such as academic underachievement or poor attendance, and design a program limited to a small target population. You may want to recruit a very small group of peer leaders the first year. In one-to-one programs, it is important to have frequent sessions with peer leaders and their receiving students.

Usually, the cross-age model generates more powerful impact through the authority vested in older, positive role models. In one-to-one programs, avoid counseling or therapeutic types of interventions and include an academic or goal-setting type of activity as a major focal point.

In developing group oriented programs led by peer facilitators, a cross-age model works most effectively in a limited number of sessions designed to produce a specific outcome. Some of the most effective issues addressed in group programs include scapegoating, child safety, substance abuse education, and career awareness workshops. The applications are vast and extensive in this group modality.

DESIGN. Your initial outcome is most critically dependent upon the precision and relevance of your program's design. Some general principles of program design need to be underscored here.

It is vital that your program be based on some valid theoretical model which applies to its mission and is reflected in its activities. You might investigate what others have done by reviewing the literature. (See Appendix B: Peer Support: A Review of the History.) Also, you should develop a set of guiding principles such as those presented in the training section of this manual. Referral guidelines, safeguards, and behavioral warning signals should be clearly delineated.

The program activities should supplement other existing activities and not be used to replace teacher or counseling staff activities. They should have meaning and protect the legitimacy of the programs. Stapling letters to go out to parents, filing, and correcting papers are examples of illegitimate, demeaning activities to be avoided.

Care and quality must guide you in choosing sensitive and competent participants. Your human resources must participate voluntarily, without subtle or overt coercion. Receivers in individual programs should be guaranteed confidentiality of privileged information.

Roles should be clearly specified as well as the criteria for entry and exit from the program. Models of these roles and criteria are provided in the Program Guides in this volume.

Documentation is another essential element of any substantive peer-assisted endeavor. Some of the elements in the paper trail include written evaluations of trainees' skills before and after training sessions, evaluation of the training, program results, individuals' outcome indicators, and parent observations of the programs' effectiveness.

Ongoing assessments should also be part of the paper trail. Please consult the Appendices for a complete set of documentation forms, designed for one-to-one or group programs. The applicable programs are listed on the heading of each form.

Adequate staffing to promote optimal program functioning must be present. A workable ratio of training and supervisory staff to peer leaders is five to one.

Adequate space arrangements will insure the optimum environments for training, group, and individual activities and advisory sessions. Be sure to include designated rooms in your proposal.

The design should insure regular opportunities for peer leaders, support staff, and receiving students to meet face to face. These conferences should promote unity, program revision, and development responsive to their needs.

Above all, a volunteer program needs flexibility and opportunities to share experiences, enjoy the activities, and promote personal growth through mutual participation.

It may be advisable to develop a course in peer leadership and issue credit for participation. The course should include the training, monitoring, and follow-up activities. Although the classroom format insures regular contact with peers and coordinators, it may compromise the program's integrity by promoting opportunism as an incentive.

Once you decide on a purpose and group or individual activities, you will want to pave the way for acceptance by enlisting support from all professional personnel involved with your program population. This would include the superintendent, principals, teachers, and guidance personnel.

For example, if you decide that your peer leaders should enter a health class to discuss peer pressure for three sessions, you will need Board of Education clearance, curriculum approval, superintendent endorsement, and teacher receptiveness. In addition, you may need written consent from the parents of peer leaders and their receivers.

Funding

Any program needs funding in order to operate. One advantage of peer support initiatives is their cost effectiveness in reaching high numbers of people at low expense. The voluntary nature of peer support assists in lowering costs. You will need some money to pay the coordinator, provide training, secretarial back-up and transportation costs.

Some of the funding resources inside and outside of the host agencies include:

• State and federal grants.
• Lions, Rotary, and Kiwanis Club donations.
• Fundraising initiatives within the setting.

• Corporate contributions.
• PTA's.

Most peer initiatives of twenty or less participants (including staff, leaders and receivers) can operate on less than $3000 for the first year and $2000 per year thereafter.

Orientation

Once you have decided upon your program design and have approval from the higher level administration, you may need up to three months to prepare the school system and community for the project.

An orientation program includes individual contacts and group contacts with all the players involved in your production. These might include student supervisors, guidance counselors, teachers, and parents. It is a good idea to prepare a brief program orientation sheet including the following:

• Information and contents of the program.
• Mechanics of the program.
• Advantages of the program.
• Peer leaders' goals.
• Receivers' goals.
• Program activities.
• Evaluation techniques.

PREPARING PRINCIPALS. Call a conference with the principals of those schools involved and focus on the following issues:

• Program format and evaluation procedures.
• Recruitment procedures.
• Budget needs and funding sources.
• Assistance in gaining board approval.
• Logistics of release time for peer leaders and recipients.
• Scheduling arrangements.
• Support in responding to teacher's attitudes.
• Vehicles to solicit high levels of involvement.
• Room assignments and transportation.

PREPARING GUIDANCE COUNSELORS. Meeting with guidance personnel from both sending and receiving schools is also important to a successful program. Here are some potential actions to be taken at meetings with guidance counselors:

• Describe guidance involvement in the recruit-

ment and selection of both peer leaders and receiving students.
• Explain how training design promotes competent peer leaders.
• Present profiles of participants.
• Discuss the importance of on-site supervision of peer leaders and the receivers.
• Describe guidance counselors' roles in the back-up referral procedures.
• Discuss the program's relationship to adjunct teachers.
• Set up ways to respond to crises that might arise at the program site.

PREPARING TEACHERS. Teacher conferences are essential to encouraging acceptance of the project. Such conferences should be held in a low-key fashion, perhaps in a casual setting.

Attempt to meet the teachers in their own academic world (if possible), eliciting their needs and showing the relationship of program goals to their concerns. After discussing all the issues and answering questions, make the following points:

• Announce that program participation is voluntary for everyone involved.
• Explain that teachers should refer candidates who would benefit from older peer models.
• Underscore the importance of mutual agreement about activities which coordinate with curriculum.
• State the program goals and roles of the teachers as potential trainers or support personnel.
• Introduce the program as a pilot with built-in safeguards and evaluations.
• Spell out teacher's time involvement out and limit to a workable schedule.
• Stress the voluntary nature of any teacher's consultation with students or peer leaders.
• Emphasize that teacher involvement is essential to the program's success.

MEETING WITH PARENTS. Before the program becomes operative, a short presentation to parents should be made at a PTA meeting or at a special orientation session for parents of the target population. The following actions should be taken:

• Provide program rationale, mission, and preventive nature.
• Describe training, supervision, and evaluation.

• Discuss Board of Education or school endorsement.
• Describe voluntary nature of program.
• Express the need for parental support in helping children benefit from program activities.
• Make sure parents have your phone number and address for any follow-up questions or concerns which might warrant further communication.
• Make sure that the parents receive feedback on the program's outcome.

It is essential that before recruiting, training, and implementing the program, you design an extensive description which includes the following sections:

• Mission statement.
• Goals and objectives.
• Planning.
• Recruitment and selection.
• Training.
• Implementation.
• Evaluation.
• Follow-up.

The program design should be carefully conceived and clearly spelled out. It is helpful to begin with a demonstration project or short-term pilot project before implementing a larger scale endeavor.

Qualifications of coordinator, supervisor, and all participants should be carefully considered in the way they relate to the program task. Standardized evaluation instruments, informal surveys, or questionnaires should be selected based on their appropriateness to the program mission and its activities.

Recruitment

In general, success or failure of your program will depend on the quality of student participants selected to do the job. Some of the criteria to bear in mind include student availability, motivation, academic grades, scheduling constraints, reliability, and well-roundedness.

All peer leaders should be good communicators, open and empathic to others. They should demonstrate ability to respect others' confidential information. Flexibility and dedication are also qualities which should be sought in any peer leader. Some peer programs enlist high risk

students as peer leaders. This practice incurs a major liability and could be potentially damaging to both leaders and receivers. Use as many of these recruitment procedures as time and resources permit:

1. Request guidance counselors, teachers, coaches, and appropriate staff to recommend high school students interested in joining a peer support program.

2. Visit a meeting of the Future Teachers Association, human relations psychology classes, or service organizations to make announcements stating the program goals and requirements.

3. Place an announcement in the school's bulletin or newspaper.

4. Design a short peer leader staff nomination form and distribute to guidance counselors, homeroom teachers, and subject teachers. (See Appendix A, Model 1.)

5. Design and distribute a short peer leader student nomination form (see Appendix A, Model 2) which includes the criteria for program participation. Distribute this form to the peer population and select candidates rated highly by their contemporaries.

6. Distribute application forms to candidates, and ask students to fill them out. (See Appendix A, Model 3.)

SCREENING AND PRELIMINARY ASSESSMENT. The methods of screening depend on the needs of the individual program. For example, if several coordinators are available, the program will accommodate a large number of students. If, on the other hand, limited resources are available to administer the program, a small group is advisable. Four to eight peer leaders is a viable range for a beginning program.

After deciding the number of peer leaders, set up screening interviews with each candidate. Ten minutes per interview is sufficient to assess each student's motives for helping, activities and interests, class schedule, available time, academic performance, areas of expertise, and ability to relate to others with sensitivity. Refer to permanent record files to gather data about students' grades, interests, and competencies. Be sure to notify students before checking his or her records.

You may decide to use a standardized instrument such as the Index of Perception to assess leader competency in human relation skills and round out your data base. (See Appendix, A, Model 4.) You may also wish to have each candidate submit a written statement explaining his/her reasons for wanting to take part in the program.

Finally, you may want to narrow your selection process in a series of rounds and then request peer references to cross-validate your impressions.

After you have selected your peer leaders, be sure to notify those candidates not chosen and offer them appropriate explanations. Issue parent consent forms to new trainees, authorizing them to participate in the program. (See Appendix A, Model 5.) Be sure this form, as well as others has been approved by your Board of Education or other executive body.

Set up training dates, and notify staff by memo. (See Appendix A, Model 6 for example of program announcement.) It is helpful to view the screening procedure as divided into three stages: pretraining, training, and post-training. Advise your leaders that they must complete these stages of scrutiny before they enter the program. Use pretraining assessments such as the Index of Perception, statement sheets, and interviews. Use observation checklists, attendance, and participation as training assessments. If you are comfortable with peer review, then ask the trainees to rate each other. A post-training assessment might include post-tests using the same pretest instruments.

In your second year, use advanced peer leaders to assist you in the training and three stage screening process.

RECRUITMENT AND SELECTION. It is important to make preliminary decisions about the qualifications and criteria for admission to the program, and state these criteria in your written program description. Entry criteria for individual and group programs differ widely, depending on selection procedures and program mission.

For example, if you are entering a classroom, the selection process is controlled by the actual class membership. On the other hand, when selecting individual students for one-to-one helping activities, you must look at each individual candidate's profile before determining his/her eligibility. Standardized instruments such as self-concept scales (Florida Key or Mooney Problem Checklist) can be used for individual selection and recruitment purposes (Purkey et. al. 1971 and Mooney, 1978). The following steps may be useful in your recruitment and selection process:

1. Make up and distribute receiving student referral forms to homeroom teachers and guidance counselors at the target schools. (See Appendix A, Model 7).

2. Place announcements in the school's daily bulletins or newspapers and visit selected homerooms to publicize the program. Make posters.

3. Stress the voluntary nature of the program if it is to be a one-to-one helping arrangement.

4. Devise an application for receiving students, describing the goals and criteria. Distribute to students who have been referred as potential candidates. (See Appendix A, Model 8).

5. Collect the applications to determine which students are interested in receiving help.

6. Check permanent records for student profiles and academic levels on standardized tests. Screen out those students who are experiencing massive school failure. These students are probably not appropriate for a peer intervention.

7. Send referring staff members a memo (see Appendix A, Model 9) and a Receiving Student Evaluation such as the Florida Key (see Appendix A, Model 10) and gather this valuable observational data on your receiver candidates.

8. Check with students' guidance counselors and teachers to validate your own impressions and round out your data base.

9. For programs requiring small group interventions, you may want to visit physical education classes to solicit volunteers who meet the criteria of a certain profile; for example, underachievers, students who wish to improve social or prob-

lem-solving skills. Often the peer leaders can visit classes and recruit directly.

After you have narrowed your population to a core group of potential candidates, call a meeting and explain the program more thoroughly. This meeting should be convened after the peer leaders are trained. Describe any matching procedures relevant to one-to-one helping programs and make students aware that their peer leaders will be matched individually based on compatible profiles.

Be sure to mention any time frames or delays which might occur between the actual selection process and the programs target date. For example, it may be possible that scheduling factors may prevent some students from participating in the program. Thus, the tentative nature at this stage should be underscored. During this meeting, distribute parent consent forms for the receiving students (see Appendix A, Model 11) and ask them to return them as soon as possible.

Be sure all receiving students who are not chosen are placed on a waiting list and notified of their status. You may want to send a letter to those on the waiting list. (See Appendix A, Model 12).

Training

A variety of training approaches are applicable to different types of peer support programs. Peer leader candidates may be trained on or off campus, during school time or on weekends, in single day time blocks or short term intervals. Recently there has been a proliferation of peer leadership courses which usually extend throughout one semester. Several commercial training guides are available and are listed in the Bibliography.

The type of training should be tailored to the goals of your particular program. However, all training programs should include a preassessment instrument to determine baseline levels of competence in a candidate's entry level communication and interpersonal skills.

In general, training approaches should include icebreakers, group building, communication guidelines and barriers, empathy training, behavioral warning signals requiring professional referral, some academic support skills, and rapport building techniques.

All training programs should include a list of goals, objectives, and guiding principles designed to accomplish a training mission. Finally, an end-of-training evaluation should be included to assess the impact on the candidates' skill development.

Useful training formats include experiential exercises, role playing, hypothetical dilemmas to solve, observation checklists and feedback mechanisms, and specific outcome indicators for each exercise.

All candidates should be required to attend all training sessions as an eligibility requirement. The professional qualifications of trainers are also paramount to the success of any training program. Thus, it is essential that trainers serve as models and guides to embody the skills they teach. Personality attributes include flexibility, creativity, endurance, and sensitivity.

Although peer leader trainers may not necessarily be mental health professionals, training in human relations skills is an important contribution to professional competency.

It is often useful to include a one or two day wilderness experience as part of the training. Outward Bound types of challenges and problem-solving dilemmas create a spirit of cooperation and build a cohesive group which rallies support and develops conflict resolution skills.

Be sure to arrange for training site availability well in advance of the initial training date. Materials, resources, audio-visual aids, and any other details should be cleared in writing.

Prior to the training, it is important to stress that each candidate's skills must meet specific criteria before the final selection and program participation is to take place. Thus, the final selection criteria should include the candidate's attendance, participation, interests, feedback and checklist data, ability to relate to others, and discrimination abilities as measured by specific instruments.

At the end of the training, the trainer should make the final selection and then meet privately with each candidate, discussing reasons for selection or denial of entry into the program.

Finally, the trainer should solicit written feedback on the quality of the training from each candidate.

Suggestions for improvement should be made. In some programs, after an initial cycle is complete, experienced peer leaders often participate in subsequent training sessions as assistants. Such a revolving model assists not only in the perpetuation of the training, but also in future recruitment, screening, and program improvement.

At the completion of the training, a celebration is often helpful in providing the necessary ritual of completion. A poster making session to publicize the program and begin recruitment often rallies the spirit. Follow-up training sessions prepare leaders for specific group oriented programs focusing upon problem-solving skills, support building, or leisure time activities in the target population.

The best format for group oriented training programs includes a rehearsal model, whereby the trainers run through a specific series of group exercises while peer leaders adapt roles of receiving students in the target population.

After each session, peer leaders use checklists to provide written feedback to trainers on trainers' effectiveness. Discussions clarify any misconceptions or unpolished details.

Typically, after a sequence of sessions is completed, the peer leader candidates then reverse roles, running the exercises as peer leaders. They too receive feedback from the rest of the group members, including the program trainer. After the two cycles are complete, the peer leaders are now ready to lead group oriented programs.

It is important that programs begin immediately after the training is complete. Thus, it is necessary to pave the way for program commencement by setting start-up dates and clearing logistical details in advance. Delays in program implementation often dampen spirit and enthusiasm in both peer leaders and receiving students who anxiously await the start of the program. A phone network of peer leaders should be set up to promote ongoing support when the program begins.

Implementation

Start-up procedures differ widely from program to program. An individual one-to-one program requires more detailed logistics than a group program. For example, after the training is complete for a one-to-one program, it is important to arrange schedules, transportation, room assignments for helping sessions, teacher supervision, student passes and release from classes, and teacher authorization. Many one-to-one programs are held during lunch periods, in small rooms, with participants sharing lunch while engaging in helpful activities. Often helpers use academically oriented activities to break the ice and develop a helping relationship.

Matching is an essential aspect of successful goal completion. In general, students are matched by same gender, personality, background, ability, interest, and scheduling availability. As mentioned earlier, it is advantageous to schedule older students helping younger recipients in one-to-one relationships.

Once matching is complete, interview and distribute letters to receiving students placed on waiting lists. Be sensitive about their feelings. Schedule meetings with the peer leaders to review profiles of their receiving students. Preliminary conferences with receiving students' teachers and their peer leaders are often arranged to discuss particular academic concerns relating to receiving students' goals and objectives.

It is helpful to schedule an introductory conference with peer leaders and their receiving students to allow both parties to meet and to decide whether or not they would like to work together.

Set up schedules and make up an Assignment Sheet and a letter to the staff at the sending school. (See Appendix A, Models 13 and 14.) Distribute assignment sheets to teachers at the receiving school and letters to sending school staff. Issue Peer Leader and Receiving Student Passes. (See Appendix A, Models 15 and 16). Peer leaders should receive appropriate ID cards to identify them to administrators and teachers. (See Appendix A, Model 17.)

Once a program has begun, it is important for the coordinator to obtain feedback from peer leaders, supervisors, and all participants.

Transportation records, attendance records, and report card data should be reviewed periodically.

Supervision

Supervision models vary widely from program to program. For the most part, each peer leader should be assigned to a competent supervisor who can meet with him or her once a week during lunch or after school to assess the program progress. Assessment should be made on the basis of careful record keeping, verifiable outcome attainment, and feedback from observing teachers.

A program checklist should be developed and reviewed by the supervisor and peer leader periodically. (See Appendix A, Model 18). Classroom performance checks should also be used to assess peer leaders' abilities to maintain high level work in their classes. (See Appendix A, Model 19.)

At times it is helpful for the supervisor to interview students who are part of the target population. Such interviews can determine logistical barriers and generate program improvements. Occasionally, it is necessary for a coordinator or supervisor to recommend that a one-to-one relationship be terminated for a variety of reasons. These might include poor attendance, unreliability of peer leader, unproductiveness, or personality conflicts between leader and receiver.

In group programs, observing teachers usually provide valuable feedback on the process and atmosphere of each session facilitated by peer leaders. Furthermore, student reaction is included in the ongoing assessment procedure during weekly meetings between peer leaders and their supervisors.

Strategy conferences both before and after group meetings are often helpful. These meetings can be held during lunch, free periods, or even on the phone. The program coordinators should also arrange for large group meetings of all peer leaders on at least a once-a-month basis. You may want to hold such meetings in the early morning hours before the official day begins.

Peer leaders should be required to attend such meetings. Often such sessions provide a format for valuable participation, support, and strategy sharing.

All peer leaders, supervisors, and program coordinators should have access to phone numbers in case of emergency. It is also helpful to provide a list of specialized professionals and community resources which can be called upon for back-up assistance.

Evaluation

The types of assessment and evaluation procedures vary widely from program to program. Some are very informal, using verbal feedback as a sole assessment procedure. Other programs include surveys filled out by both peer leaders and receiving students. As mentioned above, training evaluations include specific checklists and standardized instruments to measure communication skills of peer leaders. (See Section 2, Session 47.)

No matter what type of evaluation or assessment tool is used, it is important to keep records on each program. Data should be collected to assess the successes and limitations of any program. Changes should be made based on ongoing feedback provided through the various types of data.

Valuable measures of receivers' progress include report cards, self-concept scales, ratings of work samples, attendance records, Follow-up Interview Questions (see Appendix A, Model 21), and disciplinary records. Peer leaders may also keep logs to show progress toward their receivers' goals.

To assess peer leaders' learning, readminister the Index of Perception Scales (Appendix A, Model 4) or Conscious Communication Skills Inventories (Section 2, Session 5). Compare score changes with baseline data at the pretraining level. Ratings of performance by their receiving students are also viable assessment tools.

It is important to share information about ongoing program successes and changes to peripheral faculty members as well as the general student population. Frequently, students are asked to make presentations at faculty meetings or parent groups to provide valuable information about program details. In some programs, students often make presentations to professional conventions about their experiences and learning in their roles as peer leaders. Other programs provide demonstrations of activities and consultation to other agencies.

It may be valuable to publish articles in the school newspaper or even to put out a newsletter about the program which can be distributed to the school population. Some programs solicit ongoing referrals by placing referral boxes in popular locations such as the cafeteria. It is important to keep principals and administrators abreast of program developments through written communications and occasional conferences. Isolation and poor communication can spell disaster for any innovative program of this type.

Energizing Activities

After the initial rush from one-to-one helping sessions or the novelty of a four session group program subsides, peer leaders may fall into a routine as they do with any other repetitious activity. To keep these volunteers fresh and well-motivated, programs often build in a variety of activities to fuel the spirit:

1. Invite speakers from public agencies to conduct sessions on relevant issues such as HIV/AIDS, divorce, violence, etc.

2. Attend peer leaders' conferences and conventions.

3. Schedule joint training and idea sharing with other fledgling peer programs.

4. Invite former peer leaders and receivers to meet with current participants.

5. Invite professionals from the community to meet with participants.

6. Brainstorm and develop idea banks such as metaphors for change or approaches that work.

7. Encourage peer leaders to design new programs and recruit new peer leaders.

8. Involve peer leaders in designing and conducting new training activities.

9. Initiate fundraising activities.

10. Have a "Peer Leader of the Year" award.

11. Ask peer leaders to design buttons, T-shirts,

and pencils with logos reflecting your program's image.

12. Invite other agencies to visit your program.

13. Invite the media to cover your program activities.

14. Select and invite luncheon speakers to address your facility.

15. Plan year-end celebrations or field trips.

Program Completion

The completion process for each program differs widely in accordance with its mission and duration. For example, some closed-end groups typically run for four sessions per cycle. A one session fourth grade tobacco awareness group led by peer leaders is a relatively simple closed-end cycle which runs its own course and finishes after all the information is presented. However, an ongoing one-to-one helping relationship based on academics and social support may run for an entire academic year.

Occasionally, it is necessary for a one-to-one relationship to continue throughout following year. For example, some transitional programs which use peer leaders as guides to incoming ninth graders require extensive involvement to continue their adjustment process the following year. It is possible that a twelfth grade student guiding a ninth grade student may need to facilitate a transfer of a new peer leader at the end of the academic year.

Prior to the twelfth grade peer leader's graduation, it is important to assess the receiving student's progress and determine whether such a transfer is necessary. If a given student needs continued support, the peer leader might introduce him or her to another peer leader about one month before the end of the school year. Such a transition can facilitate a smooth transfer and continuation of services during the summer or the following year.

In all one-to-one programs, it is essential that peer leaders prepare their receivers for the completion of the program by reviewing goals, successes, and areas that need improvement. Usually, the generation of new strategies and reinforcement of positive resources are all part of the completion process.

It is sometimes useful to stage a year-end event such as a party or field trip for all program participants. As the end of the program approaches, it is important to be mindful of this impending separation and support peer leaders in dealing with their students' concerns surrounding separation.

The peer leader should provide his or her phone number to promote ongoing communication after the formal relationship has ended. Often, peer leaders continue to be in contact with their receiving students for several years. Each one-to-one relationship is different and requires a unique program completion procedure.

As the end of a program cycle draws near,

opportunities for peer leaders to reflect, brainstorm new ideas, and make contributions to future program cycles should be provided. Surveys, meetings, introduction of new peer leaders by current participants, and exchange of addresses and phone numbers will insure the program's legacy. (See Appendix A, Model 22 for Peer Leader Program Evaluation model.)

From the coordinator's perspective, it is always appropriate to provide final feedback in the form of a report to or meeting with those administrators and teachers who have been involved. A final peer leaders' meeting should also be called and some sort of celebration or even a banquet may be held as a final event. Thank you notes are often helpful in acknowledging the support of significant program contributors and participants.

SECTION 2 —
PRELIMINARY TRAINING GUIDE

Section 2 — Preliminary Training Guide

Session 1: Introduction

Time
Forty-five minutes

Goals
• To set the tone for the program and training experience.

• To identify and discuss the program's goals and suggested procedures.

(The goals and procedures can be easily modified according to the various schools' needs.)

Materials
Introduction Letters and General Guidelines for Peer Leaders.

Process
Trainer requests the trainees to divide into two groups of four member search.

Ask each group to form two circles with one circle inside the other. Distribute the Introduction Letters and General Guidelines to each group.

Each member in the center circle will then take turns reading one goal and procedure from the letter. As each person reads, he\she should give a reason as to why each is important to peer helping.

Request the outer circle to observe and listen critically as the center circle reads. Following the reading of each section, ask both groups to discuss the rationales and limitations of the contents presented. Invite members to comment on each.

Trainer moves into the observer groups to assist in modeling the observation process. Initiate criticism and comments during discussions.

Outcome Indicators
1. Trainees should point out at least two weaknesses in the announcements or questions about them. For example, their questions may include: Why are there only one or two sessions per week? The level of students' programs is not spelled out.

2. Trainees should ask for at least four clarifications, since some of the statements in the announcements are brief and incomplete.

Introduction Letter

Name_____   Date_____

Welcome to our training program. As peer leaders, you are taking on a big responsibility and probably carry with you some high expectations of yourselves. Being a peer leader is not a simple process. You don't just get instant results by pushing a button. From your own experiences you should remember how hard it was to solve some of your earlier problems, such as becoming part of a group, going on your first date, and dealing with that tough subject you hated and feared so much.

This word of warning should tell you while some learning will occur in your sessions, the real problems will be solved outside of your sessions. Therefore, you should be careful not to expect to solve your receiver's problems or to take on their burdens. The same principles apply to the groups you may lead.

This is easy to say, but hard to do. To expect too much of your student might damage your relationship with them. This training will focus on a few helpful and harmful things you can do. Remember, you are listeners who listen, not all-powerful change agents who renovate others.

The following are some goals and procedures that you should know.

Learning Goals
• To learn the skills of communicating, responding, and tutoring necessary to be an effective peer leader.

• To learn how to use your natural sensitivity to reach others. This sensitivity includes concern for your receivers, understanding their situations, and putting yourselves in their shoes.

• To learn how to evaluate and criticize this experience.

Service Goals
• To assist receivers in becoming more diversified in school and in relating to others more effectively.

• To assist students in improving grades.

• To promote a variety of positive behaviors in the groups you lead and in the individuals you see.

• To identify behavioral warning signals and initiate the appropriate referrals.

Some Activities Designed to Reach Your Learning Goals
• This three day training program will emphasize communication and tutoring skills. Once you begin your assignment, weekly advisory sessions will focus on what happens in the sessions and provide you with coaching. Those of you doing one-to-one helping may want to touch base with your receiver's teacher regarding progress in the subject you are tutoring. Always ask your receiver for permission before you contact an adult.

Page 2 - Introduction Letter

• A personal log will be kept by you on each receiver or group with whom you work. This journal will enable you to set goals for each area, evaluate how you are doing, and identify your sensitivities to the receiver's needs. The only people who will see these confidential logs will be the program coordinators. Any problems or questions they raise will be discussed in the weekly advisory sessions.

• Two specific forms, the Training Evaluation and the Program Evaluation, will enable you to evaluate the program's progress. Your weekly advisory sessions will provide opportunities for you to assess the program's worth as it proceeds.

Some Activities Designed to Promote Your Helping Goals
Your coordinators will assign you to work with individuals or groups to promote a variety of positive behaviors in school, with friends, family, and alone.

Your participation in the training program does not bind you to continue in the program. If anything arises which raises questions about your continuation, please make us aware of it. If we have questions, we will let you know.

We sincerely appreciate your interest in this program and will do anything we can to help you to have a positive, fulfilling learning experience.

Best of luck to you all,

Program Coordinator(s)

General Guidelines for Peer Leaders

Name_____   Date_____

1. When working individually in Smooth Transitions, One-to-One, or Welcome Program, be sure to set goals and monitor them periodically. Where applicable, use backup materials such as entry level surveys. When working in the One-to-One Program with younger students, decide which subject area to focus upon, first choosing the one which is most manageable and easily remedied.

Avoid choosing a subject which a student has failed for three marking periods, or one in which a student is hopelessly lost or dislikes. Use about half the session for academics in a goal-oriented approach and the other half discussing the student's other issues such as peer relationships, teacher relationships, etc.

2. When dealing with academics, ask student for permission to contact his or her teacher to check progress periodically. Also be sure to indicate that you will be seeing the student's report card to check academic progress.

3. Meet with your advisor every week to discuss how things are going with individual students or group oriented programs.

4. Each person will need a pass to leave classes and to go to a helping session. Leaders who leave school will need a Peer Leader's Pass for the duration of the program. This will permit you to leave classes on the day of your session. Your subject teachers will need to sign this pass.

5. Maintain at least a C average in your subjects. Your report cards will be routinely sent to the program coordinators. If your grades drop, teachers may recommend that you be dropped from the program.

6. Be sure to maintain your paper trail which includes personal logs, surveys, progress on goals, and written evaluations. Also written permission from teachers and any transportation records must be up-to-date and given to your advisors regularly.

7. Keep the program coordinator and advisor informed about your student's progress and be sure to make any recommendations for additional professional backup if any behavioral warning signals show up. This includes any students who exhibit distress in your group sessions.

8. Once the helping assignments are made, you will fill out a schedule for each group or individual with whom you work. You and your receivers must get permission to leave classes, lunch, or study periods for your helping sessions. If possible, we will try to schedule the sessions during nonessential classes or study periods. Sessions will be held in available rooms at the receivers' schools. Use the phones in Room #_____ to contact any necessary transportation companies.

9. You are expected to attend group support sessions. Times and places will be announced.

10. Out of respect for your receivers' privacy, you should keep all information confidential. Tell your receivers that their privacy will be protected and that you will discuss your sessions only in your advisory meetings with program staff.

The only exceptions to this confidentiality are in two areas: warning signals of self-harm and harm to others. For example, if your receiver tells you that he/she is taking drugs, drinking, or engaging in other self-damaging behavior, we will be obliged to make a referral to resources where special services can be supplied.

11. Your one-to-one sessions will continue until you, your receiver, and your advisor indicate that help is no longer needed. Either the peer leader or the receiver may decide to discontinue the relationship. Such a decision should be made on the basis of outcome completions and attitudes. For example, if your receivers or groups do not show up for sessions regularly, show disinterest, or get behind in their work, we will make the appropriate changes to fit the situation.

If you discontinue your sessions because of difficulties in the relationship, you will be given an opportunity to choose another student to help. Your group sessions will continue until the program cycle is complete.

12. Peer leaders who complete the program with interest and full participation will receive recommendations from the program coordinator for jobs and college. These recommendations will indicate that you volunteered for peer service. They will be given to potential employers and colleges of your choice.

We wish you the best of luck and hope that you will enjoy the many outreach activities that make this program so special. We encourage your criticism and suggestions for improvement.

Session 2:
Personal Collage

Time
Ninety minutes (forty-five minutes to make collages and forty-five minutes to discuss them).

Goals
• To encourage trainees to reveal experiences, attitudes, and interests represented by their collages.

• To encourage the development of trust in the group.

Materials
Large construction paper, old newspapers and magazines, pens, magic markers, scissors, tape, and paste.

Process
Trainer issues instructions as follows:

In the next forty-five minutes each of you is going to create a collage out of newspaper and magazine clippings, words, and pictures. The collages should reflect your own identity (feelings about yourselves, values, thoughts about others, attitudes, heroes, hobbies, and interests).

Trainer moves about the room assisting the trainees in getting supplies. Trainer makes his/her own collage and displays it on the wall with the others. Initiate the discussion by introducing your own collage.

After the collages are completed, instruct the group as follows:

Now that you've finished, take these next few moments to get to know each other through the collages. I'll start by introducing mine. Let's continue with the one to my left on the wall. Could you please tell the group a bit about yourself through this collage?

Perhaps you could start by telling us your name and then by talking about what the pictures, words, and colors you used represent in your life.

After the explanation of the collage, encourage the group to ask questions about it. Let students pass if they chose not to reveal private material.

Outcome Indicators
1. Trainees should discuss their hobbies, interests, occupational goals, and thoughts about freedom, dating, parents, politics, or education.

2. Trainers should look for cues indicating interest. Examples include: alertness, eye contact, changes in voice inflection from high to low, or soft to loud, and contents of collages (sports, ideals, life goals).

Session 3: Guided Fantasy

Time
Forty-five minutes

Goal
• To promote interaction and sharing of personal experiences and problems common to group members at earlier developmental stages.

Materials
Dark magic markers and flip chart.

Process
Trainer introduces the exercise as follows:

Could we please move into a circle? To help you turn your clock back in time and recall some of your earlier struggles, I'm going to ask you to close your eyes and reflect on the past. Picture yourself as a sixth or seventh grader just starting school. Imagine that you have entered the building for your first day of school.

Visualize whom you saw, what you did, and what you had to contend with.

(Give the group a minute to think in silence.)

Now, think about the challenges you experienced and who you looked to for help.

After a couple of minutes, lead the group into a discussion as follows:

I'd like you to share some of your thoughts and struggles.

Use a magic marker to record the main issues and struggles on the flip chart as they are identified by the group. Allow at least a half hour for the discussion, enough time for each participant to contribute ideas and add to others.

After about twenty minutes of discussion, point out to the trainees that their future receivers face the same issues mentioned in their group.

Have the group choose one or two struggles and trace their origin and evolution to the present. Discuss what steps were taken in dealing with the struggle and which approaches worked for various individuals.

Ask the trainees how they feel about helping students. Ask why it is advantageous that the trainees have experienced and overcome these earlier struggles.

Outcome Indicators
1. Trainees should be facing each other and be attentive.

2. The subjects raised by trainees should be followed up by others.

3. The following is a list of struggles which may be brought up by the trainees:

a. Changing classes, new schedules, and new teachers.
b. Awareness of the opposite sex and awkwardness in new relationships.
c. Disliking certain teachers and learning how to cope with classroom demands.
d. Longer and more comprehensive homework assignments in more complex subject matter.
e. Meeting new people and finding new friends.
f. Freedom versus responsibility.
g. Parental and school expectations.
h. Dealing with cliques, in-groups, and out-groups.

Session 4:
The Art of Helping

Time
Thirty minutes

Goals
• To identify and provide examples of the assumptions about effective helping relationships.

• To identify and define the three major assumptions about communication.

Materials
Assumptions about Helping Relationships Sheets, Assumptions about Communication Sheets, flip charts, and magic markers.

Process
Trainer distributes Assumptions about Helping Relationships Sheets and Assumptions about Communication Sheets to trainees and asks the trainees to form groups of eight members. Trainer distributes flip charts and magic markers to each group. Each group is instructed to review all the Assumptions and produce their own rationales for each.

Groups are given a 30 minute time limit and asked to select a time keeper, a recorder (to write the rationales on a flip chart), and a reporter to serve as a spokesperson.

After thirty minutes each reporter is asked to report the group's rationales for selected Assumptions. Then, trainer leads a discussion about each Assumption and its application to the helping process. Trainer invites question and answer dialogue.

Outcome Indicator
1. Group should provide its own examples of each of the assumptions.

Assumptions about Helping Relationships Sheet

Name_____ Date_____

1. There are two pathways of communication:

• Conscious (in the person's awareness).

• Unconscious (below the person's awareness).

2. Rapport and trust are essential to all helping relationships. Always meet another person in his or her model of the world. By studying a person and showing respect, you may develop that rapport and trust.

3. All behavior starts for good reasons. The person who got badly bitten by a German Shepherd may avoid all dogs.

4. The goal of any communication is the response you get back, regardless of the communicator's intent. You may say to someone "You look great today," and get a reply, "Does that mean I looked terrible yesterday?"

5. Resistance to your help by your receiver is a signal for you to be more flexible. If a receiving student forgets to come to your sessions three times in a row, maybe he or she is trying to tell you something about your relationship.

6. Choice is the gateway to problem-solving. Is there only one way to ask for a favor, study for a test, or make money?

7. A positive attitude enables positive responses. If you are in a nasty mood, it might affect the person whom you are trying to assist.

8. All the necessary abilities to change lie within an individual's personal history. Most people have had some success to build upon in the future (learning to dress, walk, ride a bike, read, etc.).

9. The unconscious part of the individual is an intelligent and friendly guide. It allows you to breathe, blink, avoid an oncoming car, and defend yourself against danger.

10. Physical changes and belief changes interact to create behavior changes. The way you carry yourself, breathe, move and speak influence the way you feel and act.

Assumptions about Communication Sheet

Name_____   Date_____

1. There are always two levels of communication:

• Conscious (in the person's awareness).

• Unconscious (below the person's awareness level).

2. An individual can only process seven (plus or minus two) bits of information at one time. Therefore, any overload will put the person in a receptive state of mind which makes a message more easily accepted by the unconscious part of the receiver.

3. People process and deliver information using five representational systems, also called dominant sensory channels:

• Visual (sight).

• Kinesthetic (internal or external feelings, emotional reactions).

• Auditory (sounds).

• Gustatory-olfactory (taste or smell).

• Digital (nonsensory based information).

4. Eye-accessing cues (eye movements) reveal how individuals process this information. Refined observation of eye movements can tell you which sensory channel is used to access information. The sensory channels change quite rapidly as indicated by quick eye movement.

Session 5: Conscious Communication Guidelines

Time
Forty-five minutes

Goals
• To present trainees with four principles of communication.

• To enable trainees to practice responses using these principles and to discuss potential reactions to these responses.

Materials
Conscious Communication Guidelines Statement Sheets, flip charts, magic markers, and pencils.

Process
Trainer requests the trainees to assemble in a circle and instructs the group as follows:

Read the guidelines, statements, and questions on the Conscious Communication Guidelines Statement Sheets. Then write your responses to the questions using the guideline that applies to each statement.

After allowing time for trainees to complete the response forms, trainer asks the trainees to form groups of four. Trainer distributes flip charts and magic markers to each group.

Each group is instructed to review all the Guideline Statement Sheets and develop one collective response and rationale for each statement. Groups are given a 30 minute time limit and asked to select a time keeper, a recorder (to write the responses and rationales on a flip chart), and a reporter to serve as a spokesperson.

Trainer leads a large group discussion to share the responses offered and to explore receivers' potential reactions to them.

Outcome Indicators
1. Each trainee should respond to the four statements on Statement Sheet.

2. Although the responses are subjective and not standardized, the trainees should use words that reflect opinions, feelings, and empathy. The Carkhuff Standard Statements (Carkhuff, 1969b) is an instrument helpful in assessing such words.

Conscious Communication Guidelines Statement Sheet

Name_____   Date_____

Goal
• To practice responding to others using four basic communication guidelines.

Directions
To give you some idea about how to use these communication guidelines, we are providing this self-evaluation sheet. Read each communication guideline along with the statements and questions below it. Imagine yourself in the peer leader's role and write your best response to each. Assume the statement came from a student seeking your advice.

1. Focus on the person to whom you are talking. Talk to the person, not about him/her or about what he/she said. Reflect on the subject in a personal way.

RECEIVER'S STATEMENT. "Yesterday me and my friends got really bombed on ten six-packs. I was so blasted that I was out cold for one hour. I don't even remember how I got home."

How can you respond with a personalized focus? How would you respond?

_____

_____

_____

2. Be aware of your own opinions about the issues you discuss with your students. Share your opinions, but do not be too attached to them. Present your attitudes as if they are one way of thinking, not the only way. Openness and truth are valuable but not when used in such a way as to threaten the receiver.

When threatened, the receiver will have to defend his/her point of view or actions he/she might use against parents or other authorities.

RECEIVER'S STATEMENT. "I was up till two in the morning last night studying for the spelling test. When I walked into the room, I just couldn't remember any of the words, so I very carefully snuck out my word list and placed it on my lap under the desk. Well at least I got 90% on the test, and the teacher never even saw me."

How do you view cheating?

_____

_____

_____

Page 2 - Conscious Communication Guidelines Statement Sheet

Keeping your viewpoint in mind, how could you respond to what this person said?

_____

_____

_____

_____

3. Be aware of how you're feeling at the moment you are talking to your receiver. How you feel affects the whole relationship.

RECEIVER'S STATEMENT. "I was walking home yesterday and I saw a bunch of kids in the playground. As I got closer, I noticed that they were teasing John about his pimples. He was all uptight, crying and carrying on, but they just kept on busting him. I wanted to say something but the last time I defended someone, nobody talked to me for three days, so I just kept walking."

How do you feel about (a) the situation and (b) the person's statement?

_____

_____

_____

_____

Keeping in mind these feelings, how would you respond to what this person said?

_____

_____

_____

_____

Page 3 - Conscious Communication Guidelines Statement Sheet

4. Try to put yourself in the other person's place so that you can better understand that person's viewpoint.

RECEIVER'S STATEMENT. "Last night I had to take my little sister out to trick or treat. When we got outside I saw a few of my friends and joined them. They weren't too happy about having her along. After the third house, John said, 'Let's cut through this dark alley way.' My sister got scared and started to cry so I didn't go. Boy, does she get me mad."

If you were this person, how would you have reacted?

_____

_____

_____

_____

Putting yourself in this person's shoes, how would you respond to this story as a peer leader?

_____

_____

_____

_____

Session 6:
Conscious Communication Skills

Time
Twenty minutes

Goal
• To introduce the skills to be learned and practiced in the next eight sessions.

Materials
Conscious Communication Skills Sheets.

Process
Trainer instructs the group as follows:

Read through all the Communication Techniques and Skills and try to make up an example showing how you would use each.

Allow five minutes for this process. Ask the members to take turns giving examples of each technique. Direct a discussion around the leaders' reasons for using these skills. No prolonged demonstrations should take place.

Outcome Indicators
1. An example of each technique should be given.

2. A discussion should point out the reasons for using the skills.

3. At least one receiver's reaction to each barrier should be identified as an example of how the communication process is cut off.

Conscious Communication Skills Sheet

Name_____   Date_____

Goal
• To practice identifying and using these communication skills.

Directions
Read through all the Communication Techniques and Skills and try to make up an example illustrating how you would use each technique.

1. ACTIVE LISTENING. Focus on the person to whom you are talking. Talk to the person, not about him/her or about what he/she said. Listen actively to your receiver. Show your attentiveness nonverbally by nodding, touching, leaning forward, smiling, and changing your facial expressions accordingly.

2. LISTENING FOR FEELINGS. Try to pick up on the feelings he/she is expressing. Be aware of your own feelings about what you are discussing with your receiver. Although your feelings and attitudes are important, do not be too attached to them. Present them as though they were one way of thinking, not the only way.

3. CONTINUING RESPONSES. Use positive sounds and words which may encourage more dialogue. These sounds and words may include, "uh-huh, yes, okay, oh, go on."

4. PARAPHRASING MESSAGES. Use paraphrasing to enable the receiver to clarify how his or her messages and desires correspond to what he or she is saying. For example, if someone says to you, "I had the worst day today. First I missed the bus, then I forgot my lunch, then I had to go back home to get a homework assignment, and then I got yelled at from the teacher for being late to class." A paraphrase might be, "What a day! It must have been terrible for you."

5. ENCOURAGING RESPONSES. Use encouragement by making statements that reflect your receiver's ability to handle a given situation. Statements of competence should be backed by facts, not by assumptions.

For example, if you are talking to a student who tells you he/she never passes a math test, you might question his/her use of the word "never." Just repeat the word "NEVER" to the person. You will be surprised that your receiver will spontaneously come up with counter-examples of situations where he/she has passed tests.

6. QUESTIONING. When you are confused or think that your receiver is ready to learn something new about himself/herself, questioning can help to clarify more details about a situation. For example, if someone tells you about how he/she manages to wake up in the morning for a fishing trip but usually oversleeps for school, you might ask about what it would take to wake up for school like he/she wakes up for fishing.

Page 2 - Conscious Communication Skills Sheet

7. CARING RESPONSES. Be aware of how you are feeling at the moment you are talking to your receiver. How you feel affects the impact you will have in your responses. Show that you care and understand by expressing your feelings. Try to put yourself in the person's place so that you can better understand your receiver's viewpoint. Imagine yourself in the same situation as the one the person is describing and respond with understanding.

8. CONFRONTING AND POINTING OUT DISCREPANCIES. Point out discrepancies between what your receiver wants to do and the behavior which seems to defeat his/her's purpose. For example, a student might say to you, "I want to pass history so I can avoid going to summer school." Inquire about how the person's other activities (watching TV, using the phone, etc.) the night before a test might interfere with his/her goal.

Session 7:
Conscious Communication Barriers

Time
Forty-five minutes

Goals
• To acquaint trainees with barriers to effective communication.

• To enable trainees to recognize the effects of these barriers by dramatizing their use in a one-to-one role play and demonstrating each drama to the group.

Materials
Conscious Communication Barriers Sheets.

Process
Trainer introduces the exercise as follows:

When we presented the Introduction, we made the point that in your role as peer leader, you should keep your expectations realistic. Expecting your receiver to change too fast can lead to a lot of frustration and bad feelings. The sheet I am going to hand out has some behaviors that are often used by peer leaders who expect too much.

To give you an idea of what these statements feel like to use and how they interrupt the helping process by discouraging communication, we're going to ask you to read through these ten communication barriers now.

Distribute Conscious Communication Barriers Sheets and allow five minutes for the group to read silently through them. Continue as follows:

Now that you have read them, let's try them out on each other. Break into pairs, and separate yourselves so that there is space between each pair. Each pair should demonstrate these barriers by making up a conversation using them. One person in each pair will take the part of a peer leader and the other, the part of a receiver. Take a few minutes to make up two dramas, about four sentences each.

Each pair should demonstrate two barriers, one barrier for each conversation. After the first conversation, reverse roles with the peer leader now becoming the receiver and vice versa. You will have ten minutes to make up two dramas and practice them.

Each pair gets two sheets of paper, each having two barriers to demonstrate. Move around to the pairs making yourself available to answer questions and, after ten minutes, instruct the group as follows:

Let's demonstrate your conversations to the group. There are no right or wrong answers, so just relax and get into the process. After each demonstration, let's see if we can guess which barrier was used.

Lead a general discussion on the use and effects of the barriers.

Outcome Indicators
1. Each pair should make up and demonstrate two dramas, each illustrating one barrier.

2. To check understanding of the barriers, the group should reach at least 70% accuracy in their attempts to guess those demonstrated by each pair.

3. At least one receiver's reaction to each barrier should be identified as an example of how the communication process is cut off.

Conscious Communication Barriers Sheet

Name_____   Date_____

Goal
• To practice identifying these barriers to communication.

Directions
Demonstrate these barriers with your partners by using them in your conversations.

1. TELLING OR ORDERING. "Don't touch that." "Get your assignments done immediately." Statements such as these are controlling, judgmental, and insensitive. They produce resentment and resistance from receivers.

2. WARNING OR THREATENING. "If you don't get here on time, then forget it!" "If you don't stop fooling around, you'll get into trouble." Such statements provoke the receiver to test your reactions to their opposing responses.

3. PREACHING. "You must want to go to college. It is the only way to insure a successful future." "You should be more honest." These remarks lead to guilt, anger, and shame on the part of the receiver.

4. PROVIDING STANDARD SOLUTIONS OF CHEAP ADVICE. "If you are more considerate, your parents will treat you better." Remarks like this one are rigid and often inaccurate. These comments can mean that there is only one way to do things, and that the you are "one up" on your receiver. They can turn off your receiver or make him/her dependent on you.

5. INFLUENCING OR CONVINCING. "Everyone knows that drinking at your age leads to alcoholism." This type of statement uses logic to convince the receiver that the leader is right. It puts you in a "superior" position to your receiver.

6. LABELING OR DISCREDITING. "You're a bore." "You're really stupid." Such remarks are extremely judgmental and tend to rally defensive behavior or anger.

7. INTERPRETING. "You're doing that to get attention. You really want her to like you. That's why you're cheating on her to make her jealous." Statements like these also signal a judgmental superiority on the part of the peer leader. Defensive behavior often results because the receiver may feel insulted or degraded.

8. MAKING GLIB PREDICTIONS. "Everything turns out for the better." This type of statement shows that the peer leader is denying his or her own feelings about the receiver's problems. It often serves as an excuse to get off the subject.

Page 2 - Conscious Communication Barriers Sheet

9. CROSS-EXAMINING. "How much time did you spend on your homework?" "Did you use the strategy we talked about?" Statements such as these show your distrust of the receiver. They place the receiver in the position of searching for the correct answer or the answer the leader wants to hear.

10. NOT LISTENING OR INTERRUPTING. Leader appears to tune out or speak when others are talking. This shows a major disregard and lack of concern.

Session 8: Communication Guidelines Review

Time
Fifteen minutes

Goal
• To review the communication guidelines and barriers.

Materials
Small cardboard box, Communication Skills and Barriers Sheets from Sessions 6 and 7 (each numbered skill and barrier is cut into demo strips), and pencils.

Process
Trainer puts the demo strips into two boxes — one for the skills and one for the barriers.

Trainees are asked to pick either a communication skill or barrier from the boxes, and make up an example to illustrate what is on the demo strip. For example, if a trainee receives Barrier #3, "Preaching," ask the trainee to verbalize a response such as, "You should be much more honest than you are."

If a trainee receives Skill #7, "Caring Responses," he/she should verbalize an example of this process such as, "I know that if I were facing a major exam in math with three F's on previous tests, I might feel kind of nervous."

Then trainer calls on members of the group to share their responses to each of the four statements on the Communication Guidelines Statement Sheet (see Session 5.) Statement #2 requests that the leader beware of his/her own point viewpoint about the issues discussed with the receiver. Keeping that in mind, the response should clarify the peer leader's view on cheating and the actual response to the receiver's statement.

Outcome Indicators
1. An example of each technique and barrier should be given by the trainees.

2. The trainee group should correct any faulty responses and attempt to make them more accurate.

3. By the end of the exercise, all responses should be 90% accurate.

Session 9:
Nonverbal Listening Skills

Time
Forty-five minutes (six minutes for trainer demonstrations, ten minutes for group discussions, two minutes per small group role plays, two minutes per small group discussion, fifteen minutes for large group discussion).

Goals
• To practice and recognize nonverbal listening skills.

• To disclose reasons for entering this peer support program.

Materials
Nonverbal Listening Skills Checklists and pencils.

Process
Trainers review positive and negative nonverbal signals in a two minute role play. The role play should deal with why the trainees believe kids can help others. The first minute should exemplify nonverbal signs of interest and agreement (leaning forward, smiling after sentences are uttered, changes in tones, and relating).

The second minute should focus on negatively toned, nonverbal signals: rigid body posture, gruff, short toned nonreplies, and little eye-to-face contact. After a short (ten minute) discussion, trainer instructs the group as follows:

This is an exercise to allow you to practice some non-verbal listening skills while stating your reasons for joining the program. Group yourselves into threes. Each group should find a place in the room with some distance from the other groups. Each person will assume one of three possible roles: listener, responder,

or observer. Members will take turns rotating roles until all three have been taken by each participant.

The responder should face the listener and discuss what factors led him or her to join this program. While the responder states his or her reasons for joining, the observer uses the Nonverbal Listening Skills Checklist to record information about the listener's nonverbal communication skills. You will be doing this three times, until each of you has tried out the three roles.

After about two minutes of discussion, trainer gives the stop signal, then the group spends the next two minutes discussing the listener's nonverbal signals and the responder's reasons for becoming a peer leader. Trainer distributes the checklists, signals the group to stop at two minute intervals (for role playing and small group discussion), and then assists in general discussions.

After the three groups have completed their dialogues, lead a large group discussion about the reactions to dialogues and communication skills. Each trainer should indicate strong and weak areas of nonverbal behavior in "Learned" statements.

Outcome Indicators
1. Each observer should check at least half the items indicating positive nonverbal attending behavior.

2. Discussions within small groups after each role play should be characterized by outbursts of surprise and revelations. The voices should be loud, giggly, and, at times, fast talking.

3. The large group discussions should reveal strong areas of nonverbal communication and weak areas that need work for each trainee.

Nonverbal Listening Skills Checklist

Listener _____ Observer_____

Responder _____ Date_____

Goals
• To identify some reasons for joining the program.

• To practice active attending behaviors.

Directions
Your nonverbal communication has just as powerful an impact as the words you say. Attending behavior can be the key that unlocks the barriers of mistrust and deepens the quality of the relationship.

This sheet is to be used by the observer to rate the nonverbal behavior used by the listener and the responder. Read through the categories on nonverbal behavior. As you watch the two people talking, check the lines next to the signals you see. You may check one category more than once. Remember to place checks for the listener as well as the responder. Switch roles three times.

POSITIVE SIGNALS			NEGATIVE SIGNALS		
Listener	**Responder**		**Listener**	**Responder**	
		Face and Head			**Face and Head**
		Makes frequent	_____	_____	Avoids eye-face contact
_____	_____	eye/face contact			Uses few reactive
		Expresses reactions	_____	_____	expressions to others
_____	_____	to other's messages	_____	_____	Uses few nods
_____	_____	Nods	_____	_____	Yawns
		Arms and Hands			**Arms and Hands**
		Moves with words	_____	_____	Remain motionless
		Uses flowing	_____	_____	Remain rigid
_____	_____	movements			
		Touches or reaches			**Voice**
_____	_____	toward other person	_____	_____	Talks too loud
			_____	_____	Talks too soft
		Voice	_____	_____	Talks too fast
_____	_____	Changes volume	_____	_____	Talks too slow
		Makes changes in			**Body**
_____	_____	pitch			Turns away from
_____	_____	Talks slow and fast	_____	_____	the person
		Body	_____	_____	Slumps
_____	_____	Faces the person	_____	_____	Looks rigid
		Leans forward for			
_____	_____	emphasis			

Session 10:
Listening for Feelings

Time
Thirty minutes (five minutes for Trainer Model, five minutes for large group discussion, one minute per role play, two minutes per small group discussion, and ten minutes for final large group discussion).

Goals
• To enable the trainees to practice listening for content.

• To enable the trainees to improve their recall of messages.

• To enable the trainees to recognize and distinguish between different types of feeling messages expressed by others.

Materials
Listening for Feelings Checklists, Listening For Feelings Statement Sheets, overhead projector, transparencies, and pencils.

Process
TRAINER MODEL
Trainer requests a volunteer to play the role of a younger receiver through a trial role play, using the checklists. Trainer distributes the checklists to the group and asks trainees to complete them after the volunteer reads the following statement.

VOLUNTEER (RECEIVER). "My mother won't even let me out at night anymore. I'm so sick and tired of staying in that house that I could bolt any minute."

After allowing the participants enough time to check off feelings, use an overhead projector to show a sample of a completed checklist which identifies the expressed feelings. Although the expressed feelings are variable and affected by nonverbal cues, the following feelings might be checked to illustrate expressions in the above statement:

• anger tension
• sadness hate
• frustration

Ask the trainees to compare their completed checklists with yours and attempt to reach some agreement in a large group discussion.

TRAINEES' ROLE PLAY
Checklists and statement sheets should be distributed to those playing the parts of leader and observer before each of the three dialogs (one minute each) and discussions (two minutes each). They should be filled out by the receiver and by the observer. Different perceptions should emerge.

The trainer moves around the room observing the groups during their dialogues, offering assistance. The trainer facilitates a group discussion, focusing on the difficulties encountered by group members in recalling and discriminating facts and feelings.

Trainer requests group members to divide into threes and gives the following directions:

This exercise uses role playing to give you practice identifying the feelings your receiver expresses to you. Each member of your group will have a chance to take the three different roles: leader, receiver, and observer. The leader responds as if he/she were trying to understand the problems and feelings expressed by a receiver.

The receiver assumes the role of a younger student coming to an older pupil for assistance. First the receiver silently reads through the statement sheet and then repeats the statement to the leader. While the receiver is talking to the leader, the observer checks the appropriate items on the checklist, attempting to interpret the expressed feelings of the receiver.

After the receiver has made a statement, the leader also checks off the feelings associated with the message on his/her checklist. The observer should be matching the restated message with the original and also matching the feelings perceived by the leader with his/her own feelings.

After each dialogue is role played, each three member group discusses and compares how both the messages and feelings expressed by the receiver were perceived by the leader and by the observer. Different perceptions should emerge in the small group discussions.

Outcome Indicators
1. Checklists filled out by the large group during the Trainer Model should include at least half of the feelings on the checklists posted by trainers.

2. All group members should participate by taking the three roles.

3. Small group discussions of each dialogue should last for the entire two minutes. If the trainees finish early, this may be a signal of misunderstandings or lack of involvement.

4. Trainer should check for nonverbal cues indicating trainees' levels of involvement and understanding. If puzzled faces are noted, trainer should offer further clarification.

5. Trainees' comparisons of observer and leader checklists should reveal similar perceptions.

Listening for Feelings Checklist

Leader _____   Observer_____

Receiver _____   Date_____

Goal
• To practice listening for feelings.

Directions
Feelings are just as essential parts of any conversation as the words that are used. Reading them is not an easy skill to master.

This sheet is used by students playing the parts of leaders and observers. After the receiver makes a statement, check off the feelings that you think were expressed. Compare notes on each other's impressions, and then find out what the receiver's intended feelings were. Change roles three times to give all members practice.

RECEIVER'S FEELINGS EXPRESSED:

_____Fear

_____Anger

_____Confusion

_____Sadness

_____Excitement

_____Happiness

_____Stress

_____Love

_____Hate

_____Envy

_____Frustration

_____Amazement

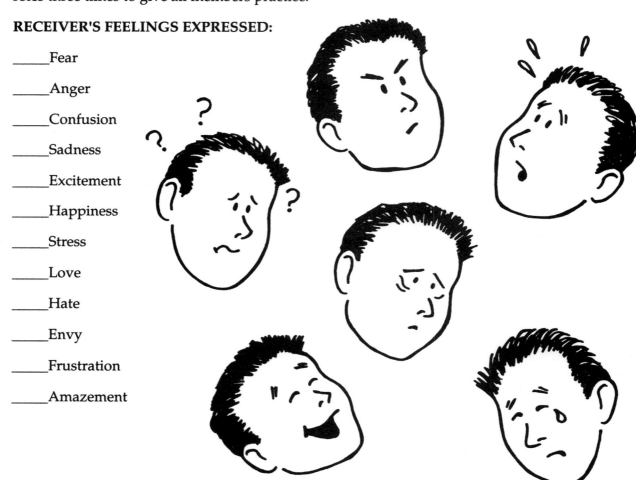

Listening for Feelings Statement Sheet

Name_____   Date_____

Goal
• To practice listening for feelings.

Directions
Use these statements as conversation starters.

1. "I can't believe it. Everything is going much better now. Last week I was able to get into my homework. I actually studied one hour for a history test and got a B+."

2. "I can't stand that kid. He always makes stupid comments in class. The next time he starts up, I'm going to destroy him."

3. "I feel like I don't know how to act with people anymore. When I am around my friends, I don't know what to say. They must think I'm really stupid."

Session 11:
Continuing Responses

Time
Thirty minutes (five minutes for Trainer Model, five minutes for large group discussion, one minute per role play, two minutes per small group discussion, and ten minutes for large group discussion).

Goal
• To enable trainees to practice appropriate verbal responses designed to encourage receivers to continue their dialogues and pursue their concerns.

Materials
Continuing Response Checklists, Continuing Response Statement Sheets, and pencils.

Process
Solicit a volunteer from the trainees' group to play the part of the receiver. Trainer introduces the exercise as follows:

This exercise is designed to give you practice in making verbal continuing responses such as "um, yes, go on." These replies often encourage the receiver to continue exploring what's important in his/her life.

To demonstrate how to use these responses and how to fill out the checklists, we will model a typical dialogue for you. (Volunteer's name) will play the receiver, and I will play the peer leader.

Trainer distributes Continuing Response Checklists to trainees and proceeds as follows:

Look at your checklists and familiarize yourselves with the best continuing responses and the phrases below them that describe the leader's reaction statement. After (name) gives the first statement, check the verbal continuing response you would use, listen to the continuing response that is used by the trainer, and check it. Then, when (name) gives the following statement, check the phrase that best describes it.

TRAINER MODEL
VOLUNTEER (RECEIVER). "I'm so bored in music class that I have to do something to keep me going."

TRAINER (LEADER). "Oh?"

VOLUNTEER (RECEIVER). "Yeah, sometimes I push the kid next to me."

Trainer facilitates a large group discussion comparing the trainees' and trainers' continuing responses on effectiveness in generating productive reactions. Trainer instructs the group as follows:

As in the last exercise, we're going to give you a chance to try the technique. Form two groups of three and put enough distance between your groups to avoid distractions. To practice giving continuing responses, each member of the group will have a chance to play three roles: leader, receiver, and observer. As the leader you should select the most natural continuing response you feel would be effective in encouraging the receiver to explore the issue.

The receiver says the statement. The leader responds with a continuing response, and the receiver continues with a reaction statement. The observer checks off the continuing response on the checklist and checks off the phrase that best describes the receiver's reaction statement. Take about one minute for each role play and one minute for discussion of the observer's impressions. Talk about the effect of the continuing response on the conversation and decide whether another response might have encouraged more dialogue.

Distribute three Continuing Response Checklists and three Continuing Response Statement Sheets to each group and signal one and two minute time limits. Move around from group to group observing and assisting participants in continuing response techniques. Then lead a short group discussion on the trainees' impressions of this exercise.

Outcome Indicators
1. All group trainees should dramatize the three roles.

2. If the small group discussions finish early, this might be a signal of misunderstanding or lack of involvement.

3. Trainers should observe for cues which indicate the members' level of involvement and understanding: active talking, contents of discussions.

4. Trainees should demonstrate their ability to use the continuing responses relevant to the receiver's statements.

5. The receiver's replies to the leader's continuing response should extend the conversation towards its goal.

6. Small group discussions should compare continuing responses and produce alternate responses.

7. Large group discussion should identify the obvious limitations of this technique.

Continuing Response Checklist

Leader _____   Observer_____

Receiver _____   Date_____

Goal
• To practice making comments that will encourage the receiver to continue the conversation.

Directions
Conversations often end unless you do something special to keep them alive.

The observer should use this checklist to record the types of continuing responses used by the leader. The observer should also put checks next to the type of reply made by the receiver after hearing the leader's continuing responses.

TYPES OF RESPONSE

_____Yes

_____Go on

_____Yeah

_____Um

_____Really

_____No response

_____Oh

_____Tell me more

RECEIVER'S REACTION

_____Goes into more detail

_____Changes subject

_____Tunes out

_____No response

Continuing Response Statement Sheet

Name_____   Date_____

Goal
• To practice making responses that will encourage the receiver to continue the conversation.

Directions
Use these statements as conversation starters.

1. "Mr. Johnston, the English teacher, kicked me out of class, and I ended up in the principal's office."

2. "It's tough to compete for the first string against three older guys."

3. "You know, my girlfriend is very sick. She just got out of the hospital because of an ulcer. When she finds out I've been seeing Judy, I'm afraid she'll get so upset that she'll end up back in the hospital."

Session 12: Paraphrasing Messages

Time
Thirty minutes (five minutes for Trainer Model, five minutes for large group discussion, one minute for role play, two minutes for small group discussion, ten minutes for large group discussion).

Goals
• To provide practice in paraphrasing messages. This fosters self-awareness by eliciting others' reactions to your communication.

• To identify intended and perceived messages and their outcomes.

Materials
Paraphrasing Messages Checklists, Paraphrasing Messages Statement Sheets, and pencils.

Process
Ask for a volunteer to play the part of a receiver. Introduce the exercise as follows:

Paraphrasing your receiver's statements can help the young person become more aware of how others receive them. We'll give you a checklist and then model one way of doing this.

There are no right or wrong ways. The most important thing is to reflect the feeling as accurately as you can.

Trainer distributes Paraphrasing Messages Checklist to each participant and proceeds as follows:

Use the checklist to evaluate the accuracy in paraphrasing the receiver's messages. (Name) will play the part of the receiver. I will play the leader.

TRAINER MODEL
VOLUNTEER (RECEIVER): "I really hate Mrs. Edwards. She always picks on me in class."

TRAINER (LEADER): "It sounds as though you must be really miserable in her class. So you're mad at her."

After the participants have checked off their check lists, lead a large group discussion focusing on how the participants would have paraphrased and how they evaluated the paraphrasing response to the receiver's statement.

Request the trainees to take the same three roles as in the previous exercises, spend one minute per role play, and two minutes per small group discussion. A five minute large group discussion should conclude the exercise.

Distribute three Paraphrasing Message Checklists and Paraphrasing Message Statement Sheets to each group and signal one and two minute time limits.

Move around from group to group observing and assisting participants in paraphrasing techniques.

Outcome Indicators
1. All trainees should dramatize the three roles.

2. The small group discussions after each dialogue should continue for the entire two minutes. Early completion signals misunderstanding or lack of involvement.

3. Trainers should observe cues indicating the level of involvement and understanding.

4. The small group discussions should produce various interpretations and distortions of the receiver's intended messages.

5. Trainees should discuss their differences in judging intended messages and the different perceptions. Some of the nonverbal signals related to feelings (presented earlier) should be identified.

Paraphrasing Messages Checklist

Leader _____   Observer_____

Receiver _____   Date_____

Goal
• To practice paraphrasing messages.

Directions
Many of you have probably had a conversation with someone else and wondered whether the other person has really understood your situation.

One way to let someone else know you're with them is to paraphrase what they have just said. This is an effective way to see if your impressions are accurate. Switch roles as in previous exercises.

This checklist should be used by the observers to record the quality of paraphrasing performed by the leader. Check whichever items describe what you have heard paraphrased.

MESSAGES ARE:

_____Left out

_____Expressed in less words

_____Added to by leader

_____Not accurate

_____Totally accurate

Paraphrasing Messages Statement Sheet

Name_____   Date_____

Goal
• To practice paraphrasing statements.

Directions
Use these statements as conversation starters.

1. "Judy didn't invite me to a party. I think I know why. Her friend Joan and I don't get along. Joan probably convinced her not to ask me. Who needs her anyway?"

2. "I hate this school. The last school I went to was much better. They treat you like dirt here."

3. "I can't wait till summer. My camp is going to be really great because I'll be in the best bunk with the older kids."

Session 13: Encouraging Responses

Time
Thirty minutes (five minutes for Trainer Model, five minutes for large group discussion, one minute for role play, two minutes per small group discussion, and five minutes for large group discussion).

Goal
• To enable the trainees to practice responses which support others. Such responses can be effective in encouraging action on the situations or problems presented.

Materials
Encouraging Responses Checklists, Encouraging Responses Statement Sheets, and pencils.

Solicit a volunteer to play a receiver in a role play. Introduce the exercise as follows:

This exercise provides practice in responding with support and encouragement to your receivers. Stating that you recognize a person's potential to solve his or her problems, you may spur some constructive actions.

As in the previous exercise, we'll model one way to use this skill. Unlike the previous one, your role play in this exercise will include a response from the receiver. The segment goes as follows:

• *Receiver makes statement.*
• *Leader responds.*
• *Receiver makes reaction statement.*
• *The observer will rate both the encouraging response and the receiver's reaction to it.*

Trainer distributes Encouraging Responses Checklist to each participant. Trainer continues as follows:

Look at your checklists. You will be rating my response to the receiver. Do I give an example of what receiver is capable of doing? Do I respond on the basis my feelings? Do I misinterpret what the receiver said? Do I respond to what I expect of the receiver? Check the rating that best fits my response.

When the receiver reacts to my response, evaluate his/her reaction to it. Did he/she continue to discuss the same subject, go off the subject, go deeper into it, express new ideas, new confidence, or more involvement? Check one or more of the appropriate ratings.

TRAINER MODEL
VOLUNTEER (RECEIVER). "I really have a tough time with math."

TRAINER (LEADER). "The work you've done today shows you can do it. Try a little harder."

VOLUNTEER (RECEIVER). "I guess I did OK today. So, I should be able to get it sometime."

After participants complete their checklists, lead a large group discussion focusing on what basis the leader responded and what type of reaction the receiver gave. Try to reach an agreement. Elicit the trainees' own encouraging responses to the same situation. Suggest that they use their own open-ended questions.

Distribute Encouraging Responses Checklists and Statement Sheets to all participants and instruct them to break into groups of three. Ask the groups to role play and rate each other. Hold a large group discussion after role play.

Outcome Indicators
1. All trainees should assume three roles.

2. The small group discussion after each role play should continue for the entire two minutes.

3. Trainer should observe for cues indicating members' level of involvement or understanding.

4. Small and large group discussions should focus on the difficulty encountered in the process of helping others to see their own potential. The differences between positive feedback based on fact and positive feedback based on opinion should be discussed.

5. Checklists should reflect a majority of effective responses and positive reactions.

Encouraging Responses Checklist

Leader _____   Observer_____

Receiver _____   Date_____

Goal
• To practice using responses that make others aware of their potential to succeed.

Directions
Stating someone's potential to solve a problem or face a challenge often boosts confidence. It is important that your examples of the person's potential be based on real evidence from the person's past. Try to simulate authentic, confidence boosting, encouraging responses. Switch roles.

Observers record the types of encouraging responses given by leaders. When the receivers react to the encouragement, the quality of their reaction should be checked on the appropriate lines.

TYPES OF ENCOURAGING RESPONSES GIVEN BY LEADER

More Effective

_____What the receiver is capable of doing

_____Leader's gut level reaction to feelings

_____Leader's expectations of the receiver

Less Effective

_____Leader's misunderstanding of receiver's statement

_____A topic which is off the track

Page 2 - Encouraging Responses Checklist

REACTION TO LEADER'S ENCOURAGEMENT

More Effective

_____On the same subject

_____Expressed deeper understanding of the situation

_____Expressed new confidence

_____Showed more involvement

Less Effective

_____Off the subject

_____Expressed confusion

_____Expressed self-doubt

_____Ran away from the problem

Encouraging Responses Statement Sheet

Name_____   Date_____

Goal
• To practice using responses that make others aware of their potential to succeed.

Directions
Use these statements as conversation starters.

1. "I tried to do my grammar homework, but I just can't get it."

2. "I never get anybody to go out with me. Everyone I ask turns me down."

3. "Sometimes I think everybody is down on me. I just can't seem to get along with anyone."

Session 14:
Questioning Skills

Time
Thirty minutes (five minutes for Trainer Model, five minutes for large group discussion, one minute for role play, two minutes per small group discussion, ten minutes for large group discussion.)

Goal
• To enable the trainees to practice using questions to gather data and clarify statements made by others.

Materials
Questioning Skills Checklists, Questioning Skills Statement Sheets, and pencils.

Process
Solicit a volunteer to play the part of a receiver. Trainer introduces the exercise as follows:

This exercise gives you practice in asking questions to get more information or to clarify statements made by others. Since you will be also asking questions of your teachers, we have included the teacher role in your practice role play.

Trainer distributes Questioning Skills Checklists to the group and continues:

This is a dialogue in which questions are used to get more information about a receiver's situation. I will play the leader and my partner will play the receiver. Take a look at your checklists. In the top section, rate my question on one or more of the categories. For example, I could ask an open-ended question, such as "Where do you live?" and also be fact oriented.

Use page 2 of the Questioning Skill Checklist to rate the receiver's reaction to my question. Was I able to get an answer? Did the answer lead naturally to another question?

Wait till I respond to my partner's reaction before rating my question.

TRAINER MODEL
VOLUNTEER (RECEIVER). "My mother won't let me see him because she thinks he's too old for me."

TRAINER (LEADER). "Do you think you know why you mother thinks age should stop you from seeing him?"

VOLUNTEER (RECEIVER). "Well, I can't understand why his age has anything to do with it. I think there are other reasons."

TRAINER (LEADER). "Well, what could they be?"

Distribute three Questioning Skills Checklists and three Questioning Skills Statement Sheets to participants and instruct them to break into groups of three and follow the same procedures as in previous exercises. Role play and rate each other.

After participants complete the checklists, lead a large group discussion underscoring how the trainer used an open-ended question and received a reaction which got more exploration. Ask what questions the others would pose to the same statement.

Outcome Indicators
1. All group members should assume three roles.

2. The small group discussion after each role play should continue for the entire two minutes.

3. Trainers should observe cues indicating trainees' levels of involvement and understanding.

4. Small group discussions should focus on items included in the checklist. The trainees should discuss goals of the questions. In addition, the receivers' reactions to the question should be identified and explored in terms of their effectiveness.

5. Completed checklists should show at least half the leader's questions to have generated productive reactions.

6. Large group discussions should focus on alternate type of questions and reactions by receivers.

7. The dangers of cross-examination of the receivers or teachers should also be explored.

Questioning Skills Checklist

Leader _____   Observer_____

Receiver _____   Date_____

Goal
• To practice asking questions to get information and improve understanding.

Directions
You'll find that sometimes lack of information can lead to major misunderstandings in communication. Use this opportunity to improve your information gathering skills through well-formed, nonthreatening questions.

Observer should check the types of questions asked by leaders. In addition, observer should check the types of receiver responses to the questions.

TYPES OF QUESTIONS ASKED BY THE LEADER

More Effective

_____Open-ended question

Less Effective

_____Yes-no question

Either Effective or Ineffective

_____Feeling question

_____Asking for explanation

_____Fact oriented (what, which, where)

_____Process oriented (how)

_____Time oriented (when)

Page 2 - Questioning Skills Checklist

RECEIVER'S RESPONSES TO LEADER'S QUESTIONS

More Effective

_____Receiver calms down

_____Receiver makes a commitment to do something about problem

_____Receiver see that his/her first statement was unrealistic

_____Receiver expresses new learning or exploration

Less Effective

_____Receiver gets upset

_____Receiver avoids problem

_____Receiver continues unrealistic line of reasoning

_____Receiver gives yes or no answer

_____Receiver avoids answering

Questioning Skills Statement Sheet

Name_____   Date_____

Goal
• To practice asking questions to get information and improve understanding.

Directions
Use these statements as conversation starters.

1. (RECEIVER). "I can't talk to John. He and I live in two different worlds because whenever I tell him how I feel about things, he gets angry or calls me a wimp."

2. (RECEIVER). "I really want to go to vocational school, but I'm afraid I'll lose my friends if I'm out of regular school."

3. (TEACHER). "John has been talking a lot in class lately. He seems to get fidgety."

Session 15:
Caring Responses

Time
Thirty minutes (five minutes for Trainer Model, five minutes for large group discussion, one minute for role play, two minutes for small group discussions, ten minutes for large group discussion).

Goal
• To provide trainees with practice responding with concern, empathy, and involvement. This skill promotes the development of trust between the leader and receiver.

Materials
Caring Responses Checklists, Caring Responses Statement Sheets, and pencils.

Process
Solicit a volunteer to play a receiver in a role play. Trainer introduces the exercise as follows:

This is an exercise to let you practice some effective ways to show your concern and involvement in another's life situation. Showing authentic concern can often improve understanding. We will demonstrate the skill together.

Trainer distributes Caring Responses Checklists to group and continues:

Look at your checklist. You are asked to rate the kind of caring response used by the leader and receiver's reaction to the response. As we role play this dialogue, check off the kind of caring response I use to show concern. Then check off the type of reaction my partner offers to the caring response.

TRAINER MODEL
VOLUNTEER (RECEIVER). "I tried to do my homework, but the phone rang, and I got involved in a long conversation with Judy. The next day when the teacher called on me in class, I had no idea what to say."

TRAINER (LEADER). "I can remember how embarrassed I was when that happened to me."

VOLUNTEER (RECEIVER). "You mean to say, you've been caught unprepared?"

After the participants complete their checklists, discuss what type of response the receiver made and compare the participants' perceptions of it. Also compare the their perceptions of the receiver's reaction. Discuss the receiver's actual reaction and other alternatives.

Distribute Caring Responses Checklists and Statement Sheets. Ask the trainees to break into groups of three and follow the same procedure as in the previous exercise. After the role plays and small group discussions, hold a large group discussion.

Outcome Indicators
1. The discussion of the Trainer Model should generate rationale for using caring responses.

2. All group trainees should assume all three roles.

3. Trainers should observe cues indicating trainees' high level of involvement.

4. Small group discussions should focus on items included on the checklist. Trainees should be discussing effective ways to show concern and alternate ways to cope with positive and negative receiver reactions.

5. Completed checklists should show at least half the caring responses to be effective.

6. Large group discussion should address the difficulties in giving caring responses and the range of reactions to such responses. Appropriate conditions for the use of caring responses should be identified.

Caring Responses Checklist

Leader _____   Observer_____

Receiver _____   Date_____

Goal
• To practice making accurate caring responses.

Directions
The observer should use this checklist to indicate the types of caring responses made by leaders. In addition, the observer should record the types of reactions made by receivers.

TYPES OF CARING RESPONSES GIVEN BY THE LEADER

More Effective

_____States how leader feels about the receiver's situation

_____Agrees with situation

_____Describes leader's reaction to the way receiver dealt with situation

_____Leader shares own experience

Less Effective

_____Leader responds in an automatic or phony way

_____Makes a general statement not really related to receiver's situation

RECEIVER'S REACTION STATEMENT SHOWS

_____Surprise

_____Relief

_____Rejection of Leader

_____Clinging dependency

Caring Responses Statement Sheet

Name_____   Date_____

Goal
• To practice making accurate caring responses.

Directions
Use these statements as conversation starters.

1. "I wish my mother would get off my back. She always gives me the third degree when I want to go out. She's always on my case."

2. "My friend was injured in the game yesterday. They took him to the hospital and the doctor isn't sure if he'll be able to play again this year."

3. "My parents just grounded me for one month because of my lame report card."

Permission to reprint for classroom use. Copyright © 1992. V. Alex Kehayan, *Partners for Change* (Program Guide). Jalmar Press: Rolling Hills Estates, CA.

Session 16:
Discrepancy Statements

Time
Thirty minutes (same divisions as in previous exercises)

Goal
• To enable trainees to practice giving feedback by pointing out discrepancies between thoughts and actions, between desires and behavior, and between behavior perceived by self and by others. Confronting such discrepancies serves to make others aware of their own self-defeating behavior.

Materials
Discrepancy Statement Checklists, Discrepancy Statement Sheets, and pencils.

Process
Solicit volunteer for role play. Introduce the exercise as follows:

This is an exercise designed to give you practice in providing honest feedback to teachers and students concerning the differences between their needs and their actions. Sometimes people want to be accepted, but their behavior causes rejection by others.

Since this technique may be valuable in your interactions with teachers, as well as students, you will have a chance to role play teachers' statements as well as students' statements.

Distribute Discrepancy Statement Checklists to students and continue as follows:

As my partner and I present this role play, use the checklist to rate us. My partner will play the receiver, and I will play the leader. Rate the way I confront the receiver. Do I show that his/her actions go in two different directions? Do I compare my attitude toward the situation with the receiver's? Do I tell the receiver that what he/she does will not enable him/her to get what he/she wants or believes in? Rate the receiver's reaction to my response. Do you see surprise, anger, arguing, or guilt? Here is a dialogue where I confront the receiver to point out the difference.

TRAINER MODEL
TRAINER (LEADER). "You're saying that you wanted to pass, but you also say that you only studied five minutes."

VOLUNTEER (RECEIVER). "I know I could have studied more, but my friend came over and we got involved in playing pool."

TRAINER (LEADER). "It seems as though you want to see your friends and still get good grades. Is there a way you could do both?"

After the participants have completed their checklists, lead a large group discussion comparing their confrontations and others' reactions to it. Ask if the style was helpful and why. Elicit other responses and possible reactions.

Distribute Discrepancy Statement Sheets and ask the trainees to break into groups of three and play the parts of teacher, leader, receiver, and observer. After role plays and small group discussions, hold a large group discussion.

Outcome Indicators
1. The discussion of the Trainer Model should show that trainees understand why the trainer confronted the receiver. The checklists should indicate that over half the trainees correctly identified the type of confrontation (related to an action that does not lead to a desired outcome). In addition, one-half the participants should have correctly identified receiver's reaction.

2. Group members should have assumed roles as teacher, receiver, leader, and observer.

3. Trainers should observe cues indicating trainees' high level of involvement.

4. Small group discussions should focus on checklist items. The discussions should also focus on effective and ineffective uses of confrontation, and the time to confront and not to confront.

5. Completed checklists should show at least half the confrontation responses to be effective.

6. Large group discussion should focus on trainees' difficulties in using confrontation and the range of reactions to it. Appropriate conditions for the use of confrontation should be identified by the trainees.

Discrepancy Statement Checklist

Leader _____   Observer _____

Receiver _____   Date _____

Goal
• To practice using discrepancy statements effectively.

Directions
This skill allows you to assist someone in learning about behavior which undermines his or her goals. It also helps you to recognize and point out inconsistencies and discrepancies.

The observer should use this sheet to check the leader's approaches to pointing out discrepancies. In addition, the observer should record the reaction of the receiver to the confrontation.

LEADER POINTS OUT

_____Receiver uses two conflicting actions

_____Receiver's attitudes are different from leader's

_____Receiver's behavior defeats personal goals

_____Receiver should decide what is most important

_____Receiver's behavior is bad, good, or untouched

RECEIVER'S REACTION TO CONFRONTATION

_____Shows surprise

_____Avoids reacting or changes subject

_____Expresses anger

_____Argues

_____Shows guilt by putting himself/herself down

_____Makes excuses

Discrepancy Statement Sheet

Name_____   Date_____

Goal
• To practice using discrepancy statements effectively.

Directions
Use these statements as conversation starters.

1. (TEACHER). "I really wanted to meet with you last Thursday, but I got tied up in a faculty room."

2. (RECEIVER). "I know I should study, but it's a real pain."

3. (RECEIVER). "I really enjoy teasing my best friend, Jane. She's such a sucker for a joke."

Session 17:
Trainee Assignment

Time
Thirty minutes

Goal
• To practice all conscious communication skills.

Materials
Combining Your Skills Checklists, pencils, and video equipment (if available).

Process
Distribute Combining Your Skills Checklists and ask trainees to get together in groups of three at home or after school before the next training session. Request that they role play and rate each other's responses in improvised discussions. If video or audio recorders are available, ask them to tape the discussions and bring them to the next session for a group critique.

Outcome Indicator
1. Reports and/or video replays show evidence of skills utilized effectively.

Combining Your Skills Checklist

Leader _____   Observer_____

Receiver _____   Date_____

Goal
• To practice Conscious Communication Skills.

Directions
Get together in groups of three at home or after school and use the checklist to practice. Role play and rate each other's responses in improvised discussions.

If camcorders or audio recorders are available, tape the discussions and bring them to the next session for a group critique.

As you observe the two people talking, check the following items to describe how you would rate the behavior of the leaders.

COMMUNICATION SKILLS

Body Language

_____Listens actively

_____Shows discomfort

Verbal Skills

_____Paraphrases messages accurately

_____Expresses continuing responses (Oh, Uh-huh)

_____Gives caring responses

_____Points out discrepancies

_____Uses encouraging responses

_____Asks questions

_____Restates receiver's feelings accurately

Page 2 - Combining Your Skills Checklist

COMMUNICATION BARRIERS

_____Telling

_____Warning

_____Preaching

_____Providing standardized solutions or cheap advice

_____Convincing

_____Labeling or discrediting

_____Interpreting

_____Giving glib predictions

_____Cross-examining

_____Not listening

_____Interrupting

Session 18: Transformative Communication Skills

Time
Twenty minutes

Goals
• To define transformative communication and differentiate it from conscious communication.

• To define minimal cues of internal states and sensory channels used to process information.

• To identify some techniques used to initiate unconscious, indirect communication in order to transform behavior.

Materials
Transformative Communication Skills Sheets and pencils.

Process
Trainer distributes sheets and discusses the contents thoroughly, providing examples and eliciting questions and dialogue from the group.

Outcome Indicator
1. Group should ask questions about these novel concepts and discuss their implications.

Transformative Communication Skills Sheet

Name_____   Date_____

1. Always observe minimal cues to determine how their changes reflect positive or negative internal states. Minimal cues include changes in:

- Facial expressions
- Muscle tone
- Skin color
- Eye movements
- Posture
- Gestures
- Breathing rate
- Location of breathing
- Rate of speech
- Volume of speech
- Body alignment (symmetrical or asymetrical).

Also observe these minimal cues carefully as you communicate with another person. The subject of conversation and your responses will effect changes in these minimal cues. They can be of great value to you in establishing and maintaining rapport.

Often you can tell what state a person is headed towards and lead him/her away from a potentially negative state and into a positive one.

2. Observe universal eye movements to provide you with valuable information about another person's dominant sensory channel used to process information. The sensory channels include:

- Visual
- Kinesthetic (feelings)
- Auditory (sounds)
- Gustatory/olfactory (taste and smell).

By observing eye patterns, you may determine the way a person is thinking: whether she/he uses sounds first to spur pictures and then feelings, or whether he/she has feelings about what is said and then later makes pictures and goes into an internal dialogue. Memorize and use your eye accessing cue charts to assist you in developing more rapport.

3. Use matching and pacing skills to communicate with a person's unconscious by using personalized biofeedback. Finely tune your own responses to pace and match the other person's:

- Breathing rate
- Pulse rate
- Tonal qualities
- Speech rate
- Gestures
- Postures

Page 2 - Transformative Communication Skills Sheet

• Skin color
• Language reflecting sensory channels.

4. After matching and pacing, you may introduce a positive change or shift of focus to initiate achievement of a person's personal goal. This assumes that you know where the other person wants to go. Using key words which match a person's eye accessing cues and then gradually changing channels can help shift the focus. For example you may want to use words such as, "Things look good, appear very clear, and seem sunny."

You might want to make a change to the kinesthetic (feeling) mode to guide a person into a more authentic feeling state. For example, use such words as, "You seem to grasp this so well that it looks like you have a firm grip on it." By leading a person into a more kinesthetic mode, you can help him/her gain access to a feeling state.

You may also lead a person who is very excited into a calm state by bringing your rate of speech up to his/hers in an accelerated way and then gradually shifting the speed to a slower rate and lower tone to help him/her calm down. This process of auditory leading must unfold quite slowly.

You may also want to prepare a person for the future by suggesting he/she imagine a new situation in which he/she can use a skill which is currently operating. For example, when someone is solving an equation quite well in front of you, you might want to say, "And you can use the same step-by-step skills that you have now on tomorrow's algebra test."

5. Negative commands can be very helpful in dealing with someone who tends to be oppositional. There are a lot of people who take great pleasure in contradicting and questioning whatever you say. When trying to assist someone who is oppositional, you may want to preface your remarks negatively. The stubborn person who needs to change his antagonistic behavior might respond well to a statement such as, "You don't want to control your outburst until you're ready." Another example would be a remark to someone who wishes to lose weight, "Don't stop eating until you're ready to be very thin."

The negative command principle can have disastrous impact if used in the wrong way. For example, using negative commands to stop behavior can only reinforce it. When someone is talking too loud you might want them to quiet down and say, "Don't talk so loud." They will have difficulty stopping because the real message is, "Talk loud." Saying "Be quiet" is much more useful.

6. Use indirect analogies, called "quotes," to express a potentially threatening message. Examples include, "There are a lot of turkeys out there who constantly interrupt you when you talk." or, "Have you ever met someone who just tries too hard?" Such indirect messages, when framed in another context, and removed from the current situation, can be useful in actually illustrating a point that you want your receiver to learn.

7. Metaphor is another indirect communication technique that might assist someone in achieving positive goals that are attainable and unprovocative.

Page 3 - Transformative Communication Skills Sheet

Remember that metaphors must relate to the person's life. They can be a disguised message using things like animals or movie scripts to illustrate ways in which people make positive changes. Always remember to build the positive solutions upon actual personal competence rather than magical occurrences. See examples in Session 24.

Introducing magic into metaphors can lead the person to an assumption that fate or destiny can substitute for personal motivation and effort. Avoid magical endings. Make sure to build into your metaphor characters who correspond to actual significant figures in your person's life.

Session 19:
Minimal Cues

Time
Ten minutes

Goal
• To demonstrate how minimal cues reflect people's inner state of consciousness.

Materials
Minimal Cues Sheets.

Process
Trainer instructs the group on the various behavioral manifestations of internal states. Such internal states may be described as fear, anger, joy, relaxation, etc. Trainer should review the subtle facial expressions, body postures, and speeds of movement which indicate a variety of internal states.

To provide a demonstration, the trainer requests one of the trainees to come to the front of room,

"Go inside himself or herself," and actually relive an experience from the past, feeling it, seeing it, hearing it, and sensing it.

As the trainee accesses the internal state, the trainer requests the audience to identify some subtle minimal cues listed on the Minimal Cues sheet.

In a second demonstration, another trainee should come to the front of the room and run through a demonstration of an internal state. Then have the other participants close their eyes, while the demonstrator makes one subtle change, such as a position of foot or hand or head tilt. Then the trainer should ask the trainees to identify the change between state one and state two.

Outcome Indicator
1. Trainees should be able to identify the manifestation of the various minimal cues such as breathing rate and location posture, head tilt, facial expressions, pulse rate, color changes, etc.

Minimal Cues Sheet

Name_____   Date_____

Goal
• To identify minimal cue changes.

Directions
Use this sheet to help you identify the subtle verbal and nonverbal minimal cues that go with each internal state: positive, negative and neutral. Your trainer will guide you through this exercise.

Breathing	**Face**
rate	lips
high	muscle tension
low	color change
deep	twitches
shallow	eye blinks
Posture	**Pulse**
bent	rate
rigid	veins bulging
head tilt	crossed legs
Speech	**Gestures**
rate	arms
pitch	legs
volume	hands
tone	movement speed

Session 20: Identification of Internal States

Time
Twenty minutes

Goal
• To learn to recognize changes in three internal states.

Materials
None.

Process
Trainer instructs the group to break up into groups of three. Each group assigns letters to each member (A,B,C). Three trials will be given.

Trainer requests person A to go into himself/herself and relive a positive experience (state one) by thinking, feeling, seeing, and hearing it. Observers identify the minimal cues silently.

Then after about thirty seconds, trainer asks person A to come back out of himself/herself and introduces a "breaker state." For example: "Picture yourself floating on a tranquil river." "Picture yourself sitting in a movie theatre watching a blank screen."

Trainer requests person A to go back into himself/herself and see, feel, and hear a neutral experience (state two) while observers B and C identify the minimal cues of that state. Trainer introduces another breaker state.

Trainer requests person A to relive a negative experience (state three) while observers B and C observe and identify minimal cues.

Trainer requests person A to go back into himself or herself and relive either one of the three states: positive, neutral, or negative. This occurs for about twenty seconds, while B and C observe and then are requested to put up one, two, or three fingers, to identify the state. Person A then assesses the accuracy of observer's selections.

Then the trainer initiates another breaker state and asks person A to go back into himself or herself and relive state one of the previous states while observers watch for minimal cues. In about twenty seconds, trainer requests observers B and C to identify which state was accessed by raising one, two, or three fingers. Repeat for a third time with A accessing one of the previous states.

This cycle is repeated until observers accurately identify A's internal state. Then the trainer requests groups to identify and discuss the cues and states. Finally, trainer requests groups to switch roles until all three members have participated as observers.

Outcome Indicator
1. When both observers in each of the groups accurately recognize and identify the internal states, the criteria have been achieved.

Session 21:
Universal Eye Movements

Time
Thirty minutes

Goal
• To introduce the eye positions which signify how information is accessed through the left and right brain hemispheres.

Materials
Eye Accessing Cues Sheets and Matching Predicates Sheets.

Process
Trainer distributes and reviews the Eye Accessing Cues Sheets and discusses how the various positions signal each information access mode used by individuals.

Trainer calls someone to the front of the room and requests audience to observe eye movements while he or she asks a series of sensory-based questions. Participants then observe the positions of the eyes and how they shift. Assuming the volunteer is right handed, the eye patterns should follow the Chart on the Eye Accessing Cues Sheet.

Trainer asks trainees to form groups of three and practice asking questions of members while observing eye movements.

Trainer introduces the concept of using predicates to match the various styles of accessing information: auditory, visual, or kinesthetic. Trainer reviews the types of verbal predicates used in signifying a person's dominant mode of accessing information.

For example, words such as look, see, visualize, focus, watch, horizon, etc. signify the visual mode of accessing. Trainer then passes out the Matching Predicate Sheet to the group to review the process.

Trainer requests groups to form pairs and hold conversations in which partners take turns matching predicates, using their Matching Predicate Sheets.

Outcome Indicators
1. In large group discussion, trainees should report identifying eye movements with 70% degree of accuracy.

2. Trainees should also report abilities to match predicates.

Eye Accessing Cues Sheet

Name_____   Date_____

Goal
• To recognize eye accessing cues accurately

Directions
The eye positions tell much about the way we think with our senses and which senses we choose to use most frequently. Use this sheet to identify which senses your partner is using to process information.

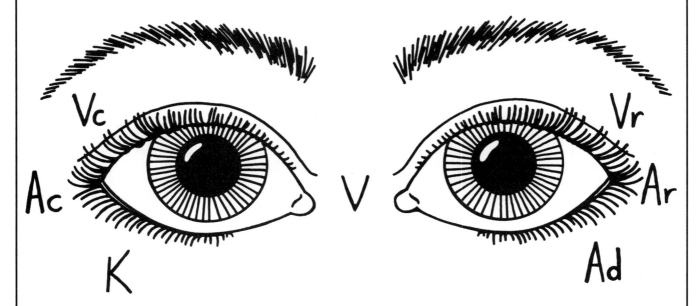

FACING THE PERSON

Vc- Visually Created: Making images of things never seen before or seeing things differently than before. "What would you look like with green hair?"

Ac- Auditorily Created: Hearing new sounds. "Imagine a bird barking like a dog."

K- Kinesthetic: Feelings emotions, having moods, touch, muscle movement. "Are you warm?"

Vr- Visually Remembered: Seeing images from past. "What is your favorite movie?" "Remember your brother's face."

Ar- Auditorily Remembered: Sounds heard before. "Can you name your favorite song?"

Ad- Auditory Dialogue: Talking to yourself. "Now stay calm."

V- Visually constructed or Remembered: Blank stare, eyes straight.

Matching Predicates Sheet

Name_____   Date_____

Goal
• To match predicates.

Directions
Use this sheet to give you some ideas about which words to use in responding to your partners and matching their sensory-based processing channels.

VISUAL (V)
• Hazy outlook
• Focus on the problem
• Clear up
• Colorful ideas
• Foresee problems
• New horizons
• Looks clear
• Scene
• Perceive
• Imagine positive outlook
• Notice
• Appear
• Watch
• Enlighten
• Sparkle
• Scope
• Sunny
• Cloudy

AUDITORY (A)
• Keep in tune
• Quiet man
• Thrash metal
• Loud mouth
• Sounds good
• Discuss
• Say
• Rings a bell
• Earful
• Scream
• Mention
• Talk
• Vocal
• Hear
• Articulate
• Resonant
• Verbalize
• Raucous crowd
• Rowdy
• Disquieting

KINESTHETIC (K)
• Feel changed
• Stumble upon it
• Trash it
• Grasp it
• Warming my heart
• Drill
• Soft
• Flow
• Stress
• Hold on
• Soft
• High pressure
• Gripping
• Firm
• Handle
• Callous
• Solid
• Heart-warming
• Rigid
• Uptight
• Chill out

OLFACTORY (O)
• Bitter pill
• Bad taste
• Sanguine
• That stinks
• Sweet smell
• Sour puss
• Delicious
• Foul
• Nauseous
• Unsavory
• Revolting
• Sugary
• Bitter sweet
• Yummy
• Delectable
• Mellow out
• Acrid

Session 22:
Demonstration of Leading

Time
Ten minutes

Goal
• To demonstrate how matching then changing one's body posture, rate of speech, tonality, gestures, and facial expressions will change another person's mood.

Materials
None.

Process
Trainer asks a member of the group to come up to the front of the room and think of two stories: one about a negative experience, and another about a positive experience. As the subject thinks of each experience, trainer asks two trainees to stand on either side of the individual.

Person A, on the left of the subject, is requested to carefully observe all the auditory signals such as voice tone, loudness, pitch, variation in tones, and speed of speech.

Person B, on the right of the subject, is asked to observe all the visual cues such as posture, gestures, head tilt, facial expression, position of feet and hands, and speed of movements.

Trainer privately instructs students A and B that they are to gradually shift the subject back toward previous positive state during the positive story.

Subject is then asked to tell the story about the negative experience for about two minutes. Then subject is asked to tell about the positive story for about two minutes.

Finally the subject is asked to retell the negative story, while person A waits for ten seconds, before introducing verbal suggestions to match the original tonality, rate of speech, and other auditory features of the positive story.

At the same time, person B asks the subject to move gradually so that body posture, gestures, facial expressions, and movement gestures the positive signals in the positive story.

Outcome Indicators
1. The subject will experience an inability to remain in the negative state as students A and B adjust auditory and visual cues to the positive experience.

2. Subject's laughter will indicate return to the positive state. This exercise should illustrate the inability to keep a negative mood while showing positive external cues. Subject should test the change by attempting to maintain a negative state while taking on the positive cues.

Session 23:
Matching, Pacing, and Leading

Time
Three minutes

Goal
• To demonstrate the way a person's negative or angry mood can be shifted by his or her peer leader. Pacing and matching posture, voice, and minimal cues can gradually shift a person to a more positive, upbeat, functional state.

Materials
Matching, Pacing, and Leading Sheets.

Process
Trainer demonstrates this process through a role play whereby trainer paces, matches, and leads a trainee from an angry state to a calm state.

Trainee distributes Pacing, Matching, and Leading Sheets and reviews concepts with group.

Trainer then requests the group to divide into pairs, assign letters A and B, and practice matching, pacing, and leading. First person A matches B during a two minute conversation, then person A and B switch roles.

Outcome Indicator
1. Participants should be able to articulate what minimal cues were matched, paced, and changed through this five minute process.

Matching, Pacing, and Leading Sheet

Name_____   Date_____

Goal
• To demonstrate the way a person's negative or angry mood can be changed by his or her peer leader. Pacing and matching posture, voice, and minimal cues can gradually shift a person to a more positive, upbeat, functional state.

MATCHING AND PACING

Directions
In pacing these minimal cues, one uses personalized biofeedback to establish empathic rapport with the unconscious parts of another human being's activity level.

• Breathing Rate
• Pulse Rate
• Voice Tones
• Voice Speed

• Gestures
• Posture
• Sensory based language (auditory, visual, kinesthetic, or digital)
• Eye blinking

LEADING

Directions
After matching, introduce changes or shifts of focus to initiate achievement of personal goals. This assumes that you know where the person wants to go.

Session 24:
Metaphor Generator

Time
Forty-five minutes

Goal
To review and integrate principles and skills of metaphor making.

Materials
Metaphor Principles Sheets and Metaphor Examples.

Process
Review metaphor principles by reading them aloud and going over the example stories. Find questions and discuss the procedure.

Divide trainees into groups of three, assigning them the following tasks on a rotating basis. Members of each triad are to assume roles as receiver, leader, and observer. The receiver is to present a small summary of his life and family, highlighting a particular area of gridlock, such as poor grades, procrastination, social risk, test anxiety, etc. The leader takes notes while the receiving student describes profile.

The peer leader then develops a metaphor, the goal of which is to assist the student in initiating a positive change based on the personal gridlock presented in his/her profile. Allow five minutes. The metaphor should include the basic allegorical components.

After the peer leader has developed the story, perhaps jotting down some notes, the peer leader should deliver the metaphor, using the stacking technique, while the observer checks to see that all the skills and procedures are followed. After the metaphor is delivered, observer provides feedback based on the Metaphor Principles Sheet.

Each metaphor generator sequence should last approximately fifteen minutes including feedback. All members of the triad should assume each role.

Outcome Indicators
1. Three accurate metaphors should be produced by each group.

2. Written feedback based on Metaphor Principles Sheet should be provided to each peer leader who indicates corrections on the metaphor notes.

Metaphor Principles Sheet

Name_____   Date_____

Goal
• To practice creating appropriate metaphors and delivering them to partners to accomplish their goals.

Directions
Use the principles below to develop an appropriate change-oriented metaphor for your partner. Interview your partner to get a personal profile. Ask about the particular hurdle facing your partner.

Then develop a metaphor that uses the following principles to match the person's life situation and promote personal change drawn from personal resources.

There are two basic types of embedded metaphors:

NEGATIVE. a story that describes severe consequences of a behavior pattern that matches the life patterns and major challenges experienced by the student. (See "Is a Lie Worth It?".)

POSITIVE. a story that represents problems, patterns, and conflicts of the student but results in a solution. The situations, characters, and patterns correspond to the student's own life. ("See Better Late Than Never" and "First Things First.")

Some principles to follow:

1. Make the metaphor as indirect as possible. Use animal stories with kids when possible. With adults, disguise the characters sufficiently so as not to make them too obvious.

2. Build in as many symbolic characters as possible, and be sure to make the theme of the problem symbolize the receiving student's real life.

3. Always make the solution or resolution of the conflict evolve from the character's personal resources even when supported or enlightened by others. Avoid "magic" solutions.

Page 2 - Metaphor Principles Sheet

4. When possible, use the technique of "stacking" to enable the student to initiate an internal search. This search enables the student to review his/her previous experience to find an event which parallels the current metaphor. It is an inward focus. When stacking, extend the beginning of the story to include lots of information.

Stacking usually precedes and concludes a metaphor. It can be a sensory overload such as the following: "I had a friend many years ago who used to live in New Jersey before he moved to Toronto, Canada, and he once told me a story about his friend whose father had an annoying habit of forgetting to...."; or "I don't know why I'm reminded of this story or whether you will find it important enough to remember, but if it's not, then you may choose to forget it. If it is important, then you can remember to remember it. It is up to you."

5. Always be careful to imply the story is fiction unless you are actually describing authentic events. Never misrepresent fiction as fact. It will destroy the trust.

6. Use a breaker state at the end of the metaphor to get the person out of the state of mind and into a new inner state. You can do this by changing the subject and talking about another experience.

Metaphor Examples

Name_____   Date_____

Negative Metaphor: Is a Lie Worth It?

BACKGROUND

This metaphor responds to the needs of a middle school child who lies excessively to avoid punishment from her mother. She has taken this lying behavior into the school and has recently engaged in some very inauthentic acts such as stealing the teacher edition of an English book and using it to do her homework and lying to friends and counselors about her grades in order to avoid disgrace.

STORY

I am reminded of a story about my cousin named Pat who goes to school in Ohio and had the opportunity to get together with me for the holidays and told a story about a friend who she was close to in her class. This was someone that she knew a long, long time ago.

Now, I don't know why I'm telling this story, but I'm just reminded of it, and the story goes like this: Pat had this friend and she and her friend were in a history class together and they were supposed to do a project for history and the project was to be done in partners. Now Pat's friend, Connie, said that she'd be willing to work with Pat on the project as her partner, but behind Pat's back, Connie went to the teacher of the history class and told her that she would be doing the project with another friend.

When Pat found out, she was very upset because Connie had lied to the teacher and also lied to my cousin. The way that Pat reacted was to withdraw from Connie and just treat her like any other kid in the school. Rather than sharing secrets and spending lots of time together, the relationship changed from closeness to just simply one of saying, "Hello." In the fall, Connie met an older cheerleader who gradually gained her trust, accepted the lies, and told her that she didn't have to be honest until she was ready to trust. After their friendship developed, Connie no longer had to be dishonest.

Positive Metaphor: Better Late Than Never

BACKGROUND

This metaphor is delivered to a seventh grade girl doing poorly in school and putting too much emphasis on social life. She tends to disregard her homework and expects the assignments to "take care of themselves." Her best friend is an honor student going into higher classes next year. This seventh grader wants to model her friend and follow the same schedule. Unfortunately, she is prevented from doing that by her poor performance, and, by necessity, must enter the basic skills courses. She is disappointed. The seventh grader loves animals.

The metaphor is designed to raise her awareness that she does have personal resources and is getting more tense by using fantasy rather than constructive action. A stacking technique is used to introduce the metaphor and create a confusion state, necessary to institute an internal search.

Page 2 - Metaphor Examples

STORY
I am reminded about a story about dolphins. Have you ever been to Sea World? I hear it's a fun place. Anyway let me tell a story about these dolphins at Sea World. Now most dolphins at Sea World are intelligent except for this one who was acting rather slow and isolated from the rest. The trainer figured that the problem was laziness and that this dolphin was not working up to his capacity. This dolphin watched while all the other dolphins were doing their training routines.

Things got so bad that the trainer had to take him out of the show because his behavior was so much slower than the others. Time passed, and the trainer decided to give this dolphin another chance. She let him go back into the show and during the next training trial, gave him a very easy trick to do which involved jumping up for a fish. Remarkably, this dolphin jumped and was rewarded with a fish which inspired him to jump higher on other trials.

It took him longer to master the difficult tricks that other dolphins could do. But in the long run, this dolphin eventually caught up and succeeded. Luckily, he was allowed to enter some of the real shows and earn the respect of his audiences.

I heard you went to the movies last weekend. So, tell me, how did you enjoy the movie?

Positive Metaphor: First Things First

BACKGROUND
This is a metaphor shared by a twelfth grade peer leader with a seventh grader at a middle school. The seventh grader was avoiding homework by letting other things get in the way. He was smart enough to do the work and perform up to grade level, but had been mildly depressed and felt somewhat turned off by the challenges of school work. The metaphor was an indirect technique used to bring some hope into his life.

STORY
You know what? I want to tell you a story. It is about a kid who's got this friend. And his friend has this problem and he goes to school somewhere, I think upstate. I can't remember where, but this friend of a friend of this boy has got a problem and so the story goes.

Once upon a time this eleventh grader was having some difficulty in school with some grades, and he was doing poorly in a few of his classes because he was neglecting to do his homework and study. He would go home after school, and he'd have a thousand things to do and let everything get in the way. One day he had this really big test that was to decide his grade for the marking period. He knew this and when he went home, he said, "Okay, Mom, you know I really don't know this, but I am going to study and I am going to pass the class. You have nothing to worry about."

She said, "Okay, fine. Do what you have to do, and I'll leave you alone."

This average teenager had other things to do. He decided go out to play basketball with his friend. Two hours later when he got home, it was already five o'clock. Now he wanted to rest for a little bit and he said, "I'll study as soon as I get a little rest." He sat down and turned on

Page 3 - Metaphor Examples

the TV. He found that his favorite show was on, so he watched it. "Now it was around six o'clock and time for dinner. He said, "Alright, after dinner, I'll start to study."

He ate dinner and got through with dinner around 7:15 and then relaxed a bit. He turned on the TV again and then found out that another one of his favorite shows was on. So he sat down and said, "Okay this is it, this is the final show. I'll study after this." The show ended at about 8:30, and then he remembered he had something really important to tell one of his friends.

He called him up and they got into this big conversation that lasted for about a half hour. Now it was 9 o'clock. He went to get out his books, and all of a sudden, the telephone rang. It was another friend of his and his friend said, "There is this really great movie playing down at the theater. Do you want to come with us? All the guys and the girls are going, and we'll have a really good time."

So he said, "I don't know, man. I have this big test to study for." He sat down and debated. He said, "Alright, forget it. I'll go to the movie. I'm sure I'll get by with the knowledge that I have." So he went to the movie, and he got home at eleven. He spent some time deciding whether or not he should still study for the test. He decided not to study for it, and he went to bed.

He woke up the next morning and went to school. He went to the class, took the test, and failed it. Now he was in big trouble, because this test produced the deciding grade for the current marking period. He didn't pass the test, and he failed for the marking period.

This continued on for quite a while until one day he sat down and he said to himself, "This is it, I'm a high school junior and I want to go to college. In order to get out of high school, I have to start studying and pass my classes."

One day his brother had a friend over who was in college, and they talked. His friend said that it was really important to get his values straight because college wasn't easy these days, and you really need good grades to get in.

This kid who was having problems finally realized that he had to get on the ball. So what he did was, instead of going out and doing all the other things that he really loved to do when he had tests or homework to do, he would limit his activities and concentrate more on studying and passing. He finally started to study. He limited his activities and didn't go out with the guys. He played ball only on weekends and cut down his TV watching and phone conversations.

Gradually he began to get a better and better feeling about himself. He passed the classes that he had to, and now he's going to college. He just turned himself around by limiting the things that he wanted to do and allowed more time for his studies which were so important in this time of life.

Session 25: Combining Your Skills

Time
Forty-five minutes (five minutes for each of three role plays, five minutes for each small group discussion, fifteen minutes for large group discussion).

Goals
• To provide practice integrating and using appropriate communication skills.

• To improvise on the interpersonal dialogues provided in the written statement sheets.

Materials
Combining Your Skills Checklists, Conversation Sheets, and pencils.

Process
Trainer introduces the exercise as follows:

This exercise is intended to give you practice using all the communication skills you have learned in actual situations. You will each be playing three roles: leader, receiver, and observer.

After you have role played the written conversation, feel free to improvise further dialogue as your observer rates your communication skills.

The trainer distributes Combining Your Skills Checklists and Conversation Sheets and signals when to begin and end each role play and when to discuss each experience within the groups. Trainer continues:

Enjoy yourselves. We will call the group together and get your reactions after you have played your roles.

Trainer initiates a large group discussion to promote feedback, sharing, and awareness of skills that need improvement.

Outcome Indicators
1. Trainers should observe cues indicating the trainees' high level of involvement.

2. Trainees should have assumed roles as leader, receiver, and observer.

3. Each pair should extend the conversations.

4. Small group discussion should be actively focused on the observer's feedback for each role play. Any discrepancies between rater's perceptions and those of leader and receivers should be discussed in small groups. Issues such as relating styles and context of responses should be brought up and resolved if possible.

5. The large group discussion should be open and free flowing. Trainers should observe that leaders used communication skills. Questions and follow-up should emerge from the group.

Combining Your Skills Checklist

Leader _____   Observer_____

Receiver_____   Date_____

Goal
• Use the checklist to rate your leader's communication skills.

Directions
As you observe the two people talking, check the following items to describe how you would rate the leader's skills.

COMMUNICATION SKILLS

Body Language
_____Listens actively

_____Shows discomfort

Verbal Skills
_____Paraphrases messages accurately

_____Makes continuing responses (Oh, Uh Huh)

_____Gives caring responses

_____Points out discrepancies

_____Gives encouraging responses

_____Questions

_____Restates receiver's feelings accurately

COMMUNICATION BARRIERS

_____Telling

_____Warning

_____Preaching

_____Providing standardized solutions or cheap advice

_____Convincing

_____Labeling or discrediting

Page 2 - Combining Your Skills Checklist

_____Interpreting

_____Giving glib predictions

_____Cross-examining

_____Not listening

_____Interrupting

Matching and Pacing
_____Rate of speech matched

_____Rate of movement matched

_____Sensory language matched

Leading
_____Rate of speech changed

_____Rate of movement changed

_____Sensory language changed

_____Uses future pacing

Imagery
_____Uses visualization to access positive problem-solving strategy

Metaphor
_____Uses positive

_____Uses negative

Conversation Sheet

Name_____   Date_____

Goal
• To practice your conscious and transformative communication skills.

Directions
Use these conversations as springboards to practice your conscious and transformative communication skills.

1. A girl has been trying to get this guy's attention. She doesn't know how.

LEADER. "How are you doing?"

RECEIVER. "Ah, things are getting to me. There's this guy that I like, but he doesn't know I exist."

LEADER. "Sounds pretty frustrating. Well, tell me more about him."

Questions:
a. How do you view this girl's problem?
b. Do you think you can solve it for her?
c. What is your objective in this situation?
d. How do you intend to pursue the situation further?

2. A boy "spaces out" during the session.

RECEIVER. "Were there War Lords at your school when you were there?"

LEADER. "No, not that I know of. What are they all about?"

RECEIVER. "Well, there's this group of guys that hang out in town. And now they got a few girls with them. They got this incredible initiation that you need to go through before you get it. So far, they've been moving around taking care of their own business."

LEADER. "What's their business?"

RECEIVER. "Well, if they need more money, sometimes they grab you and rip you off."

LEADER. "That sounds pretty scary. Who got hit lately?"

RECEIVER. "A lot of people. Some of them are my friends."

LEADER. "Have they ever threatened you?"

RECEIVER. "No." (At that point the boy looks away from you as though he has drifted into a fantasy.)

Page 2 - Conversation Sheet

Questions:
a. What could be going on in this kid's mind that's making him disconnect?
b. Do you think he might be frightened of this gang?
c. If you did think he was scared, how would you approach the situation?
d. What kind of things might you draw out of this kid in order to help him solve his problem (if he is fearful of his own safety)?

3. The boy won't open up.

LEADER. "How was your weekend?"

RECEIVER. (hesitates) "Okay, as usual."

LEADER. "Well what did you do?"

RECEIVER: "I played some football."

LEADER. "Oh you like football?"

RECEIVER. "Yeah".

LEADER. "So you're into football."

Questions:
a. Where do you go from here?
b. How might you get this boy to begin to open up?

Session 26:
Improvisations

Time
Thirty minutes

Goal
• To provide trainees with practice in role playing improvised conversations with video feedback and critical reflection from large group discussion.

Materials
Combining Your Skills Checklists from Session 25, pencils, and camcorder equipment.

Process
Trainer requests two members to volunteer to role play a dialogue between a leader and a receiver. Video operator tapes the drama (optional). The large group should be observing the discussion and making notes based on the Combining Your Skills Checklist. After about five minutes, two trainees will pick up the dia-

logue where the first two left off. A third pair should continue and complete the sequence.

Video operator plays back the sequence, stopping before each response from the leader. At this point, ask the participants to state how they would respond to the same situation.

Continue this process until the dialogue is completed. If no video equipment is used, trainer holds a critical discussion after each pair has worked together (at approximately five minute intervals).

Outcome Indicators
1. Four of the eight communication skills should be practiced effectively during the role play sequence.

2. The group should be able to critically analyze the communications, discussing which skills were used well. The barriers should also be discussed and alternative responses posed.

Session 27: Recognizing Warning Signals and Conditions

Time
Forty minutes

Goals
• To recognize potential warning signals and conditions that may lead to suicide.

• To identify potential peer leader responses to others who exhibit warning signals.

• To identify the potential reactions and outcomes of peer leader responses.

Materials
Warning Signals and Conditions Sheets, flash cards (cue signals and conditions on each card).

Process
Trainer distributes Warning Signals and Conditions Sheets to group and allows ten minutes for each member to read them.

Then each trainee, one at a time, selects a flash card with a behavior description on it. He/she must then give an example of the behavior to the group and receive corrective feedback.

If a person chooses Behavior #1 (sudden changes in behavior or emotional expressions), an example might include: "My student is usually very calm and slow-paced, but during our session today, he was hyper and couldn't stop talking."

Then elicit from another group member a way to respond to the behavior. For example, the peer leader might ask the receiver what he/she has been eating or drinking, or ask whether something distressing has happened.

Outcome Indicators
1. Each group member should provide an accurate example of one behavior and one appropriate response.

2. Group should actively criticize the responses and generate possible counter-reactions by receiving students.

Warning Signals and Conditions Sheet

Name_____   Date_____

Goal
• To provide examples of the signals and conditions and suggest appropriate professions for referrals.

Directions
Use these signals and conditions to find examples of real life illustrations and then suggest a professional who might help.

WARNING SIGNALS

1. Sudden changes in behavior or emotional expressions (withdrawn or aggressive).
2. Disturbed sleep patterns (insufficient, excessive, or interrupted).
3. Feeling statements that suggest depressed or hopeless state ("Life is not worth living").
4. Loss of interest in normal activities.
5. Risky or daredevil behavior that involves physical danger.
6. Sudden drop in school or job performance.
7. Total detachment from some important experiences.
8. Inability to express plans for future.
9. Changes in eating or weight patterns – either more or less.
10. Drug or alcohol abuse.
11. Giving away prime possessions.
12. Preoccupation with death thoughts.

CONDITIONS

1. Recent loss of a job, or a loved one.
2. Severe medical problem or illness.
3. Recent neglect or rejection by important figure or care provider.
4. Previous suicide gesture or attempt.
5. History of alcohol abuse or chemical dependency.
6. Approaching anniversary of loss of important person or event.
7. Occurrence of several major life changes coming in a short time span.

Session 28:
Improving Study Skills

Time
One hour

Goal
• To practice assessing study skills deficits and formulating plans of action.

Materials
Video camcorder (optional), Study Skills Improvement Guidelines, Study Skills Checklists, Action Plan Sheets, and pencils.

Process
Trainer distributes Study Skills Improvement Guidelines, Study Skills Checklists, Action Plan Sheets, and pencils.

Trainer introduces the exercise as follows:

Please take five minutes to read the Study Skills Guidelines. (Pause). Are there any questions? We will use these guidelines when developing Action Plans to assist receiving students.

Please get into a circle. This experience is designed to prepare you to help others in determining their strengths and weaknesses in study skills and to help them improve. One way to start is to use yourselves as examples and assess your own study skills.

Assuming you are in a role of receiver, read through the Study Skills Checklist and indicate which weaknesses you encounter in your own work.

Trainer requests that two volunteers role play a dialogue, assuming the parts of leader and receiver. Instruct the participants to:

1. Go over the checklist.

2. Discuss the weaknesses and strengths based on checklist results.

3. Develop an Action Plan based on Study Skills Improvement Guidelines.

This sequence can be videotaped and played back to the entire group. After this has been accomplished, lead a discussion revolving around the activities and strategies shown in the dramatization.

Outcome Indicators
1. Role play should demonstrate clear communication skills and mutually planned objectives.

2. Large group discussions should focus on strengths and limitations of the role play sequence. Group members should determine the validity of the mutually prescribed objectives based on the goal-setting criteria. In addition, the members of the group should suggest improvements and discuss additional strategies.

3. All trainees should make up hypothetical information and complete checklists.

Study Skills Improvement Guidelines

Name_____   Date_____

Goal
• To learn the steps in developing a study skills improvement plan.

Directions
1. Complete Study Skills Checklist.
2. Analyze time-budgeting problems.
3. Analyze note-taking problems.
4. Explain available services of the program.
5. Explain which bad habits and poor attitudes surfaced in the analyses and on the Checklist.

Goal Setting
1. List with the receiver the important qualities, habits and traits which you and he/she have decided address.
2. Set challenging but realistic goals that the receiver wants to reach.
3. Consider the possible blocks and obstacles to these goals.
4. Discuss ways to get around blocks.
5. Devise short term plans of action for each goal. The action plan should be designed to maximize the chances to reach the goal and minimize the chances of failure.
6. Devise a long term, realistic plan that's not too hard or not too easy. The challenge should be exciting to the receiver.

Questions to Ask Teachers
1. Discuss with your receiver the most appropriate questions to ask the teacher.
a. What kinds of tests are given?
b. How often will tests be given?
c. On what do you base your grades?

Note-taking
1. The following guidelines can be helpful in improving note-taking procedures:
a. Use large pages.
b. Use separate pages for each subject.
c. Use outline form.

Study Skills Checklist

Leader _____   Observer _____

Receiver _____   Date _____

Goal
• To practice developing a study skills strengths and weaknesses profile for your student.

Directions
This checklist is based on your observation of your receiver's study skills behavior in math, English, or social studies. After you have been working with the student for three or four sessions, complete this form by placing the appropriate number next to each phrase.

1. Often   **2. Sometimes**   **3. Never**

_____Student lacks the necessary materials to finish work.

_____Student is easily distracted.

_____Student puts obstacles in the way of work.

_____Student demonstrates short attention span.

_____Homework is done right after it is assigned.

_____Student reviews notes periodically.

_____Student looks at heading and titles before reading the text.

_____Student tends to skip the graphs, tables, and figures when reading text.

_____When taking tests, student frequently spends too much time on the first half of the test and does not complete the second half.

_____Student engages in last minute cramming.

_____Student memorizes material without understanding it.

_____Student seems to have difficulty in picking out the most important parts in reading textbook assignments.

Page 2 - Study Skills Checklist

_____Student experiences difficulty in choosing the right way to study for a test.

_____Student wants to drop out of school.

_____Student dislikes teachers.

_____Goal of student is to receive just passing grades.

_____Student feels teachers are too demanding and require too much work.

_____Patterns of grades show drop-off after first marking period.

Student's note-taking activities are as follows:

_____Sloppy

_____Disorganized

_____Out of sequence

_____Too extensive

Action Plan Sheet

Leader _____   Observer _____

Receiver _____   Date _____

Goal
• To establish a study skills improvement plan.

Directions
Use this form to establish an improvement plan with your receiver.

The things I see as my most important needs in developing better study skills are:

1. _____

2. _____

3. _____

To help me solve my problems with study skills, I will take the following actions:

PROBLEM   **ACTION**

1. _____   _____

2. _____   _____

3. _____   _____

4. _____   _____

5. _____   _____

Session 29:
Introduction to Tutoring

Time
Thirty minutes

Goal
• To explore and apply tutoring techniques.

Materials
Tutoring Guidelines, paper, and pencils.

Process
Trainer introduces a teacher who will discuss the general tutoring principles with the group. The teacher may call for a volunteer from the group and demonstrate a modeling procedure described in number three of the Tutoring Guidelines. Teacher will explain how students learn best (by rote, by repeating, by doing) and will demonstrate teaching approaches to enhance learning. After the teacher demonstrates his/her application of general guidelines, he/she asks the large group to discuss the demonstrated principles.

Outcome Indicator
1. Trainees should ask questions, discuss approaches, and describe their own learning strengths and weaknesses.

Tutoring Guidelines

Name_____   Date_____

Goal
• To present tutoring guidelines to peer leaders.

Directions
Use these guidelines when assisting your receivers in their academic subject areas.

1. Communicate clearly with your student. Use some of the suggested procedures in your Conscious Communication Guidelines in Session 6 to enhance your abilities to help.

2. Use informal methods to find your student's academic level in math and verbal areas.

a. To evaluate math levels, give an informal test of sample items which range from simple to difficult.

• Observe the way the student organizes figures.
• Note what skills are lacking.
• Check to see which parts of the work are understood.
• Check for computation errors. Note what operations are faulty (multiplication, division, and others).
• Look for difficulties in understanding concepts.
• Check how the student approaches the problem, and whether he/she understands it.
• Go over the informal assessment with your student, asking him or her to try to identify errors.

b. To evaluate reading abilities, have the student read out loud.

• Listen for smoothness in oral reading.
• Check word attack skills.
• Check recall.
• Check word knowledge.

c. To assess writing skills, ask the student to write a sentence about why he or she wants assistance or what he or she expects to get out of the program. Discuss the reasons and goals.

• Check the punctuation.
• Check level of vocabulary.
• Check spelling.
• Check penmanship.
• Check grammar.
• Check organization.

d. To assess work in the target area (math, English, history, geography), ask your consulting teacher to give you a copy of the student's work. This sample can serve as a baseline with which to compare new samples taken every month.

Page 2 - Tutoring Guidelines

3. Always model the techniques you are teaching your student. Then ask the student to practice the technique. For example, in reading skills, you might want to demonstrate:

• Scanning for information.
• Reading for facts and sequence.
• Skimming.
• Reading for main ideas.
• Reading for inference.
• Reading for oral expression.

4. Games can be helpful in drilling students. Examples include:

• History: Quizmo.
• Math: Multiplication War.
• Spelling: Scrabble, Football Spelling, Hangman.
• Vocabulary: Dial-a-Word.

You can make many of these games with your students.

5. Flexibility can enhance the learning process. Be prepared to try new techniques. People learn in different ways.

Session 30:
Test Taking

Time
Thirty minutes (ten minutes for role play, twenty minutes for discussion).

Goals
• To introduce the group to the "thought mill" technique of brainstorming.

• To give the trainees practice in helping their receivers prepare for tests.

Materials
Test Preparation Guidelines, magic markers, flip charts, paper, and pencils.

Process
Ask the group to break into two small groups (four to six members). Request group members to read the Test Preparation Guidelines silently.

Distribute Test Preparation Guidelines, magic markers, flip charts, paper, and pencils. Introduce the exercise as follows:

This exercise is designed to give you practice in using the "thought mill" technique of brainstorming. The exercise stresses methods to use in preparing your receivers to take tests.

Now that you have formed two groups, you will be given some tasks to complete in ten minutes. I will let you know when to begin and end.

Your tasks are to describe three ways to apply the guidelines to the helping situation and criticize and eliminate any nonessential guidelines which you feel have been left out. Each group should designate one member as a recorder to jot down ideas as they come

up and another member as a reporter to describe what happened after the exercise is completed.

The thought mill technique is used to generate ideas and creative solutions to problems. All ideas should be heard without criticism no matter how outrageous they seem. The recorder should write down all ideas given.

At the end of the session, the group should spend about two minutes ranking its ideas in order of importance and then discussing them in that order with the large group. The trainer will let you know when to begin and end the exercise and when to discuss your ideas in the large group. Have a good time.

The trainer signals the beginning of the exercise and signals the ten minute time limit. Trainer holds large group discussion, observes, and records the suggestions on a large piece of newsprint posted on a visible wall.

Trainer should move around the room monitoring thought mill guidelines and should provide assistance.

Outcome Indicators
1. During large group discussion, the members should be attentive, spontaneous, and show respect for each other by listening without interrupting.

2. Members should observe the guidelines for thought mill presented by trainer.

3. Two new ideas should be added to the Test Preparation Guidelines and two should be deleted in large group discussion.

4. The improvements and changes should be recorded and displayed to the group.

Test Preparation Guidelines

Name_____   Date_____

Goal
• To present these pointers for effective test taking to peer leaders.

Directions
Use these guidelines when working with your receivers to assist them in improving their test taking strategies.

Practice tests

1. Use practice tests in conditions similar to those of real examinations. Time yourself.

2. Arrange the questions in the same order as the material appears in the chapters, notes, and lectures.

3. Answer the questions without referring to the books.

Rules for taking tests

1. Read directions. Find out where the most points are given for various items.

2. Silently read through all the test questions before answering them.

3. If you don't understand a question, check it, move on and then return to it at the end of the test if you have time.

4. When answering an objective question, never leave any spaces blank. Fill them in with guesses. Remember that the first answer you give is most likely to be the correct answer.

Session 31:
Identifying Stress Triggers and Signals

Time
Forty-five minutes

Goals
• To acquaint trainees with some of the internal warning signals of stress.

• To enable trainees to recognize the effects of stress on the body and mind.

• To enable trainees to assess how they respond to challenges that trigger stress.

Materials
Stress Triggers Checklists, Warning Signals Checklists, balloons, 6' tubes, and pencils.

Process
Trainer introduces the exercise as follows:

Stress has been defined as the amount of wear and tear on the body. It is an internal state which often comes from two opposite forces occurring simultaneously. The first is arousal and the second is restraint. Stress can be triggered by both positive and negative events. Stress reactions can be short-lived or prolonged. The three stages of a stress reaction are:

1. ALARM: Bio-alarm goes off, glands secret hormones, and body reacts.

2. ADAPTATION: Your body returns to a more normal flow.

3. BREAKDOWN: You become exhausted, sick, or severely depressed.

The result is a kind of internal gridlock that burns up your energy. It is not the outside forces that cause the stress, but the way you react to them.

There are stress reactions to outside events and stress reactions to internal states. Some people thrive on the internal state of stress and seek outside activities to trigger arousal states.

Some outside events are beyond our control. These include illness, changes in family, and certain types of accidents. Other outside events are challenges that we may accept, reject, or delay.

Many of these challenges are positive at first glance, and often entice us to accept them because of potential benefits they might bring to us. They might include such things as running for student council, going out for a sport, or entering a race. Some might pose values conflicts such as how to confront a close friend whom you think may have cheated or stolen from you.

Some challenges appear positive and others appear negative. Some trigger stress immediately and others produce delayed stress reactions.

This exercise is designed to acquaint you with the way you take on challenges that produce immediate or delayed stress.

Trainer requests a volunteer to play the part of the stress receiver. Then the trainer requests each trainee to list one stress trigger on a piece of paper. Ask trainees to indicate whether it is:

• In Control
• Outside of Control
• Immediate
• Delayed

Allow five minutes for thought and writing. Give the stress receiver a balloon attached to a six inch tube and instruct him/her to blow one full breath each time he/she accepts a stress trigger from the audience member. Remind the receiver that some of the triggers will be out of his/her control. These are unavoidable and must be accepted. The others may be accepted or rejected.

Ask each trainee to come to the front of the room and deliver the trigger in the most persuasive way possible to the stress receiver at the front. See how many triggers it takes to bring the receiver's balloon to the breaking point. Discuss the metaphor of early warning signals, regulation, and incremental increases brought on by triggers.

Initiate a large group discussion on how trainees make decisions about accepting stressful challenges and how both voluntary or unavoidable stressful events effect their level of functioning.

Then continue with the following:

This is an exercise designed to acquaint you with your own stress warning signals and the events which trigger stress reactions.

I am going to pass out Stress Triggers Checklists and Warning Signals Checklists. These checklists include some of the most prevalent conditions that tend to produce stress. Please add the Stress Triggers that were identified in the previous exercise. Take the next ten minutes to review the triggers and signals, and check the ones which affect you.

Distribute Checklists. Allow ten minutes for the group to read through them silently. Hold a large group discussion of how the triggers and signals impact the trainees in their own lives. Be sure to allow members to pass on personal information that is too threatening or painful to share publicly.

Make sure you emphasize the need to check out any physical symptoms with a physician before assuming they are just stress reactions.

Outcome Indicators
1. Group discussion should yield acknowledgements of triggers and signals by each member.

2. Trainees should share life situations revolving around common stressors.

Stress Triggers Checklist

Name_____   Date_____

Goal
• To identify your life conditions that might trigger stress.

Directions
Use this checklist to identify those conditions which are impacting your life.

MOST GENERALLY ACCEPTED TRIGGERS

_____Loss of special person   _____Parent substance abuse

_____Poor grades   _____Conflict with opposite sex

_____Parent pressure   _____Family problem

_____Peer pressure   _____Teenage pregnancy

_____Physical changes   _____Personal substance abuse

_____Parental divorce or separation _____Difficulty relating to others

_____Fears about future   _____Financial trouble

_____Lack of friends   _____Overload

_____Loss of job

ADDITIONAL TRIGGERS

_____

_____

_____

_____

_____

_____

_____

_____

Warning Signals Checklist

Name_____   Date_____

Goal
• To recognize the effects of stress on the body and mind.

Directions
Use this checklist to identify personal warning signals of stress impacting your life.

_____Cold hands	_____Stomach problems
_____Fast breathing	_____Diarrhea
_____Sweaty hands	_____Frequent urination
_____Muscle tension	_____Sleep disturbances
_____Furrowed brow	_____Irritability
_____Tremors or tics	_____Headaches
_____Panic attacks	_____Sadness
_____Anxious feelings	_____Apathy
_____Blushing	_____Impatience
_____High blood pressure	_____Phobias
_____Nonmedical physical symptoms	_____Respiratory problems
_____Feeling disconnected from life	_____Drinking or drugs
_____Distractible	_____Plagued by repetitious thoughts
_____Short-tempered	_____Suicidal thoughts

Session 32:
Self-Support Strategies

Time
Forty-five minutes

Goal
• To acquaint trainees with some of the self-support strategies useful in coping with stressful situations.

Materials
Self-Support Strategies Sheets.

Process
Trainer instructs the group as follows:

Read through all the Self-Support Strategies and try to make up an example showing how you would use each.

Allow ten minutes for this process. Ask the members to take turns giving examples of each strategy. Direct a discussion around the trainees' reasons for using these skills. No prolonged demonstrations should take place.

Outcome Indicators
1. An example of each strategy should be given.

2. A discussion should point out the reasons for using the strategies.

Self-Support Strategies Sheet

Name_____   Date_____

Goal
• To identify strategies which may be useful to you in coping with stress.

Directions
Use this list to identify those strategies which are relevant to you in your life. Make up examples of how they may be used.

TIME MANAGEMENT
1. Use your bio-clocks when planning activities. Schedule more demanding activities when your energy level is usually high.

2. When faced with difficult projects, break them down into pieces so they are not so overwhelming.

3. Reward yourself after each task by giving yourself a treat, making a phone call, exercising, or doing other nurturing activities.

4. Develop checklists or graphs to monitor yourself and see your progress.

5. Try to set up plans to deal with problems as they occur. Avoiding problems only brings on more stress.

6. Set deadlines for your projects.

STRESS REDUCTION
1. Go to bed to sleep, not to worry. If you are stressed, get up and read a book, watch TV, etc.

2. If you can't sleep, try this exercise: Imagine yourself at a chalkboard with a tray next to it. Imagine that on the tray are a piece of chalk and an eraser. Imagine yourself picking up the chalk, reaching out to the board, and writing the number 100. Then slowly bring your arm down to the tray, leave the chalk and pick up the eraser.

Lift the eraser slowly to the board and erase the 100. Then slowly bring the eraser down to the tray, pick up the chalk again and move it to the board. Write the number 99 and continue slowly. Drop one number each time you run through the cycle.

3. Avoid self-medication, tranquilizers, drinking, or other substances.

4. Take a break and move to another location to interrupt the stress pattern.

5. Set goals that are within your reach.

6. Use rehearsal techniques to run through an upcoming challenge the way in which you would like to deal with it.

Page 2 - Self-Support Strategies Sheet

7. Beware of attempting to control situations that are totally out of your control. Instead practice ways of dealing with them more effectively.

8. Use tension outlets that work for you such as exercise, pillow fights, screaming, writing a journal, etc. Make sure they don't produce more stress.

9. Schedule regular talk time to clear the air with high stress producing individuals.

10. Call your friends to get support.

11. See a funny movie, talk to a funny person, read a funny story, or think of a funny experience.

12. Use hobbies, sports, and artistic outlets.

13. Practice deep breathing low in the abdomen. Move your breath slowly downward, deepening each breath and lengthening the intervals. Imagine pure air coming into your lungs and cleansing your mind.

14. For a headache, pretend to surround the area of pain with a rubber band. Gradually stretch the rubber band very slowly moving the pain down your arms, into your fingers, and out your fingernails.

Do this in slow motion, breathing deeply from the abdomen, with every breath making the pain thinner and weaker as it flows out your body.

15. Visualize a calm scene with all its colors, sounds, and sights.

16. Imagine yourself being in the scene and run it in slow motion until you get to the most enjoyable part. Then step into the picture.

17. Use symbols to connect with the most relaxing experiences or inner state.

18. Use biofeedback, stress cards, or commercially produced tapes which contain self-hypnosis scenarios.

19. Visualize the people who evoke stress reactions in a new, compromising, or outrageous setting. Use visualization to change them into cartoon-like characters with pink mustaches and purple ears. Make them appear in black and white instead of in color. Or imagine them far away or out of focus.

20. Visualize and experience a positive state when you were in charge and had it together. Imagine yourself being in the scene and run it in slow motion with all its sights, sounds, colors, smells, and people.

Page 3 - Self-Support Strategies Sheet

Think of your own special code or symbol that you can use to remind yourself to get back the power state. The symbol might be a color, name, code, or vision that ushers in the positive state you need to act effectively when under stress.

In a variation of the above, try a visual overlay technique. Use the power state scenario to cover up an image of a negative situation that evokes stress. Move the positive scene over the stress scene very slowly, until it covers over the negative image. This technique can do a lot to take the edge off a stressful situation.

In another variation of the above, notice the posture you were in as you were experiencing the positive state. Try to move yourself into the same posture. Change your breathing to match the power state. Also change the way you were moving to match the power state. You will be surprised how much your physical state can change your mental state from a negative to a positive mode.

21. Try listening to your favorite music and making up new lyrics that guide you through a difficult situation. "I'm going to make it through this mess, the way I did last time." It sounds silly, but it will work with the more light-hearted.

Session 33:
Your Resource Network

Time
Twenty minutes

Goal
• To set up a peer leader support system which shares coping strategies that might be useful to receiving students and peer leaders.

Materials
Resource Network Sheets and pencils.

Process
Ask the group members to recall some situations they have been through and challenges they have overcome. These may include going through a parental separation or divorce, losing a special friend, passing a difficult subject, making a speech, or overcoming a conflict with a friend.

Ask those members willing to support others going through similar problems to share experiences and coping strategies. Distribute the Resource Network Sheets, and ask trainees to list names, phone numbers, experiences, and coping strategies.

Photocopy the sheet, and distribute it to the group with a follow-up suggestion that trainees may find a way to share these experiences and coping strategies with others and report back to the group periodically.

The personal support group may be used to assist peer leaders in coping with their own problems and reaching out to their receiving students.

Outcome Indicators
1. Trainees should list at least one experience each.

2. Group members should list at least one coping strategy used to deal with the situation.

Resource Network Sheet

Name _____   Date _____

Directions
Please fill in your name, phone number, situation, and coping strategies.

Name	Phone #	Situation	Coping Strategies You Will Share
1.			
2.			
3.			
4.			
5.			
6.			
7.			
8.			
9.			

Session 34:
Pathways to Solutions

Time
Forty-five minutes

Goals
• To acquaint trainees with strategies to resolve conflicts.

• To enable trainees to recognize the effects of these strategies by dramatizing their use in a one-to-one role play.

Materials
Pathways to Solutions Sheet, Sample Situations Sheets, and pencils.

Process
Trainer introduces the exercise as follows:

When we presented the General Announcements, we made the point that in your role as peer leader, you should keep your expectations realistic. Expecting your receiver to change too fast can lead to a lot of frustration and bad feelings.

Pathways to Solutions are strategies to assist your receivers in finding realistic solutions to their problems. To give you an idea of what they feel like to use, we're going to ask you to read through these strategies.

Distribute Pathways to Solutions Sheets and allow five minutes for the group to read through

them. Clarify any questions about how to use the model. Continue the discussion by saying:

Now that you have read them, let's try out the seven strategies on each other. Break into pairs and separate yourselves so that there is space between each pair. Each pair should demonstrate these strategies by making up a scenario and using them. You may use the Sample Situations Sheets for examples. One person in each pair takes the part of a peer leader and the other, the part of a receiver. Take a few minutes to make up two dramas. Each pair should demonstrate the sequence of strategies for each scenario.

The leader should assist the receiver in running through the sequence until the desired outcome is reached. After the scenario, reverse roles with the peer leader now becoming the receiver and vice versa. You will have twenty minutes to make up and practice two dramas.

Each pair receives Sample Situations Sheets. Move around to the pairs making yourself available to answer questions and monitoring time lines. Then lead a general discussion on the use of the strategies.

Outcome Indicators
1. Each pair should make up two scenarios and demonstrate the strategies for each.

2. To check understanding of the strategies, the group should reach at east 70% accuracy in their attempts to attain desired outcomes.

Pathways to Solutions Sheet

Name_____   Date_____

Goal
• To present problem-solving strategies.

Directions
Use these pathways to address challenges in your own life.

1. What is the problem?

2. What do you want? What do you think might happen when you get it?

3. Is it in your control?

4. Is it inside or outside yourself?

5. How do your beliefs affect this goal? What do you value?

6. What are the roadways to get a positive result?

7. Is the outcome what you expect?

EXAMPLE OF HOW TO USE THE MODEL

1. Problem: You're worried about going to high school next year.

2. You want to be accepted by peers in high school.

3. Yes!

4. Both. Outside: The students will act the way they normally act. Inside: Your attitude will influence them to accept or reject you.

5. Maybe you believe that if you project an attitude of confidence, you will be accepted. Maybe you believe that you can be just as accepted at high school as you were in middle school. Maybe you find your co-curricular activities as important to you as acceptance by others.

6. Knowing whom to talk to, when to speak, and what to say are all roadways to gaining acceptance. You also need to build on the friends you already have, check reactions from others and be flexible in the way you talk. Acting confidently but not arrogantly and, most of all, acting as though you like you like yourself tend to bring acceptance from others.

7. You follow the roadways and after a few weeks, you gain acceptance from others.

Sample Situations Sheet

Name_____   Date_____

Goal
• To develop alternate outcome strategies to resolve conflicts.

Directions
Break into helping pairs. Assume roles of guide and partner. Run through this sequence of strategies using a real or imagined situation which poses a problem for you. Switch roles and repeat the sequence.

SAMPLE SITUATIONS

1. Deal with someone is who constantly exploiting you or using you.

2. Deal with someone close to you who constantly unloads on you.

3. Overcome put-downs.

4. Overcome procrastination.

5. Decide whether to enter or exit a relationship.

Session 35:
Friends or Lovers

Time
Thirty minutes

Goal
• To develop alternate outcome strategies to resolve conflicts.

Materials
Friends or Lovers Story Sheets.

Process
Trainer sets the stage for this event by asking students to recall a situation in which they were affected by a rumor about someone very close to them. Then spend the session engaging the group in formulating alternate outcome strategies

Distribute Friends or Lovers Story to the group, and allow ten minutes for trainees to read and think about the story. Then lead a brainstorming activity to generate possible strategies that Roger (the student in the story) might use in dealing with this situation.

Outcome Indicators
1. Through the group discussion, at least five alternative reactions for Roger should be enumerated by the group.

2. The group should also describe potential outcomes of each reaction.

3. The group should develop a hierarchy of the most desirable responses to this particular situation.

Friends or Lovers Story Sheet

Name_____   Date_____

Goal
• To develop alternate outcome strategies to resolve conflicts.

Directions
Read the story and decide how you might respond to the situation if you were Roger. Discuss your responses with each other.

STORY
Roger and Ginny have been seeing each other for a year. They are very serious. Roger's best friend, John, has just broken up with his girlfriend, Lauren, and is feeling very lonely and depressed. Roger and John have been best friends for five years. They are also on the track team together and their parents are also close friends.

One day Roger is in the locker room and notices people staring at him knowingly. Later that day he overhears somebody in school telling another that Ginny and John were seen together three times in one day: once at the local convenience store, again at a fast food restaurant, and later walking down the street. Roger looks puzzled and walks away from the conversation.

Session 36:
Who's to Blame?

Time
Forty minutes

Goal
• To introduce the concept of projection and determine how our values influence the way we perceive responsibility and blame as they apply to interpersonal relationships.

Materials
Who's to Blame? Story Sheets, paper, and pencils.

Process
Trainer distributes copies of Who's to Blame? Story Sheets and reads the story aloud to the group.

Ask the students to rate the characters from most to least admired. Lead a discussion during which the group members are asked to explain their preferences. Ask each member to explain why she or he identified the characters as desirable or undesirable.

Outcome Indicators
1. The discussion should be lively and all members should be involved.

2. The implications of each character's actions should raise questions and facilitate dialogue about the origins of blame and denial of personal responsibility.

3. General application to all relationships as well as peer leaders' roles in helping others should emerge as part of the discussion.

4. The role of personal values should be applied to the outcome strategies developed by the group.

Who's to Blame? Story Sheet

Name_____   Date_____

Goal
• To identify your problem-solving approaches.

Directions
Read the story and then list the characters from most to least admired by you. Discuss your reactions with the group.

STORY
Ron and Debbie attend the same high school and have known each other for since elementary school. They have been going out for two years.

Debbie has been spending a lot of time with Ron and looks forward to his frequent phone calls. She has a few close friends and sees them at cheerleading activities, school clubs, and other in-school events. After-school time and weekends have been devoted exclusively to seeing Ron.

Ron has a few close friends but rarely sees them after school. His friends are gradually disowning him because they resent all the time he spends with Debbie.

One day after school Ron meets Debbie and announces that he no longer intends to spend Saturdays and Sundays with her. He explains that his valuable friendships are too important to lose.

Debbie is very upset and hurt. The next day she sees Ron's friends in school and tells them off. Ron finds out and becomes very angry with her for interfering with his friendships. They have a very serious falling-out, and the relationship is ruined.

Session 37:
Refusal Skills

Time
Two hours (Break in-Break out, twenty minutes; Red Flags, fifteen minutes; Exit Mode, twenty minutes; Internal Resources, fifteen minutes; Symbol Check, five minutes; Red Alerts, fifteen minutes; "I learned..." ten minutes).

Goals
• To introduce the skills to be learned and practiced.

• To practice your refusal skills.

Materials
Refusal Skills Guidelines.

Process
Trainer introduces the exercise by using ice-breaker exercise, Break in-Break out. Trainer instructs the group as follows:

Form a circle and chain of hands. One group member gets in the middle of the circle and tries to break out.

Any member of the hand chain may decide to let him/her out. Or the group can ban together to keep the prisoner in the middle.

It is advisable to let the action continue for three minutes. Try technique with three or more people. The exercise is designed to illustrate coercion from group pressure. Use this as a metaphor to illustrate the effect of peer pressure on the individual.

Escaping the control of others requires using finesse, flexibility, and trial and error approaches. Explore the feelings and frustration produced by the power of peer bonding. Explore how it felt to escape the circle, the feelings towards the person who provided the escape route, and the after effects of the break out.

Trainer introduces Red Flags (situations to avoid). Ask the group to reassemble and hold a brainstorming session to identify typical actions and situations where saying no is a good idea. Examples would be when someone wants you to

go to a dangerous neighborhood, commit a crime, harass or injure someone else.

Ask one person to write down the possible ways to avoid potentially dangerous situations. Reproduce and distribute refusal skills to the group. Allow fifteen minutes for this exercise.

Trainer initiates small group discussions to identify Exit Modes. Ask the group to form groups of four and come up with creative ways to say no to potentially harmful situations. Emphasize the fact that there are no wrong approaches.

Trainer asks the group to share their refusal skills, and then writesthem on paper, reproduces the skills, and distributes them to the group. Allow fifteen minutes.

Trainer instructs trainees to read the refusal skills and make up an example showing how to use each.

Allow five minutes for this process. Ask the members to take turns giving examples of each technique. Direct a discussion around the leaders' reasons for using these skills. No prolonged demonstrations should take place. Distribute the Refusal Skills Guidelines and ask the groups to critique the offerings and compare them to their own refusal skill resource bank.

Trainer encourages the group to identify internal resources. Explain that we all use an array of personal resources that make it possible for us to refuse to comply with coercive peer pressure.

To identify these states of mind in different people, divide the group into concentric circles in a fishbowl motif. Ask the members of the inner circle to brainstorm about their own types of inner states which empower them to refuse to comply with other's expectations, both positive and negative. For example, most participants know how and when to procrastinate on a task or a dangerous request. Set up roles for the outer group such as: recorder who writes down the states, a reporter of the states, and an observer of leadership roles. Then ask the outer group members to add their own examples of resources.

EXAMPLES OF INTERNAL RESOURCES

1. Positive attitude that validates your position.

2. Holding power to cling to your ideas.

3. Inner strength.

4. Awareness that the consequences of giving in are not worth it.

5. Sufficient hostility towards those who are trying to force you to do something against your will.

6. Confidence.

7. Self-respect.

Allow fifteen minutes for this exercise.

Trainer asks the group to develop a symbol check. Ask the group members to think of their own special codes or symbols to remind themselves of trigger resources and attitudes that empower them to say no. The symbols might be a color, name, code, or vision that reminds them to refuse. Allow five minutes for this exercise.

Trainer sets up three role plays of typical Red Alert situations where a definite refusal is called for. Role play the peer group's techniques of applying pressure, and have members take turns using their symbols to access personal resources and refusal skills. Ask the group to form a consensus on which strategies work best for each situation. Allow fifteen minutes for the role plays and discussions.

Trainer initiates a round of sentence completion to reinforce the skills generated from the workshop. "I learned..." might be an appropriate vehicle to review the experience. Distribute refusal skill strategies to the group, and set up a phone network for further support. Use the resource network from Session 33.

Encourage the trainees to use the skills for themselves and teach their receiving students these skills. Allow ten minutes for this exercise.

Outcome Indicators
1. An example of each technique should be given.

2. A discussion should point out the reasons for using the refusal skills.

Refusal Skills Guidelines

Name_____   Date_____

Goals
• To introduce the skills to be learned and practiced.

• To practice your refusal skills.

Directions
Below are some examples of ways to exit high risk activities. They have been developed by peer leaders. Use these to compare and add to the bank you just made.

REFUSAL SKILLS

1. Invent an excuses: "I have other things I have to do."

2. Use delay tactics: "I'll do it when I'm in the mood."

3. Distance yourself: walk away to avoid facing the situation.

4. Shift the blame and try to make the pressure group feel guilty.

5. Act ignorant about how to do something.

6. Identify the other things that are more important to do at the moment.

7. Give alternate solutions to the situation: You don't have to rip off the mall to get a boom box. You can ask your grandparent, shovel snow, do a job, etc. It is much safer.

8. Get away from the situation as soon as possible.

9. Take control of the situation: "I don't want to get high. I want to meet my girlfriend at the roller coaster now."

10. Ask your friends to justify why you should do what they want you to: "What is in it for me?"

Session 38:
Confrontation Guidelines

Time
Twenty minutes

Goal
• To introduce the skills to be learned and practiced in the next exercise.

Materials
Confrontation Guidelines.

Process
Trainer instructs the group as follows:

Confrontation is one of the most difficult and delicate forms of communicating with another person. It should only be used as a last resort. It should not be used with someone whom you know to be violent or out of control. This exercise is designed to provide some approaches to effective confrontation. Read through all the Confrontation Guidelines and try to make up an example showing how you would use each.

Allow five minutes for this process. Ask the members to take turns giving examples of each guideline. Direct a discussion around the leaders' reasons for using these guidelines. No prolonged demonstrations should take place.

Outcome Indicators
1. An example of each guideline should be given.

2. A discussion should point out the reasons for using the skills.

Confrontation Guidelines

Name_____   Date_____

Goal
• To practice your confrontation skills.

Directions
Use these guidelines to practice effective confrontation skills with your partners.

1. Be flexible in setting up your expectations about the outcome of the confrontation.

2. Remember that timing and location are critical to a successful confrontation. Privacy and easy access to each other will usually improve the impact, unless you are concerned about a physical confrontation.

3. Let the person you are confronting knows what an inconvenience he caused you.

4. Talk directly to the person you are confronting.

5. Talk clearly and calmly unless the person is unable to listen. Then wait till the person is in a more receptive state.

Example: I really need to tell you something very important.

6. Always pace and match the person whom you are confronting.

7. Refer directly to the issue.

Example: Remember when we were supposed to meet at the mall last Friday?

8. Explain how the person's behavior affected you. Use "I" messages.

Example: I get furious when you keep me waiting.

9. Always listen actively to the others person's viewpoint. Put yourself in his or her shoes.

10. Ask for cooperation and openness. This will test the person's flexibility.

Example: Will you hear me out? Would you be willing to change the way you treat me?

11. Summarize what you need to resolve the problem.

Example: I need to know that you will avoid unloading your bad days on me.

Session 39:
Confrontation Barriers

Time
Forty-five minutes

Goals
• To acquaint trainees with barriers to effective confrontation.

• To enable trainees to recognize the effects of these barriers by dramatizing their use in a one-to-one role play and demonstrating each drama to the group.

Materials
Confrontation Barriers Sheets.

Process
Distribute Confrontation Barriers Sheets and allow five minutes for the group to read silently through them.

Trainer introduces the exercise as follows:

This exercise will give you a chance to experience the negative results of faulty confrontation. Read through the barriers and think of ways they might apply to situations from your lives.

Now that you have read them, let's try them out on each other. Break into pairs, and separate yourselves so that there is space between each pair. Each pair should demonstrate these barriers by making up a conversation using them. One person in each pair takes the part of a peer leader and the other the part of a receiver.

Take a few minutes to make up two dramas, about four sentences each. Each pair should demonstrate two barriers, one barrier for each conversation. After the first conversation, reverse roles with the peer leader now becoming the receiver and vice versa. You will have ten minutes to make up two dramas and practice them.

Each pair gets two sheets of paper, each having two barriers to demonstrate. Move around to the pairs making yourself available to answer questions and, after ten minutes, instruct the group as follows:

Let's demonstrate your conversations to the group. There are no right or wrong answers, so just relax and get into the process. After each demonstration, let's see if we can guess which barrier was used.

Lead a general discussion on the use and effects of the barriers.

Outcome Indicators
1. Each pair should make up and demonstrate two dramas, each illustrating one barrier.

2. To check understanding of the barriers, the group members should reach at least 70% accuracy in their attempts to guess those demonstrated by each pair.

3. At least one receiver's reaction to each barrier should be identified bas an example of how the communication process is cut off.

Confrontation Barriers Sheet

Name_____   Date_____

Goal
• To demonstrate the barriers to effective confrontation.

Directions
Below is a list of common approaches that can cause the failure of a well-intended confrontation. Use them to make up a drama to demonstrate at least one barrier.

1. Avoid setting up unrealistic expectations about the outcome of the confrontation. If you realize you can't get what you want by confronting, then try something else — like a directly stated letter.

Example: He is going to pay me back all the money by tomorrow!

2. Avoid letting your anger build up to a rage state.

Example: You have gone too far this time...I've had it.

3. Avoid telling others about the upcoming confrontation. The impact will be diluted if the person hears your complaints from others.

Example: You won't believe what he did. When I find him, he'll pay.

4. Avoid confronting a person in a crowd or among his/her valued friends. It will rally defensiveness and neutralize the effect.

5. Avoid labelling the person you confront or the behavior that angered you.

Example: How could you do such a dumb thing? Your so retarded.

6. Avoid asking set-up questions.

Example: Don't you have any common sense?

7. Avoid ultimatums and threats.

Example: This one is going to cost you.

Page 2 - Confrontation Barriers Sheet

8. Avoid accusations.

Example: I know you told Judy what I said about her!

9. Avoid why questions. They usually invite distortion or deception.

Example: Why on earth did you do that?

10. Avoid beating around the bush.

Example: Some people have been saying that you really want out.

11. Avoid ordering specific resolutions to the conflict.

Example: You'd better apologize to her immediately or you'll wish you were dead!

Permission to reprint for classroom use. Copyright © 1992. V. Alex Kehayan, *Partners for Change* (Program Guide). Jalmar Press: Rolling Hills Estates, CA.

Session 40:
Combining Confrontation Skills and Barriers

Time
Twenty minutes

Goal
• To recognize and practice confrontation skills and demonstrate barriers.

Materials
Confrontation Skills and Barriers Checklists, Confrontation Skills and Barriers Situation Sheets, and pencils.

Process
Trainers review confrontation skills and barriers in a two minute role play. The first minute should exemplify confrontation skills and the second minute should focus on confrontation barriers. After a ten minute discussion, trainer instructs the group as follows:

This is an exercise to allow you to become aware of confrontation skills and barriers. Group yourselves into threes. Each group should find a place in the room with some distance from the other groups.

Each person will assume one of three possible roles: receiver, confronter, observer. Trainees will take turns rotating roles until all three have been taken by each participant.

The responder should take a minute to develop an imaginary confrontation scenario. The responder should face the listener and discuss what factors led him or her to make this confrontation. While the confronter confronts the receiver, the observer uses the checklist to record information about the confronter's confrontation skills and barriers.

You will be doing this three times, until each of you has tried out the three roles.

After about two minutes of discussion, trainer gives the stop signal and the group spends the next two minutes discussing the confronter's skills and barriers and the receiver's responses.

Trainer distributes the checklists, signals the group to stop at two minute intervals (for role playing and small group discussion), and then assists in general discussions. After the three groups have completed their dialogues, lead a large group discussion about the reactions to dialogues, skills, and barriers.

Outcome Indicators
1. Each observer should check at least half the items indicating confrontation skills.

2. Discussions within small groups after each role play should be characterized by questions and responses. The voices should be loud, giggly, and, at times, fast-talking.

3. The large group discussions should reveal strengths and weaknesses in confrontation for each trainee.

Confrontation Skills and Barriers Checklist

Listener _____   Observer _____

Responder _____   Date _____

Goal
• Use the checklist to rate your leader's confrontation skills and barriers.

Directions
As you observe the two people talking, check the following items to describe how you would rate the behavior of the leaders as you see it.

CONFRONTATION SKILLS	**CONFRONTATION BARRIERS**
_____Has flexible expectations	_____Sets unrealistic expectations
_____Talks directly	_____Lets rage build-up
_____Talks clearly and calmly	_____Labels or discredits
_____Paces and matches	_____Asks set-up questions
_____Refers directly to the issue	_____Issues ultimatums and threats
_____Explains effect of behavior	_____Makes accusations
_____Listens actively to the other person's viewpoint	_____Asks "why" questions
_____Asks for cooperation and openness	_____Beats around the bush
_____Summarizes resolution	_____Orders specific resolutions

Confrontation Skills and Barriers Situation Sheet

Name_____   Date_____

Goal
• To practice your confrontation skills and demonstrate barriers.

Directions
Use these situations as springboards to practice your skills and demonstrate barriers.

1. Someone assumed that you said something about his/her sister and you really didn't. He/she is angry at you and you want to confront the false assumption.

2. Your friend has become very conceited and obnoxious in the last few weeks and is very critical of you and others.

3. Your parent is unloading his/her bad days on you during dinner, and you have reached your limit.

4. You have heard that your best friend is attempting to steal your boyfriend/girlfriend.

Session 41:
Response Enhancers

Time
Forty-five minutes

Goal
• To acquaint trainees with group response enhancers.

Materials
Response Enhancers Sheets and pencils.

Process
Trainer introduces the exercise as follows:

The following response enhancers are intended to help you lead groups effectively, get their attention, and develop rapport.

We will use the next forty-five minutes to review the enhancers together. We will do a round as each of you reads one of the response enhancers. I will model each technique to show you how it is used.

After trainer models each enhancer, hold a large group discussion to deal with any questions about the techniques. Then divide the group into small discussion groups, and instruct each group to spend about 15 minutes coming up with ways to use the enhancers.

Outcome Indicators
1. The discussion of the Trainer Model should generate rationales for using response enhancers.

2. Small group discussions should focus on the response enhancers.

3. Small group discussion should address the difficulties in using the enhancers. Appropriate conditions for the use of response enhancers should be identified.

Response Enhancers Sheet

Name_____   Date_____

Goal
• To identify how these Response Enhancers may be used in your program.

Directions
After trainer has modeled these Response Enhancers and you have discussed them in the large group, break up into small groups to discuss how they can be used by you in your programs.

1. SEATING FOR EYE CONTACT
Arrange chairs to promote eye contact without obstruction. In large groups, use concentric circles. Also use fishbowl techniques where an outside group observes the inner group and reacts to questionnaire or processing activity.

2. GOAL SETTING AND OUTCOME EVALUATIONS
Tell the students the desired outcomes of the session and how the group will verify the outcomes.

3. REACTION ROUNDS
Ask each member to respond to the activity by sentence completion round robin "one liner" responses triggered by "I learned or I discovered..."

4. ROLE PLAYS
Set up role play situations illustrating the points of your discussion or activities. Role play peer pressure situations, boy-girl situations, teacher-student confrontations, etc. Have the group observe and react.

5. FEEDBACK FORMS
Structure each activity with question sheets to generate written responses from group. That way no one gets off without tapping into the process, at least internally.

6. RESPONSE GROUPS
Ask each group to chose a person to report to the large group. Groups of four usually break barriers in responding to the material you present.

7. CHOICE WHIPS
When doing role play or other group activities calling for continuous responses from members, ask members to choose the next responder.

8. BRAINSTORMING ROUNDS
Ask the group to list all the issues areas, points to make, causal factors, and categories. Allow no negative reactions or put-downs. Encourage the group to take off on ideas.

9. LOADING ZONES
Every group has its negative responders who tend to be oppositional. To make an alliance with these head shakers, load all negative material into their zones of the room. You can do this by

Page 2 - Response Enhancers Sheet

stating the counter-argument opposing your point directly to the group members who appear to show signs of being negative. Examples are: "You might agree with that, but..." or "This may sound different, but..."

10. MATCH AND PACE YOUR AUDIENCE
Use matching and pacing skills to communicate with a person's unconscious by using a "personalized biofeedback." Finely tune your own responses to pace and match the other person's:

• Breathing rate

• Tonal qualities

• Speech rate

• Gestures

• Postures

• Language reflecting sensory channels

11. NEGATIVE COMMANDS
Negative commands can be very helpful in dealing with someone who tends to be oppositional. There are a lot of people who take great pleasure in contradicting and questioning whatever you say. When trying to assist someone who is oppositional, you may want to preface your remarks negatively.

The stubborn person who needs to change his antagonistic behavior might respond well to a statement such as, "You don't want to control your outburst until you're ready." Another example would be a remark to someone who wishes to lose weight, "Don't stop eating until you're ready to be very thin."

The negative command principle can have disastrous impact if used in the wrong way. For example, using negative commands to stop behavior can only reinforce it.

When someone is talking too loud you might want them to quiet down and say, "Don't talk so loud." They will have difficulty stopping because the real message is, "Talk loud." Saying, "Be quiet" is much more useful.

12. QUOTES
Using "Quotes" to convey a message that may be potentially threatening or inappropriate to say directly is a novel way to speak in metaphor. Some examples are, "There are a lot of clunkers out there who constantly interrupt you when you talk." "Have you ever met someone who just tries too hard?"

Offering an example of the negative behavior practiced by group members can be useful in actually illustrating a point that you want your receivers to learn.

Page 3 - Response Enhancers Sheet

13. DIRECTIONS
Encourage group members to talk to the group, not to the leaders. Stand near disruptive or silent members. Move isolates near friendly members.

Praise all responses that are relevant. Move around the room as you present.

14. LIGHTEN UP
Be sure to have fun and enjoy the experience.

Session 42: Icebreakers

Time
• Two and a half hours

Goals
• To prepare peer leaders to serve as effective group leaders in a variety of program contexts.

• To demonstrate appropriate use of icebreakers and warm-ups used in group leadership.

• To provide practice integrating and using appropriate warm-ups and icebreakers for group experiences.

Materials
Group Leadership Checklists, Icebreaker Sheets, materials listed under each icebreaker, and pencils.

Process
Trainer introduces the event as an opportunity to sample a variety of group process warm-up exercises to build cooperation and rapport with group members.

Trainer models each of the activities briefly, using peer leaders as assistants in the process. Then, trainer asks peer leaders to break up into groups of six. Two peer leaders colead the icebreaker of their choice with an audience of four peer leaders.

Two peer leaders observe the process, fill out the Group Leadership Checklists, and share their reactions to the leaders at the close of each activity. Follow time lines appropriate for each activity.

Then assemble the group and lead a large group ten minute discussion to process skills used and areas of improvement needed.

Outcome Indicators
1. Small group discussion should be actively focused on the observer's feedback for each role play. Any discrepancies between rater's perceptions and those of receivers should be discussed in small groups.

Issues such as relating styles and context of responses should be brought up and resolved if possible.

2. The large group discussion should be open and free-flowing. Trainers should observe that leaders used group management skills. Questions and follow-up should emerge from the group.

3. The group should be able to critically analyze the communications, discussing which skills were used well.

Group Leadership Checklist

Listener _____   Observer_____

Responder _____   Date_____

Goal
• To prepare peer leaders to serve as effective group leaders in a variety of program contexts.

Directions
As you observe the leaders conducting the session, write the numbers which best describe their skills and the activities in the session.

1. Excellent   **2. Adequate**   **3. Needs Improvement**

LEADER'S SKILLS

1._____Is prepared

2._____Shows involvement

3._____Listens well

4._____Communicates effectively

5._____Uses rapport skills

6._____Shows support

7._____Shows tolerance

8._____Provides sensitivity

9._____Promotes interaction

10._____Has clear goals and directions

11._____Makes sure voice tone and body language is congruent with verbal messages

12._____Paces and matches members

13._____Stays on task

14._____Tolerates differences of opinion

Page 2 - Group Leadership Checklist

ACTIVITIES AND CONTENT

1._____Are relevant

2._____Are useful

3._____Reflect real life situations

General comments_____

_____

_____

_____

_____

Areas to improve _____

_____

_____

_____

_____

Icebreaker Sheet

Name_____   Date_____

Goal
• To practice using icebreakers.

Directions
Practice these icebreakers in small groups, using your response enhancer skills. Your observer should fill out the Group Leadership Checklists and offer you feedback after you have led one exercise.

1. HAVES AND HAVE-NOTS
Divide group into two sections. One section, the Haves, has everything they could possible want while the other group, the Have-nots, has nothing except themselves. Ask the Have-nots to think of some important physical, mental, material, and spiritual needs. Within a five minute time period the Have-nots must try to get as many needs as possible from the Haves without any verbal communication. The Haves may or may not decide to meet their demands. Total time: ten minutes.

2. NAME GAME
Ask each person to say his or her name with an appropriate label, sound, or gesture. The do a "round" with each person repeating the name and label or gesture around the circle. Total time: fifteen minutes.

3. TINKER TOY PROJECTS
Divide into two groups, and ask each group to create a project with a can of tinker toys or box of plastic building blocks. Give five minute time limits, enforce no talking rule, and ask each group to name the project after five minutes. Process the experience asking who led, who followed, why, and how. Ask about changes in leadership and why people followed others. Ask about the competition between and within groups, and get reactions to the effect of time limits on performance. Total time: fifteen minutes

4. STRING MAZE
Materials include blindfold, chalk or magic marker, Question Sheets (Section 8, Human Relations, Session 2), and tape or string.

Leader tells the group members that they are to participate in an experiment to see how they can influence each other's performance. Leader asks one person to volunteer as the performer.

With a long piece of string or tape laid straight on the floor, extending from one wall to the opposite wall, leader instructs the performer as follows:

Your task is to keep your feet on the line as you walk from one side to the other. You will be wearing a blindfold. The group will guide you.

Leader asks other students to assemble on each side of the line, leaving sufficient space for the performer to walk without colliding with observers. Leader puts blindfold on performer.

Page 2 - Icebreaker Sheet

TRIAL 1 - Leader instructs group to give negatively toned verbal feedback (i.e.,"You're way off." "Come on, can't you do better than that?" "You're off the mark"). As performer walks the line, negative reactions are given by observers. Leader instructs one participant to count the number of times the performer's foot touches the line during the first trial. A tally should be kept on the board.

TRIAL 2 - As performer walks the line, observers are instructed to give positive verbal feedback (i.e., "You are getting close." "You're on it." "You're doing great"). Again throughout this process, an assigned participant counts the number of times each foot touches the line and records this number of touches on the board. Scores are tallied.

Repeat the process with different performers walking the line. Leader distributes Question Sheets and allows five minutes for performers and observers to respond in writing.

Then the leader holds a five minute discussion on the different conditions and how they affect the performers' behavior as well as that of the observers. The discussion should focus on how positive and negative feedback affects students' performance in other areas of their lives. Total time: twenty minutes

5. TASK GROUPS
Assign one or more groups tasks to complete with time limits and optional rewards for correct completion. Assign roles for group members such as recorder, spokesperson, time keeper etc.

6. NEEDS AUCTION
Materials include chalkboard, play money, Needs Auction Question Sheets. (See Section 11, Session 3). Leader divides up unequal amounts of play money to distribute to the class.

Begin this event by requesting students to brainstorm a few desirable qualities, values, traits, and skills. List these on the board and then ask the group to select ten of the most popular needs or attributes.

Distribute play money to the students and hold a mock auction during which participants have to establish which needs are important and how much money they want to spend. They then bid for these desirable things and talents. The process will show the group what qualities are of high and low value.

Keep a record of the selling price of each need and the name of each person who bought it. Make a chart with which to generate discussion at the end of the auction.

Distribute Question Sheets, request group to write its responses, and hold a general discussion emphasizing how needs are satisfied and what positive qualities students already have as personal resources.

Page 3 - Icebreaker Sheet

Then set up a Support Network by asking members to list qualities, talents, and skills that they are willing to share with others, and their names and phone numbers. Photocopy the sheet and distribute to the class.

Encourage students to find ways to share these skills with others, and report back to the group periodically. Total time: thirty minutes

6. BREAK IN-BREAK OUT
Group forms a circle and holds hands. Member in the middle tries to break out. One member spontaneously decides to let him/her out. Illustrates coercion from group pressure.

Alternate: Member on the outside tries to break in. The person(s) who let in the invader have broken the group's integrity and must form a new group with the invader. Total time: fifteen minutes

7. SCAVENGER HUNT
Set up a short list of experiences, qualities, and profiles for each member to find and report on during an all group discussion. Seekers may look for people who drink soda for breakfast, Capricorns, chocolaholics, iguana owners, nature lovers, etc. Total time: twenty minutes.

Session 43:
Referral Guidelines

Time
One hour (twenty minutes for the review and forty minutes for the role plays.)

Goals
• To identify the behaviors that require professional backup.

• To review suicidal or depressive warning signals.

• To identify the available professional resources in the school and community.

• To rehearse two typical referral sequences, practicing the communication skills.

Materials
Referral Guidelines, Combining Your Skills Checklists (see Section 2, Session 25), and pencils.

Process
Trainer distributes Referral Guidelines to the group and allows time for members to review them quietly.

After about ten minutes, trainer asks each student to read a trigger behavior and give an example of it.

For example, for #1, student might say "My student always tells me he can't understand how his teachers explain the classwork. He gets confused."

After each example, ask a trainee to name an appropriate professional who could serve as a resource. When all the triggers have been reviewed by the group, reinforce the need to document all referrals by first checking with a program staff member and then writing an entry into a log kept on each receiving student.

Ask the group to review Warning Signals and Conditions (Section 2, Session 27) and compare

with the Referral Guidelines.

Then, trainer asks the trainees to divide into two groups. Each group must assign a recorder, time keeper, a moderator, three actors to play leaders, two actors to play receivers, and one actor to play the professional. Trainer instructs each group that they have fifteen minutes to create a three stage role play of a referral process with a receiver.

Stage one: Helper tells the receiver that he or she will be referred to another professional for further assistance with a given problem.

Stage two: Using different actors to play roles, leader provides background and seeks advice from the professional and makes the referral.

Stage three: Using different actors to play roles, leader follows up with the receiver after the referral has been made and deals with the reactions from the receiver.

After fifteen minutes, each group is asked to demonstrate the three part role plays, while the other trainees observe and rate the leaders on Combining Your Skills Checklists. Moderator introduces the three stages setting the stage for each one as the as they unfold.

After each group presents its role plays, trainer holds a discussion focusing on the difficulties involved in deciding to make a referral and the dilemmas and strategies that unfold in the process.

Outcome Indicators
1. Each trainee should write an example of a trigger behavior from everyday life and an appropriate backup professional.

2. Nine trainees in each group should participate in assigned roles.

3. Discussion should focus on the practical implications and difficulties in seeking backup assistance for receivers.

Referral Guidelines

Name_____   Date_____

Goal
• To identify situations which warrant a referral to a professional.

Directions
The following is a list of behaviors which should trigger a referral to a professional. Give examples of these situations to help you clarify what they look like in real settings.

1. Complaints that classes are too difficult.

2. Learning difficulties such as letter reversals, eye movements, etc.

3. Illegible handwriting.

4. Low reading and math levels.

5. Poor coordination.

6. Slow copying with distortion.

7. Distorted comprehension of instructions.

8. Short attention span.

9. Distractibility.

10. Evidence of stomach, bladder, or intestinal problems.

11. Visual difficulties.

12. Hearing problems.

13. Complaints of physical pain.

14. Excessive fatigue.

15. Other medical symptoms or complaints.

16. Complaints of possible pregnancy.

17. Stuttering.

18. Lisp or speech difficulties.

19. Expressions of mistrust.

Page 2 - Referral Guidelines

20. Poor communication.

21. Oppositional behavior.

22. Prolonged poor academic performance.

23. Unusual mood changes.

24. Excessive lying.

25. Emotional outbursts.

26. Excessive absences.

27. Threats of violence.

28. Thumb sucking.

29. Irrational fears.

30. Obsessional thoughts.

31. Expressions of futility.

32. Expressions indicating child abuse or sexual abuse from adults or siblings.

33. Eating disorders.

34. Alcohol or substance abuse behaviors.

35. Expressions of suicidal intent.

36. Giving away of property.

37. Disclosure of previous suicide attempts.

38. Sudden surge of happiness after prolonged depression or despair.

39. Loss of interest in activities.

40. High risk or accident prone behavior.

Page 3 - Referral Guidelines

REFERRAL RESOURCES

1. Peer Program Coordinator.

2. Guidance Counselor.

3. Special Services Personnel.

4. School Nurse.

5. Speech Therapist.

6. Teachers, by their area of academic expertise.

7. Student Assistance Counselor.

8. Other trained staff members who may offer support.

9. Community resources such as self-help groups, volunteer organizations, and academic support groups.

Session 44: Processing and Discussing

Time
Fifty minutes (twenty minutes to review concepts and thirty minutes to discuss program impact on teachers.)

Goals
• To review some of the principles and clarify questions about the training process and all distributed materials, so as to illuminate and reinforce the skills.

• To state and discuss teachers' reactions to the program and its participants.

Materials
None.

Process
Trainer arranges trainees in a circle. A discussion reviews, questions, and summarizes Conscious and Transformative Communication skills.

Then the trainer presents a statement about the characteristics of some teachers in many school environments. The following is a list of characteristics which trainers may want to mention:

1. Some teachers are lonely and frequently isolated because they have little support from other professionals.
2. When problems arise in their classes, some teachers are often unable to discuss such issue with supervisors.
3. Some teachers are under enormous tension because of the intense situations occurring in classrooms.
4. Teachers are often overburdened with clerical work.
5. Some of the pressures experienced by teachers stem from students, parents, and administrators.

6. Teachers have little time for themselves within the school setting.

Trainer leads a general discussion of how this intervention might affect these teachers. Some of the issues that might be raised are:

1. Questions teachers might have about why they are being chosen for this project.
2. The controversy over using students as non-professional counselors.
3. The inconveniences that may be imposed on teachers.
4. Competition that may result between teachers and leaders in working with receivers.

Some of the strategies that may be used in dealing with the resulting tensions incurred by this process are:

1. Showing respect for teachers.
2. Listening actively to their feelings and problems.
3. Presenting the program as an aid to teachers.
4. Making sure that the conferences are scheduled at the teachers' convenience.

Outcome Indicators
1. All students should demonstrate active listening skills during the discussion (as stated on the Conscious Communication Skills Sheet, Section 2, Session 6).

2. Questions and lively discussion should indicate engagement in process, and content should show participants' understanding of the process.

3. At least one-half of the students in the group should state potential reactions of teachers. These may include fears, angers, and irritations.

4. At least one-half of the students should express empathy toward these teachers, while making statements reflecting teachers' needs for additional assistance.

Session 45:
Ethics Code

Time
Forty-five minutes

Goal
• To review the National Peer Helping Association's Code of Ethics for Peer Helpers and create a code of ethics applicable to the needs of the program population.

Materials
National Peer Helpers Association (NPHA) Code of Ethics For Peer Helpers, flip charts, magic markers, paper, and pencils.

Process
Trainer asks the trainees to form two groups in separate areas of the room. Ask members to assume roles as recorder, time keeper, and reporter. Trainer distributes NPHA Code of Ethics For Peer Helpers, flip charts, magic markers, paper, and pencils. Twenty minutes is allotted for this exercise.

Group one is assigned to review the introduction and ethics 1, 3, and 5, while group two is assigned to review ethics 2, 4 and 6. Groups must develop their own code of ethics using the basic tenants from the NPHA Code. They may modify, add, or delete the principles as they see fit.

After twenty minutes each group introduces its versions to the large group, using the materials and invoking leadership from each group's reporter.

Outcome Indicators:
1. The group must complete a code of ethics that is agreed upon by the majority.

2. The code must follow the principles of the NPHA code, with modifications appropriate to the program needs.

3. The code must be approved by the program advisor.

National Peer Helpers Association Code of Ethics for Peer Helpers*

Name_____   Date_____

Peer Helpers shall be people of personal integrity. As a minimum, the NPHA believes the Peer Helpers Code of Ethics shall contain the following and be evidenced by a commitment to and the pursuit of:

1. A philosophy which upholds peer helping as an effective way to address the needs and conditions of people.

2. The individual's right to dignity, self-development, and self-direction.

3. Supervision and support from the professional staff while involved in the program.

4. The development of a nurturing personality which:

• Reflects a positive role model and healthy life style (ie., development and observation of a set of norms which guide behavior while in the program).

• Rejects the pursuit of personal power, elitist status, or gain at the expense of others.

• Strives to exemplify the peer helping philosophy in all life situations.

5. Maintenance of confidentiality of information imparted during the course of the program-related activities. While confidentiality is the norm, certain exceptions shall be referred immediately to the professional staff. These exceptions include the following:

• Situations involving real of potential danger to the safety or well-being of the peer helper, helpee, or others.

• Child abuse, sexual abuse, and other situations involving legal requirements of disclosure.

• Sever family dysfunction, psychotic behavior, extreme drug or alcohol abuse, and any other problems beyond the experience and expertise of the peer helper.

6. Personal Safety

Peer helpers must recognize, report, and know techniques to deal with potential threats to their emotional of physical well-being.

* A code of ethics is an agreement among those who commit to the program as to the norms which shall guide their behavior during their involvement in the program. The code of ethics on this page is a duplicate of the National Peer Helpers Association Code of Ethics.

Session 46:
Farewell Feedback

Time
Thirty minutes (for 15 member group)

Goals
• To provide closure to the training events.

• To enable individuals to receive personal feedback from group members.

Materials
Paper, pens, pins, stamped, self-addressed envelopes.

Process
Trainer requests each trainee to write three positive attributes about himself/herself on a piece of paper. Then, with the assistance of another member, each trainee pins the paper to his/her back.

Trainer asks members to mill around, writing down one positive quality about that person on each trainee's paper (pinned on his/her back) until all are complete. Trainer should also participate. Trainer requests each member to remove and read the paper on his/her back. Trainer allows five minutes for members to savor the feedback privately.

Trainer distributes one envelope to each trainee and requests him/her to self-address it.

Two weeks later trainer mails the envelopes filled with positive feedback to each member. This step serves as a positive follow-up to the training event.

Trainers should be careful to include papers for missing members.

Outcome Indicator
1. All trainees should offer written feedback to each participant.

Session 47:
Training Evaluation

Time
One hour

Goals
• To present an overview of the training to helpers.

• To answer any final questions.

Materials
Video tape, VCR, Training Evaluation Sheets, Personal Assessment Sheets, and pencils.

Process
Trainer presents a brief summary of the training design and exercises. Play back some tapes of previous exercises. Call for any final questions. This event should turn into a general discussion.

Trainer readministers Index of Perception (see Appendix A, Model 4) and compares results with pretest.

Trainer distributes Training Evaluation Sheets, Personal Assessment Sheets, and pencils and instructs the trainees to complete them. Trainer leads a short discussion to critique the training program and give feedback to the group members on their contributions.

Outcome Indicator
1. All group members should be interacting, asking questions, and responding to each other.

Training Evaluation Sheet

Name_____   Date_____

Directions

This is not a test. There are no right or wrong answers. We are using this evaluation to improve the existing helping program. Please respond by checking or writing. You may check more than one item if appropriate.

1. Do you feel that the training sessions helped you to communicate with others?

_____Helped a lot   _____Doubt that they helped

_____Helped a little   _____Did not help

2. How interesting did you feel these training activities were?

_____Very   _____Not very

_____Fairly   _____Boring

3. Please check below the training activities which you think should be used in training future peer leaders.

_____Group flashback (your own experiences at previous school)

_____Self-disclosure exercises (collages)

_____Trainer modeling

_____Conscious communication guidelines and barriers

_____Role playing ways to handle typical situations using communication skills

_____Transformative communication skills (matching, pacing, eye movements, anchoring, metaphor)

_____Warning signals that require referrals

_____Trainee role playing dealing with personal problems

_____Study skills role plays

_____Stress management activities

_____Personal empowerment activities (getting positive states)

Page 2 - Training Evaluation Sheet

_____Pathways to solutions

_____Refusal skills

_____Confrontation skills

_____Group leadership skills

_____Referral guidelines

4. Please list any additional types of activities which you feel could prepare leaders to help others.

_____

_____

_____

5. Do you feel the training helped you to deal with situations you confront in real life?

_____Most of the time   _____Not at all

____ Some of the time   _____All the time

6. What do you think was most helpful?

_____

_____

7. What could you have done without?

_____

_____

8. Comments

_____

_____

Personal Assessment Sheet

Name_____   Date_____

Directions
To get an idea of what this experience means to you, and what you discovered about yourself, please fill out this personal assessment.

Write numbers 1, 2, or 3 on the lines below.

1. Good   **2. Adequate**   **3. Needs Improvement**

1._____Closeness to others

2._____Personal involvement in process

3._____Expressive abilities

4._____Leadership confidence

5._____Group management skills

6. My strengths_____

_____

_____

_____

7. My limits_____

_____

_____

_____

8. I learned _____

_____

_____

_____

Page 2 - Personal Assessment Sheet

Names of other participants to whom I can turn for support:

Name   **Phone #**

_____   _____

_____   _____

_____   _____

_____   _____

_____   _____

_____   _____

Session 48:
Peer Leader Selection

Time
Two hours

Goals
• To determine which trainees qualify to be selected as peer leaders.

• To select peer leaders.

Materials
Video tape, VCR, checklists used in training, tapes of role plays, and attendance records.

Process
This selection process may be initiated using a committee, panel, or single trainer. **It should be done privately, and results should be announced to the trainees during individual interviews.**

1. Peer leaders should be selected from the trainee group on the basis of their:

• Attendance

• Participation and interest

• Checklist information

• Taped role plays

• Ability to relate to other trainers, trainees, and teachers

• Discrimination abilities as measured by the Index of Perception

2. Trainers should meet privately with unselected trainees to explain reasons for denying their entry into the program. Strategies for self-improvement should be suggested. Those not selected should be encouraged to reapply next year.

Outcome Indicator
1. A core of peer leaders should be selected from the trainee group.

Session 49:
Program Selection

Time
Forty-five minutes

Goals
• To present an overview of the prevention programs to the peer leaders.

• To answer questions about the programs.

• To encourage the peer leaders to select their program preferences.

Materials
Lined paper for sign up sheets and Program Descriptions (see Introduction, pp. 6-7).

Process
Trainer distributes Program Descriptions to the peer leaders, answers questions about the programs, divides the leaders into groups of six, and asks the groups to discuss the programs and select preferences. On a lined sheet of paper, peer leaders should list four programs in order of priority.

Trainer should stress the importance of personality factors, leadership qualities, and matching of expertise to the various program models.

Trainer should explain that he/she will review the selections and make the final assignments in accordance with logistical considerations and appropriate matching.

Outcome Indicators
1. All group members should be interacting, asking questions, and responding to each other.

2. All group members should sign up for four programs.

Session 50: Poster Making

Time
Forty-five minutes

Goal
• To publicize the program with posters revealing the peer leaders' personal reflections on the training, the group, and peer leadership.

Materials
• Poster board, magazines, pens, magic markers, scissors, tape, and crayons.

Process
Ask peer leaders to create posters about the program out of clippings, words, and pictures. Posters should reflect personal spirit of peer helping as well as the themes of the eleven programs.

Outcome Indicators
1. Peer leaders should discuss changes in attitudes, themes of the program, feelings, and goals.

2. Peer leaders should use communication skills as observed by trainer.

3. Group unity should be shown in common themes on posters, messages, and the numbers of posters produced. Interaction, leadership, and role definition should reflect cohesiveness.

SECTION 3 —
SMOOTH TRANSITIONS

SECTION 3 — SMOOTH TRANSITIONS

Description

Trained juniors and seniors assist incoming students in their adjustment to high school. They serve as positive role models to guide these younger students through the first months of their new high school environment. The partnerships are intensified through a one day program of problem-solving activities which serve as metaphors for overcoming adversity in a new environment. After a few months at the high school, the ninth grade partners find their own activities and support networks. They no longer need to continue the intense guidance of their peer guides, and the frequency of contacts naturally diminishes.

Goals

• To facilitate students' positive transition to the high school milieu.

• To prevent partners from entering a negative peer subculture which promotes self-damaging behavior such as substance abuse.

• To promote academic adjustment; involvement in positive, cocurricular, organized activities; and social relationships developed around self-enhancing activities.

Planning

Coordinator secures permission from appropriate administrators to identify middle school students who appear to be mildly at risk for underachievement, self-damaging behavior, participation in negative peer culture, or abdication of responsibility as they enter their high school transition period.

Then, coordinator confers with the school principal who may assist in requesting relevant staff members to identify potential at-risk students. It is also necessary to arrange for dates, times, and available room resources for the orientation meeting which should be held in May or June of the current academic year.

Selection

PEER GUIDES. Selected high school students who have been trained as peer leaders are enlisted to develop partnerships with the younger students at the middle school and then to guide them on a one-to-one basis through their entry into the high school milieu. Matching criteria include interests, background, same gender, and abilities.

PARTNERS. Middle school students who

require support in their high school transitional adjustment are selected by middle school staff members. Students who agree to enter the program are then screened by appropriate staff members. The program goals are explained to the potential candidates during a screening interview.

Training

Peer leaders should have completed regular training program of communication and learning support techniques. These are sufficient to enable them to guide younger students through the first weeks of the ninth grade.

They should observe experienced peer guides and a coordinator run through the orientation segment of the program. Then they should rehearse the sessions while being rated by the experienced leader and coordinator. After review and revision, peer leaders are now ready to conduct their part of the orientation.

Parental Permission

All younger students (partners) will require written consent from their parents. (See Appendix A, Model 11.) Sometimes a phone call or meeting is necessary to field questions and clarify program goals.

Implementation

This process is intended to inspire collaboration, initiate partnerships, promote positive identity, and develop working relationships. In the spring, a group of high school peer leaders enters the middle school for a two hour orientation program with the younger students. They go through structured experiences designed to promote cohesiveness.

Some activities should be led by you, others by newly assigned leaders, and others by experienced leaders who have already been through the program the previous year but will not serve as guides this year. You will need to make up a roster of the peer guides and their partners for distribution. These rosters and the Support Network Sheets are distributed to promote ongoing contacts over the summer.

In September of the following year, after the partners enter high school, they are greeted by the high school guides on the first day of school for a one hour orientation session, supervised by appropriate staff members. The next organized activity is a one day group activity, for example, an outing into the woods. Outward Bound or similar problem-solving experiences, limited to a one day program, are very helpful in initiating trust and cooperation.

After the organized activity, student guides make themselves available to these newly initiated partners to offer academic and social support throughout their transition to the high school milieu. These contacts are voluntary and informal.

Program coordinator arranges ongoing supervision of the guides to provide professional advice and backup on a biweekly basis. Such meetings may be held in the morning before classes begin or during lunch. Constant monitoring and feedback is encouraged and problem-solving techniques are developed through the natural supportive group process of the high school peer leaders. Supervisors encourage guides to make referrals if behavioral warning signals appear in their partners.

Evaluation

The program is evaluated on the following dimensions:

• Partners' ratings of their guides as positive role models at completion of first marking period.

• Partners' ratings of the usefulness of the experiences provided by the orientation program.

Instruments may include the following:

• Partners' Orientation Day Evaluation.

• Smooth Transitions Guides' Evaluation Sheet — after first marking period.

• Smooth Transitions Partners' Evaluation Sheet — after first marking period.

• Work Sample Rating Form (Appendix, Model 20).

• Ninth grade report cards and attendance tally.

Follow-Up

After one marking period, contacts diminish if report card grades and other adjustment indicators show that ninth graders are ready to function independently.

Paper Trail

1. Receiving Student Parent Consent Form.   *(See Appendix A, Model 11.)*

2. Peer Leader ID Card Prototype.   *(See Appendix A, Model 17)*

3. Peer Leader Pass.   *(See Appendix A, Model 15.)*

4. Receiving Student Pass.   *(See Appendix A, Model 16.)*

5. Group Leadership Checklist.   *(See Section 2, Session 42.)*

6. Facts and Myths about High School Sheet.   *(See p. 182.)*

7. Resource Network Sheet.   *(See p. 183.)*

8. Partners' Orientation Day Evaluation Sheet.   *(See p. 184.)*

9. Smooth Transitions Partners' Evaluation Sheet.   *(See p. 185.)*

10. Smooth Transitions Guides' Evaluation Sheet.   *(See p. 187.)*

Trainees' Observation of All Sessions

Time
Two hours

Goals
• To familiarize new trainees with the Smooth Transitions Orientation Day Program by observing the coordinator and/or advanced peer guides from previous years's program conducting the session.

• To review the Orientation Day evaluation and make necessary revisions for the next cycle.

Materials
Group Leadership Checklist (see Section 2, Session 42), and pencils.

Process
Two peer guide trainees and one adult trainer observe the two-hour orientation session while completing one checklist for each exercise.

In the first year of the program, the sessions are led by the coordinator with the peer leaders serving in the role of guides. In the second year of the program, the sessions are led by the coordinator and two advanced peer guides from last year with the new peer leaders serving in the role of guides.

After the session closes, trainees attend a process conference with the coordinator and peer leaders who conducted the session. Coordinator and leaders provide feedback and clarify any concerns. Trainees and leaders review receiving students' Smooth Transitions Evaluation forms.

Both leaders and trainer work together to revise the program for the next cycle. Then the new trainees rehearse conducting the sessions while experienced leaders and coordinators provide feedback and criticize their leadership.

Outcome Indicators
1. Trainees should complete Group Leadership Checklist.

2. Trainees should offer feedback to coordinator and peer leaders who conducted the session.

3. All should review the Partners' and Guides' Evaluations and participate in the program revision.

4. Trainees should rehearse the orientation session and make necessary adjustments in their leadership style.

5. Experienced coordinator and peer leaders should rate the trainees as competent before they conduct their own session.

LEADER'S GUIDE

Session 1, Part 1: Orientation*

Time
Five minutes

Goal
• To provide younger students with a short overview of the Smooth Transitions Program and the orientation activities.

Materials
None.

Process
Prior to this activity, coordinator should match students with their guides based on personality profiles and same gender criteria.

Coordinator introduces new peer guides, support staff members, and young partners to each other. if this is the second year of the program, the coordinator introduces as leaders advanced peer guides from last years' program, new peer guides, support staff members, and young partners to each other.

The partnerships are arranged in pairs and asked to sit at tables (with two to three pairs seated at each table). Then, coordinator provides a short overview of the program's goals and the activities of the day is given by the coordinator. Allow time for questions from the group.

Outcome Indicator
1. The group should be attentive to the overview. Members' questions will indicate interest level.

*Led by coordinator or advanced peer guides.

LEADER'S GUIDE

Session 1, Part 2: Name Tags*

Time
Twenty minutes

Goal
• To foster awareness of feelings, needs, and positive qualities shared with the entire group.

Materials
3 x 5 index cards and pencils.

Process
Coordinator or two advanced peer guides introduce the exercise as follows:

This is an exercise designed to help you get to know each other. In the upper left-hand corner of a 3 x 5 card, jot down a very special place that gives you positive feelings. It may be a place you remember from the past, or somewhere you spend time in the present. (Pause.) Now, in the bottom left-hand corner, write down the name of someone you admire. (Pause.)

In the top right-hand corner, jot down what you consider to be the nicest day of your life. It may be a day of the week, a day that gave you great pleasure in the past, or your ideal vision of a good day. (Pause.)

In the bottom right-hand corner, jot down an event or experience in your life that you think of as a personal triumph or success. It could be learning to ride a bike, a first date, or anything that you are proud of in the smallest or biggest way. (Pause.) Now, in the middle of the card, jot down a title of the movie of your life. Imagine some famous producer has offered to make a film about you. Write down the title that you would choose.

Coordinator or peer guides instruct two pairs of partners and guides (four people) to spend a minute of uninterrupted time introducing each other through their name tags. Each person gets one minute to question her or his partner to clarify any words on the card. Students may pass on any question they choose not to answer. If time remains, partners and guides should switch groups of four and repeat the process in a different group.

Outcome Indicators
1. All partners and guides should have an opportunity to introduce themselves through their cards.

2. Laughter and discussion should indicate some self-disclosure activities through which the partnerships familiarize themselves.

*Led by coordinator or advanced peer guides.

LEADER'S GUIDE

Session 1, Part 3: Facts and Myths about High School*

Time
Fifteen minutes

Goal
• To enable partners to clarify their assumptions about the high school, demystify myths, and distinguish between rumor and truth.

Materials
Fact and Myths about High School Sheets and pencils.

Process
Coordinator or peer guides distribute Facts and Myths Sheets to the students. Partners are instructed to read the fifteen statements and indicate whether they are true or false by placing a check in the appropriate column.

Then the coordinator or peer guides initiate a discussion on each of the facts and myths to rule out rumors and identify some of the actual high school experiences they must face in the coming year.

Outcome Indicators
1. All partners should complete the forms.

2. Partners should ask several questions about high school.

3. Group discussion should focus on the continuum ranging from truth to exaggeration to falsehood.

*Led by new advanced peer guides.

Session 1, Part 4: Silent Cooperation*

Time
Thirty minutes

Goals
• To provide an opportunity for two groups of six (three partnerships) to cooperate and learn about leadership, interdependency, and support while competing with another group.

• To enable partners and guides to develop cooperative relationships.

Materials
Construction toys, tables, and chairs.

Process
Coordinator or peer guides request two groups of six (three partnerships) to occupy two different tables. Then the coordinator or peer guide distributes construction toys and selects two advanced peer leaders to serve as monitors and judges.

Coordinator or peer guides introduce the exercise as follows:

Each group must construct a creative project that is attached and can stand on its own. There is to be no talking, and everybody must participate. I will observe the groups, watching for any talkers, and will judge the final projects. Any talking will be counted against the whole group. You will have fifteen minutes.

Coordinator monitors time. After fifteen minutes, judges confer and announce the winning creation. Each group is asked to have a lively discussion on the process.

Discussion should focus on behavior of active members, passive members, rule breakers, helpers, intruders, and spies. Effects of frustration should also be discussed. Further discussion should focus on how each project reflects its group's identity.

Outcome Indicators
1. Two projects, one for each group, should be completed.

2. A lively discussion describing the process should produce some insights about cooperation, competition, creativity, and group roles.

*Led by coordinator or advanced peer guides.

Session 1, Part 5: Pairing and Sharing*

Time
Fifteen minutes

Goal
• To offer partners and guides an opportunity to share in a personal experience and discover how it reflects on each person's pride, self-awareness, self-concept, and new learning.

Materials
None.

Process
Coordinator or peer leader introduces the exercise as follows:

This is an exercise designed to give you practice in getting to know each other. Each of us has, at one time or another, gone through a struggle or a particularly exciting experience that was meaningful.

I would like you to break up into pairs (partners and guides) and move yourselves in different locations throughout the room. (Pause.) Please spend the next five minutes sharing a personal experience of any type with each other.

High school guides should go first, spending their time describing an experience which is important to them in any way. Partners should listen, and at the end of five minutes may ask as many questions as they wish about the experience. High school guides can either answer the questions or pass.

Then partners spend five minutes sharing an experience with their high school guides and repeat the same process.

After about fifteen minutes, instruct the group to form a circle with partners and their guides seated next to each other. Then initiate a discussion, identifying what it was like to share these experiences with each other. A round robin should unfold with each member completing the statement, "I learned..."

Outcome Indicator
1. Supervising adults should monitor the entire process and watch for facial expressions and body language indicating interest. Lots of laughter should demonstrate positive effects, feelings, and sharing.

*Led by coordinator or advanced peer leader.

LEADER'S GUIDE

Session 1, Part 6: Resource Network*

Time
Fifteen minutes

Goals
• To identify group members' interests, skills, and common activities so as to share them among the group.

• To create a phone chain and communication network to share these skills and interests.

Materials
Resource Network Sheets and pencils.

Process
Coordinator or peer leader introduces the exercise as follows:

Today you have learned much about each other through your activities. You have learned about some of your heroes, nice experiences, personal successes, and titles of your own movies.

You have also learned some facts and myths about high school, and some ways to deal with these experiences when you enter high school. You also have learned how to cooperate without talking and how to build creative projects. Finally you have talked a little bit about your lives and shared some personal information.

Based on all these things that you know, it's time now to identify yourselves and list some of the

interests and skills that you are willing to share with each other. I am going to pass out a Resource Network Sheet on which you can sign your name, put your phone number, and list any of the skills or mutual interests that you would be willing to share with someone else.

For example, if there is a math expert in the group, please offer your skill to those who despise math. You may also want to learn how to scuba dive or grow vegetables over the summer. Many of you may have some talents in gardening or other summer activities. I will begin by putting down my name, phone number, and some of my skills and interests that I am willing to share over the summer.

Distribute the sheets, allow time for the group to fill them out, and then collect them. Complete the event as follows:

We are looking forward to seeing you in the fall at the high school. We wish you all a great summer.

Outcome Indicators
1. All group members should fill out the Resource Network sheets.

2. Network sheets should be photocopied and distributed to the entire group for use during the summer.

*Led by coordinator or advanced peer leader.

Session 1, Part 7: Orientation Day Evaluation*

Time
Ten minutes

Goal
• To provide an opportunity for partners to give feedback and suggestions for improvement of the orientation day.

Materials
Partners' Orientation Day Evaluation Sheets and pencils.

Process
Coordinator or peer leader introduces the session as follows:

Now that we have been through this introduction, we would like to get some of your reactions to it so that we may modify it in the next year. Please fill out the Partners' Orientation Day Evaluation Sheets. You needn't write your names on them. Just write the date and feel free to write any suggestions which you might think would benefit the program.

Thank you very much for attending this one day session. It was a pleasure working with all of you and getting to know some of you better. We are all looking forward to picking this up next year. We will be meeting on the first day of your high school career during lunch time.

Outcome Indicator
1. Group members should complete the evaluation form.

*Led by coordinator.

Session 2: Wilderness Day*

Time
One seven-hour day

Goal
• To enable the guides and their partners to form working relationships.

Materials
Wilderness Challenge equipment.

Process
Take partners and their guides on a one day outing that includes obstacles, games, and group problem-solving activities, such as hurdles, rock climbing, and ropes courses.

Outcome Indicator
1. Group should show evidence of cooperation, support, and interdependence.

*Led by trained wilderness expert.

Subsequent Sessions

Guides and partners continue contacts personally and by phone as necessary. Your coordinator will hold periodic group events such as Breakfast Clubs and excursions to encourage unity and get reactions.

You are urged to keep in touch with partners at least once a week for the first marking period. You may want to refer them to specific teachers or peers who have expertise in particular subject areas which require attention. Collect work samples periodically and ask your advisors to have them rated. Your advisors will also collect report cards and information from teacher observation forms and share this with you.

Regularly scheduled advisory sessions between guides and coordinator should be used to monitor the program and assess your partners' progress. Use your sessions to review progress and get advice on how to help them adjust. Remember that your part-

ners should be aware that your discussion of their personal issues will be limited to the peer support program staff, except in cases of emergencies. Make appropriate referrals of any students who show behavioral warning signals.

After the first marking period your coordinator will ask you to give your partner the **Smooth Transitions Partners' Evaluation Sheet** and have him/her turn it in to the coordinator's office. Although it is confidential, you may want to get some general reactions about issues common to all from your coordinator and partner.

At the end of the second marking period, your coordinator will distribute and collect the **Smooth Transitions Guides' Evaluation Sheets** and then hold a general meeting to review the program and suggest changes for next year.

Facts and Myths about High School Sheets

Name_____   Date_____

Directions
There are many things you hear about high school before you go there. Some of these things are true and some are false. See if you can guess which ones are real and which ones are not.

True or false?

1. Older kids will push you into the boys' bathroom and shove pot down your mouth.

2. Kids will take your lunch money because you are a freshman.

3. It is easy to find your way around the high school.

4. All freshmen are beaten up by older kids.

5. There is a day called Freshman Friday when freshmen are picked on by older kids.

6. The work is so hard that you will fall flat on your face.

7. Some teachers are nice and will help you with your work.

8. Adjusting to high school is not easy and will take some time.

9. You can smoke in the halls and nobody cares.

10. It is easy to cut classes without getting caught.

11. Chances are good that you will be stuffed in a locker by an older kid.

12. Older kids make you throw out their garbage in the cafeteria.

13. If you don't dress in the latest trends, you'll be made an outcast by teachers and classmates.

14. Some seniors will deliberately give you the wrong directions.

15. You can only go to your locker during certain periods.

Resource Network Sheet

Name _____   Date _____

Directions
Please fill in your name, phone number, and skills that you are willing to share with others.

Name	Phone #	Skills and Interests
1.		
2.		
3.		
4.		
5.		
6.		
7.		
8.		
9.		

Partners' Orientation Day Evaluation Sheet

School_____ Grade _____

Guide _____ Date_____

Directions

You have just completed a one day orientation with your high school guides. We want to thank you for being part of this experience and hope that you have gained some support from each other. Please take a couple of minutes to offer your reactions.

Please read each statement and write the number 1, 2, or 3 on the lines below.

1. Excellent   **2. Adequate**   **3. Needs Improvement**

1._____Leaders were prepared.

2._____Information provided was relevant and complete.

3._____Leaders were involved and listened actively.

4._____Leaders were supportive and responsive to any difficulties with the exercises.

5._____The exercises gave me a chance to learn about myself and other people.

6. I learned _____

_____

_____

7. Please write below any suggestions or comments which might improve the Orientation Day in the future.

_____

_____

_____

_____

8. Please read the statement below and check yes or no.

I think all students should have this program. Yes_____ No_____

Smooth Transitions Partners' Evaluation Sheet

School_____ Class_____ Grade _____

Guide(s) _____ Date_____

Directions
We would like to know what you think of Smooth Transitions. Please read each statement and write the number 1, 2, or 3 on the lines below.

1. Often   **2. Sometimes**   **3. Never**

1._____My guide saw me.

2._____We spoke to each other.

3._____My guide was helpful.

4._____My guide understands me.

5._____I look up to my guide.

6._____The program was helpful.

7. Please read the statement below and check yes or no.

I think this program would help other students and should be expanded.

Yes_____ No_____

8. Write down your suggestions on how to improve this program.

_____

_____

_____

_____

_____

_____

_____

Page 2 - Smooth Transitions Partners' Evaluation Sheet

9. Please read each statement about the Wilderness Day activities and circle the words that best describes your experience.

The activities we did relate to these parts of my life: (Circle as many as you want.)

a. Cargo net: school, friends, home, sports, work

b. Group ski: school, friends, home, sports, work

c. Islands: school, friends, home, sports, work

d. Trust Fall: school, friends, home, sports, work

e. Ropes Course: school, friends, home, sports, work

10. What changes did the Wilderness Day make in your relationship with your guide? (Circle one.)

Closer   More Distant   None

11. Write a sentence describing what you learned about yourself.

_____

_____

_____

12. Describe how you have used what you've learned in facing new experiences.

_____

_____

_____

Smooth Transitions Guides' Evaluation Sheet

Guide _____   Date_____

Partner _____

Directions
We would like to know what you think of Smooth Transitions. Please read each statement and write the number 1, 2, or 3 on the lines below.

1. Often   **2. Sometimes**   **3. Never**

1._____I made contact with my partner.

2._____It was easy to reach my partner.

3._____My partner contacted me.

4._____My partner discussed his/her problems with me.

5._____The program was helpful.

6. I think this program would help other students and should be expanded.

Yes_____ No_____

7. Write suggestions on how to improve this program.

_____

_____

_____

8. Please read each statement about the Wilderness Day activities you did and circle the words that best fit for you.

The activities we did relate to these parts of my life: (Circle as many as you want.)

a. Cargo net: school, friends, home, sports, work

b. Group ski: school, friends, home, sports, work

c. Islands: school, friends, home, sports, work

d. Trust fall: school, friends, home, sports, work

e. Ropes course: school, friends, home, sports, work

Page 2 - Smooth Transitions Guides' Evaluation Sheet

9. What changes did the Wilderness Day make in your relationship with your partner? (Circle one.)

Closer   More Distant   None

10. Write a sentence describing what you learned about yourself.

_____

_____

11. Describe how you have used what you've learned in facing new experiences.

_____

_____

_____

_____

SECTION 4 —
WELCOME

SECTION 4 —
WELCOME

Description

This program uses trained peer guides to orient transfer students who enter the school and community. It is intended for middle and high school levels. Peer guides meet with their partners at least three times to give them valuable information about the school and community and to assist them with their academic and social adjustment.

Partners and guides meet during lunch or before or after school to assess the transition process, initiate any positive contact or networks, and provide ongoing support. Frequency of contact diminishes as entering students reach their transitional goals and become part of the school culture.

Goals

• To facilitate entering students' positive transition to the high school milieu.

• To prevent maladaptive coping and alliances with negative peer subcultures.

• To promote positive academic and social adjustment, maximum use of talents and resources, and appropriate channelling of interests to productive activities.

Planning

Coordinators should clear this program with top level personnel such as the Superintendent of Schools and the Board of Education. Meetings should be held with school administrators, guidance director, counselors, department heads, and any other personnel who might be helpful in facilitating new students' transitional adjustments. The goals and objectives should be stated clearly. Written authorization for the program should precede implementation.

Selection

PEER GUIDES. Peer guides should be selected on the basis of their interest in this program. All of them should be trained in the communication skills of peer guiding. Students who are selected for this should be empathic, knowledgeable about the school, and well integrated into the school culture.

RECEIVING STUDENTS. Transfer students should be referred by guidance counselors, teachers, and other students. They may also be self-referred. Clear access to the program should be provided through a central receiving source such as a box for referrals in the school or a contact person in the guidance office.

Selection of these new students should be based on their willingness to participate, their need for information, and their academic profiles. Peer leaders and their partners should be matched on gender, interests, and background. Peer leaders should be at least one grade ahead of their receiving students.

Training

All peer guides should be trained in communication skills and referral guidelines. Clear warning signals for referrals should be reviewed. Trainees should observe experienced guides conducting their sessions. In addition, peer guides should spend one forty-five minute session with the coordinator or designee to go over the program's materials and format. These should include the Procedure Checklist, Entry Survey, and school-supplied information. The coordinator or designee should outline the sequence of events and field any questions about time lines or available scheduling opportunities.

Parental Permission

All peer guides and transfer students should have signed parental permission before they start the program. (See Appendix A, Models 5 and 11.)

Implementation

The sequence of events in the program shall proceed as follows:

1. Transfer student is referred to program coordinator.
2. Program coordinator selects appropriate peer guide using matching criteria.
3. Peer guide initiates contact with newly arrived student partner.
4. Peer guide follows the sequence of procedures on the procedure checklist.
5. After approximately four to six weeks, the guide gives out the Evaluation Sheet and goes over results with coordinator.
6. If the partner appears oriented and is performing well after four to six weeks, the peer guide no longer needs to continue meetings, unless behavior warning signals require further interventions.

Evaluation

Peer guides and program coordinator should use the Evaluation Sheets as a first level assessment of the program's impact.

Follow-Up

Program coordinator should follow up the partner's progress by checking report card information and any disciplinary reports. If warning signal behaviors are observed, referral to appropriate professionals should be made. Otherwise, in about four to eight weeks, frequency of contacts should diminish naturally as the new student becomes adjusted.

Paper Trail

1. Receiving Student Parent Consent Form. *(See Appendix A, Model 11.)*

2. Peer Leader ID Card Prototype. *(See Appendix A, Model 17.)*

3. Peer Leader Pass. *(See Appendix A, Model 15.)*

4. Procedure Checklist for Guides. *(See p. 194.)*

5. Welcome Program Entry Survey. *(See p. 196.)*

6. Welcome Program Evaluation Sheet. *(See p. 199.)*

Trainees' Observation of All Sessions

Time
Three hours

Goal
• To familiarize new trainees with the Welcome Program by observing a peer guide conducting the orientation and subsequent sessions.

Materials
Combining Your Skills Checklists (see Section 2, Session 25), Procedure Checklist for Guides, Welcome Program Entry Surveys, Welcome Program Evaluation Sheets, and pencils.

Process
One peer leader trainee observes each experienced guide conduct all sessions while completing one checklist for each session.

After each session closes, trainee attends a process conference with the coordinator and guide who conducted the session. Coordinator and leaders provide feedback to the experienced guide and clarify any concerns. Trainee and guide review receiving students' Welcome Program Evaluation Form.

Guide, trainee, and trainer revise the program for the next cycle. Then the new trainees rehearse conducting the sessions while experienced guide and coordinator provide feedback and criticize their leadership.

Outcome Indicators
1. New trainee guide should observe all sessions conducted by an experienced guide.

2. Trainee should complete one Combining Your Skills Checklist for each session.

3. Trainees should offer feedback to coordinator and peer leaders who conducted the session.

4. All should review the Welcome Program Evaluation and participate in the program revision.

LEADER'S GUIDE

Procedure Checklist for Guides

Directions
Use this checklist to guide your newly arrived partner. Meet regularly with your supervisor to determine the actions you have taken to help this new student.

Name_____ Date_____

Partner _____ Grade _____

Homeroom_____ Phone _____

____1. Provide a copy of school-related information and policy sheets and review entry.

____2. Provide orientation materials (school map, locker routine, schedule and room locations, school store and cafeteria routines).

____3. Provide Welcome Program Entry Survey.

____4. Go over all classes and teachers, making partner aware of particular expectations and streamlined approaches to deal with their classes. If necessary, call in backup guides who know the teachers.

____5. Review any dress codes, attendance, discipline, substance abuse policies, and all support services such as hotlines, peer support programs, and counseling services.

____6. Describe academic program options and refer partners to guidance counselor for detailed information and entry criteria.

____7. Review partner's Welcome Program Entry Survey.

____8. Bridge transactions where necessary. For example, if you find out your partner might respond to a peer tutor and your school has such a program, bring the student to the program coordinator.

____9. Assist partner in preliminary goal-setting.

____10. Make partner aware of clubs, athletic activities, and organizations that match interest profile indicated on Entry Survey. Provide introductions to these groups if necessary.

LEADER'S GUIDE
Procedure Checklist for Guides continued

____11. Describe community resources such as recreation facilities, cultural centers, volunteer and job opportunities, local stores, restaurants, and malls.

____12. Introduce partner to positive role models who might match interests and interface compatibly with cultural background.

____13. Arrange periodical follow-up meetings and phone contact information.

____14. Continue follow-up conferences during lunch and free time as long as necessary.

____15. Give your partner the Welcome Program Evaluation Sheet.

Welcome Program Entry Survey

Name_____   Date_____

Partner _____   Grade _____

Homeroom _____   Phone _____

Directions
Please take the time to fill out this survey about your interests and activities. It will help your guide to assist you in your entry to our school system.

1. Check the categories which best describe your previous school.

_____Rural   _____Suburban   _____Urban

_____Under 1,000   _____Under 2,000   _____Under 5,000

2. List some characteristics of your previous school that you find appealing.

_____

_____

_____

_____

3. List some things about your previous school that you did not like.

_____

_____

_____

_____

4. List the changes you need to make as a result of moving to this community.

_____

_____

_____

Page 2 - Welcome Program Entry Survey

_____

5. List your favorite subjects.

_____

_____

6. List subjects most difficult for you.

_____

_____

7. List some of your interests below.

a. Sports_____

_____

b. Hobbies _____

_____

c. Cocurricular activities and clubs _____

_____

_____

d. Academic programs such as mentorships, community service, college credit course, etc.

_____

_____

e. Music _____

_____

f. Leisure time activities _____

_____

Page 3 - Welcome Program Entry Survey

8. What type of peer group activities do you enjoy? _____

_____

_____

9. Describe your peer group in the previous school.

_____

_____

_____

10. Describe the types of students you would like to meet here.

_____

_____

_____

_____

11. What are your future goals after graduation? _____

_____

_____

12. List any new interest or projects you would like to develop this year.

_____

_____

13. List any things your peer guide can do that might be helpful to you.

_____

_____

_____

Welcome Program Evaluation Sheet

School _____   Grade _____

Directions
We would like to find out if the Welcome Program was helpful and if there should be any changes. To give us your reactions, complete this evaluation and return it to your guide.

Please read each statement and write the number 1, 2, or 3 on the lines below.

1. Excellent   2. Adequate   3. Needs Improvement

My guide:

1._____Helped me learn about the new school.

2._____Introduced me to students.

3._____Linked me with people who could help me with my homework when necessary.

4._____Directed me to people who could help me get involved with school activities.

5._____Was attentive to my needs.

6._____Showed that he/she cared.

7._____Was reliable and on time for our meetings.

8._____Followed through with activities and suggestions.

9. My guide can do the following things to improve:

_____

_____

_____

_____

Page 2 - Welcome Program Evaluation Sheet

10. The program needs to improve in the following ways:

_____

_____

_____

11. The things I liked about the program are:

_____

_____

_____

_____

SECTION 5 —
ONE-TO-ONE

SECTION 5 —
ONE-TO-ONE

Description

One-to-One enables trained high school peer leaders to meet with younger elementary and middle school students individually to assist them in their educational and social development. This program combines personal support with tutoring approaches.

The tutoring allows a peer leader to support a younger student and cultivate a helping alliance around a specific, subject oriented task. The program merges both affective and cognitive domains to reduce a threat sometimes felt by students who reject traditional counseling services.

The academic assistance occurs in one subject area at the beginning of each session, and continues in that particular subject until major improvement is noted.

These sessions are held at the receiving student's school at the beginning of the school day, during lunch, or at the end of the school day. The sessions last approximately 45 minutes and sometimes develop into an informal partnership.

High school peer leaders assist their younger recipients in developing desired outcomes, strategies to attain them, and utilization of sup-port resources. Relationships usually continue until the receiving student's goals are completed or another type of referral is warranted.

Goals

FOR RECEIVING STUDENTS:
• To improve academic performance in one target subject area.

• To formulate appropriate desired outcomes, develop strategies to attain them, and improve social competence.

FOR PEER LEADERS:
• To apply their own sensitivity to others in helping relationships.

• To sharpen communication and tutoring skills.

Planning

Program coordinator begins by constructing a program description and fact sheet which includes mission, goals, objectives, training, process, and evaluation. Use the format of the program description and fact sheet contained in Model 5 in Appendix A, as a guide. Assess your receivers' population, carefully delineating the student profiles to be addressed. Older students (peer leaders) are more equipped to work with younger students than same age peers.

Receiving students most receptive to older peers are usually withdrawn, socially isolated, marginal achievers, with average or above average intelligence, and standardized achievement scores no lower than ten percent below local mean percentiles. Acting out, rebellious, delinquent students, or extremely depressed youngsters usually require professional interventions.

Approach central administrators in your target setting and secure their written approval. Then present the program to building supervisors for approval. Make sure that your local educational agency has given its written endorsement.

After receiving approval, call together potential referring teachers and guidance personnel, and distribute Receiving Student Referral Forms which outline the criteria for admission into the program (see Appendix A, Model 7). Distribute program fact sheets, and make it clear that peer leaders will not be supplying professional counselors' services but will serve as adjuncts, functioning in a limited capacity to enhance the educational development of these students.

Enlist the teachers' support in making referrals as well as serving as potential advisors to these peer leaders who meet with younger students. Be sure to explain that the program is voluntary for all participants, including peer leaders and receiving students. Set up a trial period of perhaps twelve weeks during which a pilot project may operate with a limited number of students. Use evaluation methods indicated in Section 1 — Program Development. These might include report card grades, work sample improvements, attendance improvements, and self-esteem inventories. Use the pre-to-post evaluation model.

Selection

PEER LEADERS. Peer leaders should have completed the communication skills training and demonstrated patience and understanding. They should have two available periods per week to help others.

RECEIVING STUDENTS. Check the receiving students' permanent records to screen out severe problems. Distribute Receiving Student Application Forms (see Appendix A, Model 8).

Interview a select number of students, and distribute parent consent forms.

It may be necessary to invite parents in for a meeting to describe the general principles of the program. In any event, be sure to supply the parents with a fact sheet indicating all the program components. Highlight the preventive nature of this program which ultimately aspires to interrupt negative patterns before they lead to more serious, self-damaging behavior.

It is important to screen the referred student population by checking permanent records to eliminate students who have severe illnesses or disciplinary problems. Acute learning disabilities may also pose problems meeting criteria.

Interview and select six to ten students as a pilot group. Explain to those who were not selected that their profiles are more suited to other interventions. Place some others on a waiting list. Be sure to make recommendations to guidance and teachers regarding program options for these students who are inappropriate for the program.

Matching

Before matching peer leaders with their younger students, determine the subject area where help is needed. Match older peer leaders and receivers according to peer leaders' proficiency in the specific subject areas where assistance is needed. Once you have matched candidates with competent students, pair them according to gender.

Subdivide gender and subject group according to common interests and hobbies. These subdivisions should yield a group of potential older and younger student pairs. From these pairs, select a group of peer leaders who could be released from their nonessential classes or lunch periods. Be sure that available periods of receivers and leaders are matched. Using after school time can ease the scheduling pressure.

After assignments are made, schedule individual conferences with the peer leaders to go over academic and social profiles of the receiving students.

Training

All peer leaders participating in One-to-One

should be trained in three days of communication, tutoring, and referral skills. Use the regular training format as a guide. Initiate a twenty minute session to prepare peer leaders to meet their younger receiving students.

Parental Permission

All peer leaders and receiving students should have signed parent permission before they start the program. (See Appendix A, Models 5 and 11.)

Implementation

Issue passes to both younger students and their peer leaders. (See Appendix A, Models 15 and 16.) These passes will enable them to be released from lunch period or whatever designated period is available.

Create an Assignment Sheet and issue to all teachers and personnel who are affected by the schedule changes of both leaders and receivers. (See Appendix A, Model 13.) This might include teachers who supervise lunch periods, physical education teachers, or guidance counselors.

Send a memo to all teachers of peer leaders, advising them of these activities. (See Appendix A, Model 6.) In addition, issue a Peer Leader Identification Card to each peer leader with his or her name and phone number. (See Appendix A, Model 17.) The card should be carried by the peer leader. It officially authorizes his/her presence in the receiving school's facility. Be sure to set up procedures to transport the older peer leaders to the target school.

Arrange a ten minute group meeting of all peer leaders and receiving students. The meeting should cover the following:

• Introductions and personal backgrounds.

• Times and places of helping sessions.

• Clear contracts between leaders and receivers,

• The existence of a four-week trial period and the procedures for evaluating progress.

After the group meeting, break into pairs to allow leaders and receivers to meet and to decide whether they would like to work together.

You might schedule these meetings for a ten minute interval. After these interviews have taken place, check with both younger and older students to find out whether they agree to work together.

After the assignments have been made, letters should go out to those eligible applicants who were not placed in the program. The letter should advise them that they will be on a waiting list, in case more resources become available. (See Appendix A, Model 12.)

Send a memo to the teachers of all participating receiving students asking them to fill out Receiving Student Evaluation Sheets to get a baseline self-esteem rating. (See Appendix A, Models 9 and 10.)

SESSION 1. This session offers an opportunity for peer leaders to practice rapport skills and information exchanges with each other. The Coordinator leads a type of rehearsal of the first session with feedback discussion of their concerns.

SESSION 2. Each peer leader should spend the second session assisting the receiver in filling out the Self-Evaluation Sheet.

SESSION 3. Peer leaders should assist receivers in forming Action Plans. Peer leaders should get permission to discuss academic goals and strategies with receivers' teachers.

SUBSEQUENT SESSIONS. Leaders and receivers should work on goals, discuss progress, and select new goals.

INTRODUCING LEADERS TO REFERRING TEACHERS. Arrange a meeting of referring teachers and peer leaders so that they may introduce themselves to each other. The peer leaders and referring teachers may share information about the receiving students and identify general goals and strategies.

Prior to the meeting, send a memo to all peer leaders and referring teachers. The memo should state the purpose, time, and place of meeting. At the meeting, distribute Assignment Sheets and Passes. (See Appendix A, Models 13, 15, and 16.) Ask teachers and peer leaders to break into pairs with one teacher and one peer leader in each pair.

Each pair should:

• Introduce themselves.

• Discuss reasons for participating in the program.

• Review academic and social goals for the receiving student and devise strategies for achieving them.

• Arrange a day and time for weekly ten minute conferences to discuss progress.

• Record such on Program Checklist. (See Appendix A, Model 18.)

Distribute copies of the checklist to referring teachers, peer leaders, and receiving students.

Supervision

Supervision is an essential component, reflecting the basic core of any student helping program. It is strongly suggested that you set up a supervision schedule with a trained coordinator or advisor to meet with peer leaders individually once a week.

These meetings can be set up before or after each helping session. Early mornings are sometimes the only available time during the day when advisors and peer leaders can touch base. Schedule these individual supervision sessions for approximately twenty minutes. Go over goal formulation, progress towards goals, and dynamics of each helping session.

Use brainstorming techniques to trouble-shoot and to access resources who might enhance the helping process. These include teachers, parents, outside community members, and others who have areas of expertise in particular subjects. Identify and refer any students who show behavioral warning signals.

The following activities are suggested for the first supervisory session:

1. Go over samples of receiving student's work.

2. Discuss goals and strategies.

3. Discuss the qualities of the helping relationship.

4. Elicit any questions about strategies and problems in the helping relationship and in the working relationship between peer leader and consulting teacher.

5. Review the relevant techniques learned in training.

6. Distribute schedule of supervision seminars.

7. Work out any administrative issues, such as room assignments and scheduling details.

8. Distribute blank 8 x 10 composition notebooks to be used as logs.

9. Fill out Program Checklist. (See Appendix A, Model 18.)

Schedule a once-a-month group meeting of all peer leaders participating in the One-to-One Program. These conferences can create a support network to offer suggestions regarding specific trouble spots and best responses to them. This collaborative sharing of ideas and strategies can promote a successful outcome of the program. Be aware of the confidentiality aspect, making sure that no privileged information leaves these sessions without receiving student's permission.

If possible, schedule ongoing follow-up training conferences with the peer leaders at mutually acceptable times.

Learning objectives for the ongoing training program are as follows:

• To reinforce and enhance communication and tutoring skills.

• To reinforce and increase skills in giving and receiving feedback.

• To review referral procedures.

Occasionally, it is helpful for a peer leader and/or coordinator to meet with a given student's teacher to intervene, where a particular conflict ensues. Such a meeting should be held with the informed consent of the receiving student. Discussions between teacher, peer leader, and coordinator clarify goals and procedures or initiate new goals or strategies when necessary.

Gathering and Recording Data

PEER LEADER DATA. To measure changes in the behavior and level of skills as a result of participation in the peer support program, coordinators should record baseline data on peer leaders.

Measure initial levels of discrimination, record baseline scores on the Pre-Training Peer Leader Competency Assessment, retest each six weeks, and compare scores. (See Appendix A, Model 4.) Elicit evaluative feedback about the training sessions, and consult the Training Evaluation Sheet. (See Section 2, Session 47.)

After four weeks, administer One-To-One Student Evaluation Sheet to obtain feedback regarding the receivers' levels of satisfaction with their peer leaders. Tabulate scores and note which areas appear to need improvement. iscuss these areas with peer leaders and receivers in order to determine strategies to increase the program's effectiveness.

RECEIVING STUDENT DATA. The following data may be obtained from permanent record cards, the Receiving Student Evaluation filled out by teachers, work samples, and report cards. Pre and post-test data on receiving students should be gathered.

At the program's inception and at two-month intervals, work samples should be collected by peer leaders. Select a group of teachers who are not part of the program to rate pre and post-intervention work samples. (See Appendix A, Model 20 for Rating Form.) Each marking period, students' grades in target subjects should be recorded.

At the beginning of the program and at twelve week intervals, Receiving Student Evaluations should be distributed and collected. Coordinators should take responsibility for collecting this data from subject teachers. (See Appendix A, Model 10.)

When report cards are issued, coordinators should record and compare attendance and grades.

Data Analysis
The data lends itself to analysis using methods ranging from informal to statistical. Various methods may be used, depending on the availability of time, personnel, and budgetary resources.

Regardless of whether covariance analysis, percentages, or significance tests are used, bear in mind that mean differences of baseline and post-test scores between groups should be compared. Single group score change comparisons are often deceptive and provide unreliable results.

Be sure to provide feedback to all involved staff members at regular intervals throughout the program. Keep everyone informed of changes in schedules for teachers, peer leaders, and receivers. This feedback can best be accomplished by sending written progress reports to involved staff members and administrators.

If the program duration is one semester, it is often helpful to schedule one or two group conferences with teachers and administrators to provide information and receive suggestions for change.

Hold group advisory sessions with peer leaders and coordinators to evaluate data, discuss teacher-peer leader relationships and any other program issues. In a sense, these meetings can serve as a support system through which the peer leaders can air their frustrations resulting from program pressures.

PEER LEADER DATA. This data collection will assist you in assessing the level of helper effectiveness as perceived by receivers and shown on specific skill measurements.

Peer Leader Sensitivity
To measure indices of peer leaders' sensitivity to receiving students' personal problems and struggles, retabulate affectively toned words in their log entries. Compare amount of affectively toned phrases with baseline and with two month assessments.

Discrimination
To measure discrimination, readminister Peer Leader Competency Assessment to peer leaders. Compare baseline pretest scores with post-test scores, and calculate differences in scores. Compare difference in scores.

Receivers' Satisfaction with Peer Leader

To evaluate the receivers' perception of their peer leaders, compare the levels of satisfaction as measured by pre and post-tests on One-To-One Evaluation Sheets.

RECEIVING STUDENT DATA. This data collection step enables you to assess receiving student progress and the impact of the peer intervention on their behavior and attitude.

Receivers and Control Group Attendance

Check report cards to compare attendance. Record the days that receiving students were absent. Compare current marking period's attendance with attendance during the previous marking period. Comparisons can be made in terms of numbers of absences for each group, percentages of increased school attendance, or more sophisticated measures.

Grades

Check report card grades for current marking periods. Locate target subjects for receivers' group. Record pre and post-test differences in grades for each student. Compare changes.

Work Samples

Check quality of work samples for each receiver. Select objective teachers to rate the work samples from the pre to post-tests. Note score changes and compare differences between individuals. (See Appendix A, Model 20 for Rating Form.)

Self-Concept

Score Receiving Students Evaluations and compare pre and post-test results in asserting, coping, investing, and relating categories. Compare score changes and differences between individuals. (See Appendix A, Model 10.)

Steps for Winding up the Program

TRANSFER. If, by the end of the year, it is felt that a student needs continuous assistance for the following year, and the peer leader in charge is graduating, an unobtrusive transfer should be made. The peer leader should introduce a younger trained peer leader who matches interest level, schedules, and other profile criteria mentioned earlier.

A transition period of about three weeks where the new peer leader participates in sessions is a helpful way to ease the transfer process.

REASONS FOR TERMINATION. If it is clear that the peer leader and receiving student are experiencing difficulties within the helping context, early termination of the arrangement may be a potential option. Such indicators might include poor attendance, personality conflicts, lack of goal completion, lying and inauthenticity, and verbal requests to terminate the relationship from either peer leader or receiving student.

At this point, if such a need arises, the coordinator should meet with both students to determine the appropriateness of termination or transfer to another student.

END-OF-PROGRAM PARTY. Arrange with administration to provide funds for refreshments for an end-of-the-year party. Send a memo to teachers of leaders and receivers to allow these students to be excused for the last hour of school. The memo should be sent out two weeks prior to the party. Send invitations two weeks in advance to the leaders and receivers. Plan to have games and refreshments. Ask leaders to aid in buying the refreshments.

If weather permits, have the party outside. All group activities such baseball, frisbee, and other games are helpful in generating spirit and group unity.

Spend about fifteen minutes with the entire group in a circle. Ask them to make statements about how they saw the program, what they derived from their experiences, and how the program could be improved. Record their suggestions. Ask peer leaders to provide receiving students with addresses and phone numbers and to assure them that they will be available for informal gatherings.

PEER LEADER EVALUATION. To elicit evaluative feedback from leaders regarding the program's effectiveness, administer the Program Evaluation. Note any patterns in answers to questions and record recommended changes for next year's program. (See Appendix A, Model 22.)

FINAL PEER LEADER MEETING. Call group meeting of all leaders to discuss the program's assets and limitations. Go over the Program Evaluation Sheets and elicit recommendations for improvements.

FINAL MEETING WITH CONSULTING TEACHERS. Call a group conference with the consulting teachers and administrators to gain evaluative feedback on the management, concepts, and selection aspects of the program. Elicit recommendations for changes. Be cautious and open to criticism.

FINAL RECEIVING STUDENT MEETING. Confer with each receiving student and use the receiving student Follow-up Interview Questions to gather information on the program's effectiveness. (See Appendix A, Model 21.)

SUMMARY REPORT AND THANK YOU LETTER. Compose an informal report and letter of appreciation. This document should reflect qualitative and quantitative results of the program based on data collected on leaders, receivers, and control group subjects.

The letter should also include workable program changes suggested by any group involved in the program's process. Include your expression of gratitude to teachers, administrators, and students who aided in the program's operation.

Paper Trail

1. Receiving Student Parent Consent Form. *(See Appendix, Model 11.)*

2. Peer Leader ID Card Prototype. *(See Appendix A, Model 17.)*

3. Peer Leader Pass. *(See Appendix A, Model 15.)*

4. Receiving Student Pass. *(See Appendix A, Model 16.)*

5. Receiving Student Parent Consent Forms. *(See Appendix A, Model 11.)*

6. Assignment Sheet. *(See Appendix A, Model 13.)*

7. Program Checklist. *(See Appendix A, Model 18.)*

8. Pre and Post-Training Peer Leader Competency Assessment. *(See Appendix A, Model 4.)*

9. Receiving Student Work Sample Rating Form. *(See Appendix A, Model 20.)*

10. First Session Guidelines. *(See p. 213.)*

11. Self-Evaluation Sheet. *(See p. 215.)*

12. Action Plan Sheet. *(See p. 217.)*

13. Monthly Action Plan Follow-Up Sheet. *(See p. 219.)*

14. One-to-One Evaluation Sheet. *(See p. 221.)*

Orientation

Time
Twenty minutes

Goals
• To practice behaviors and express tensions related to the first helping session experience.

• To offer feedback regarding peer leaders' helping skills.

Materials
First Session Guidelines.

Process
Coordinator distributes First Session Guidelines to trainees and leads a practice session.

Outcome Indicators
1. Peer leaders should participate by taking two roles: leader and receiver.

2. Peer leaders should role play and discuss the exercise with the group to refine and improve their skills.

LEADER'S GUIDE

Sessions 1, 2, and 3

Your training in the basic communication and academic assistance skills adequately prepares you for this program. Your coordinator or trainer will provide you with a practice session to prepare for your first helping session.

Your coordinator or advisor will arrange for your partner assignments, issue passes, arrange transportation, and establish times and places for your helping sessions. He or she will notify your teachers if you need to miss classes. You will receive an ID card and passes for yourself and your receiving student.

You will have a ten minute group meeting of all peer leaders and receiving students. The meeting will cover the following:

• Introductions and personal backgrounds

• Times and places of helping sessions

• Clear contracts between leaders and receivers.

The contract will include a four week trial period with procedures for evaluating progress.

After the group meeting, you will break into pairs to decide whether you would like to work together. After these interviews have taken place, your advisors will check with you and your partners to get your decisions.

Your sessions will be held weekly on the same day at the same time and place. Exchange phone numbers with your receiver in case either of you is ill or needs to cancel for some other reason. At the end of each session, you may want to give your receiver

a pass to get back to class without any difficulty. Your advisor will provide you with passes if necessary and help you with transportation arrangements. Plan to meet your advisor each week.

SESSION 1. Your first helping session will be introductory and follow the guidelines outlined in your practice session.

SESSION 2. You spend the second session assisting your receiver with the Self-Evaluation Sheet.

SESSION 3. Assist your receiver in forming an Action Plan Sheet. It is a good idea to get permission to discuss academic goals and strategies with the receiver's teachers.

SUBSEQUENT SESSIONS. You and your receivers should work on goals, discuss progress and complete Monthly Action Plan Follow-Up Sheets. After about one month, your advisor may ask you to give your receiving student a One-to-One Evaluation Sheet. Get it filled out and review it with your advisor to check your performance as a peer leader.

Meeting with Referring Teachers
Your advisor or coordinator may arrange a meeting with referring teachers to go over receivers' strengths, weaknesses, goals, and strategies to improve performance.

Advisory Sessions
During your weekly advisory sessions you will be reviewing Self-Evaluation Sheets, Action Plan Sheets, and Monthly Action Plan Follow-Up Sheets. You and your advisor may plan strategies to help your receivers. These include finding other people to help and suggesting other projects to expand

LEADER'S GUIDE
Session 1, 2, and 3 continued

your receiver's interests and skills.

Your advisor will collect work samples and periodically have them reviewed by teachers (anonymously) and share the changes in quality with you. Teacher observations and report card information will also be shared.

You and your advisor will also review your Program Checklists and information on the personal logs you keep. Should any warning signals come up, your advisor can be of help in making a referral to the appropriate professional.

Peer Leaders' Conferences
Your coordinator will schedule occasional conferences for all program participants to trouble shoot, offer support, and keep each other informed.

Occasionally, it is necessary to reassign receivers to other leaders. This step may be taken if you and your coordinator feel the relationship is not useful to your receiving student for some reason. It is also possible to complete the sessions when all your mutually established goals have been met.

Steps for Winding Up the Program
Usually One-to-One lasts for one academic

year. As you near the end of the year, it is good to let your advisor know if you and your receiver should continue for another year.

Often some year-end celebration with receivers and leaders finishes off the program on a positive note. You can plan this with your advisors or at the peer leaders' conferences.

It is critical to give your receivers the opportunity to evaluate your skills as a helping person. Therefore, be sure to give them the One-to-One Evaluation Sheet and then go over the completed copy with your advisor.

If you are graduating, it is a good idea to exchange summer addresses and phone numbers with your receiving students before school ends.

A follow-up meeting with referring teachers is sometimes helpful in getting feedback about the program and its effects.

Your cooperation in all these details can make the difference between partial or full impact of your efforts.

First Session Guidelines

Name_____   Date_____

Goals

• To practice behaviors and express tensions related to the first helping session experience.

• To offer feedback regarding peer leaders' helping skills.

Directions

This is an exercise intended to give you practice in using helping skills during the first helping session. Separate into groups of two.

1. One person takes the role of peer leader and the other plays the part of receiver. The leader uses the guidelines for support.

2. Use your imagination to create a typical dialogue which might unfold during the first session. The trainer will signal when five minutes are up.

3. Spend the next five minutes discussing what was helpful, missing, and not helpful. After the first role play, change your leader-receiver roles and try it again.

Sequence of Session

1. Introduce yourself. Make eye contact, smile, shake hands. Pace and match.

2. Tell the student why you're here. Discuss the fact that both of you have volunteered.

3. Explain that the session time will be divided between tutoring in one subject area and discussion about whatever he/she wants to talk about (school, friends, home).

4. Mention that with the exception of expressed intentions of self-harm or physical harm to others (such as using or dealing), your conversations will be kept in confidence. The only persons with whom the student will be discussed are the trainers and the peer advisory group.

5. Your role is to work with the student to help him/her to deal with school and social life more effectively. Discuss your role openly. This discussion may be a little uncomfortable, but certainly better than confusion on both sides at a later point.

6. Inform the student that the first four weeks will be a trial period.

At the end of that time you will both evaluate whether the receiving student is getting anything out of the experience and whether you should continue.

7. Tell him/her that you are unable to be a spokesperson to teachers, parents, and friends. The object is to develop his/her own ability to communicate.

Page 2 - First Session Guidelines

8. Tell him/her a little about yourself: why you are here and what your interests are. Encourage him/her to tell you about himself/herself. From that point on, it would be good to focus on the other person. If silence goes on for a while, talk about how it seems uncomfortable at first when you don't know one another.

9. Discuss the student's good and bad subjects. Then decide on which subject you will be working.

10. Inform your student that he/she must see the teacher of the class missed in order to get the homework assignment. If the person is upset, put him/her at ease by reflecting on his/her feelings and pacing and matching to establish rapport. Avoid making promises you may not be able to keep. If the person is quiet, it is probably because he/she does not know what to say.

11. At the end of the session, ask if there is anything that you left out or that may not be clear. Summarize the arrangement and tell the receiver that you are looking forward to seeing him/her next week.

Self-Evaluation Sheet

Name_____   Date_____

School_____   Class _____

Leader _____

Directions
Use this form to evaluate your current functioning in school and decide what you want to improve.

1. Subjects which need attention:

_____

_____

_____

2. Problems with these subjects:

a. Homework _____

b. Understanding materials _____

c. Teacher(s) _____

d. Class notes _____

e. Tests _____

3. Reasons for poor performance: _____

_____

_____

_____

Page 2 - Self-Evaluation Sheet

4. Barriers to overcome: _____

_____

_____

_____

5. Evidence that I have solved similar problems before:

_____

_____

_____

_____

Action Plan Sheet

Name_____   Date_____

School_____   Class _____

Directions
Use this form to plan an approach to setting goals and accomplishing them.

1. Desired outcomes: _____

_____

_____

_____

2. Action to be taken to improve my work:

a._____

b._____

c._____

3. Times and places to meet with peer leader:

_____

_____

_____

4. Times and places of contacts with support resources:

_____

_____

_____

Page 2 - Action Plan Sheet

5. Actions to be taken by leader to assist me:

a._____

b._____

c._____

6. Main Subject:

Focus _____

_____

7. Other Subject:

Focus _____

_____

Monthly Action Plan Follow-Up Sheet

Name_____   Date_____

School_____   Class _____

Directions
Write down the responses below to review your progress over the last month.

1. Desired outcomes:

   _____

   _____

2. Actions I took to improve my work:

   a._____

   b._____

   c. _____

3. Times and places of peer leader contacts:

   _____

   _____

   _____

4. Actions taken by peer leader to assist me:

   a._____

   b._____

   c. _____

Page 2 - Monthly Action Plan Follow-Up Sheet

5. Assistance by others:

a. Name _____Action _____

b. Name _____Action _____

c. Name _____Action _____

6. Subjects worked on: _____

_____

_____

7. Other areas:_____

_____

8. Changes for next month: _____

_____

_____

One-to-One Evaluation Sheet

School _____ Grade _____

Directions
This is a survey to get your reaction to this helping program. Since the program is new, we would like your help in finding out how it is going and whether there should be any changes.

Please read each statement and write the number 1, 2, or 3 on the lines below.

1. Often   **2. Sometimes**   **3. Never**

1.____My peer leader shows up on time.

2.____I show up on time.

3.____The peer leader seems to be interested in me.

4.____My peer leader seems to be bored.

5.____We both work on one subject and then talk about life.

6.____I come prepared with all homework and notes in the subject in which I am being helped.

7.____I find that I only do my homework when I work with my peer leader.

8.____I am not getting enough work done during the first half hour.

9.____I like talking with my peer leader.

10.____I think I can trust my peer leader.

11.____My peer leader seems to understand how to help me with my work.

12. My peer leader can do these things to improve:

_____

_____

13. The things I like best about the program are:

_____

_____

_____

SECTION 6 —
PEER INTERVENTION NETWORK (PIN)

SECTION 6 —
PEER INTERVENTION
NETWORK (PIN)

Description

Recently, peer support programs have helped people to overcome educational underachievement. The literature offers compelling evidence that group interventions have had positive impacts on student behavior and academic performance.

Candler and Goodman (1979) have shown that groups at the middle school level have been supportive to each other in dealing with crises. Kohl (1979) has used group strategies to facilitate problem-ventilation and improve time management, organizational skills, and study skills in students.

The increasing plethora of underachieving students entering our middle schools poses a major national dilemma. Leaving the security of elementary schools, middle school students confront a variety of the same anxiety producing school thrusts students into a new atmosphere of multiple roles and conflicting expectations. Many become educational casualties as a result of poor transitional adjustment. They often end up in special educational programs.

Peer Intervention Network (PIN) is designed for small groups of bright underachievers who are having difficulty in their adjustment process to the middle school setting. These are the students who feel inadequate, engage in passive, resistive behavior, and then often become the nation's dropouts, delinquents, substance abusers, and alienated youth. PIN is a group effort to reverse this negative trend.

It operates a small support group with specific roles to encourage self-directed goal formulation and positive pattern development. A PIN group can be led by professionals, experienced peer leaders, or by a peer/professional partnership. Typically, the most viable approach to leadership is the coleader model.

Usually, a peer intervention group operates for a three to four month period, during which its members change their roles from dysfunctional to functional receivers. The group unfolds as a joint effort to promote positive outcomes in its members. Once a majority of members reach their goals, the group disbands. Thus, it may be called a focused-criterion group.

Goals

• To facilitate academic, social, and emotional adjustment to the middle school setting.

• To promote goal-setting activities which are designed to remediate specific academic problems.

• To promote positive social problem-solving approaches.

• To enlist the assistance of other students in developing a support network.

Planning

The most auspicious time of the school year to launch such a program is between November and February. This time period enables the counselor to collect adequate data on student achievement as well as sufficient time to promote behavior change before June.

Use Description, Goals and Objectives, Selection and Implementation sections from this guide as a fact sheet for distribution to key administrators and peripherally involved teachers of the target population.

Photocopy Receiving Student Parent Consent Forms (see Appendix A, Model 11) PIN Fact Sheets, Self-Evaluation Sheets, Action Plan Sheets, and Teacher Feedback Sheets. Prepare them for distribution.

Present all information to the Board of Education and the Superintendent. If necessary, secure written approval. After top level approval has been secured, meet with the school principal.

Run through the idea informally from a positive viewpoint, suggesting that there may be a population of underachievers who could potentially lower the school's achievement scores on standardized tests, overload support programs, and become potential disciplinary problems as they advance in age. Describe the rationale of the program and solicit permission to identify such a population with the help of teachers.

Secure a written directive from the principal, authorizing you to start a pilot project. Call a meeting with teachers and guidance personnel, outlining the program's goals, asking for their assistance in referrals, recruitment, and program operation.

Such approval might include their willingness to offer special help and support to students who solicit their services. Request their cooperation in filling out a Teacher Feedback Sheet which

supplies information on students' classwork, homework, and behavior.

Ask teachers if they would be willing to confer with you and the peer leader to assess progress and make necessary strategy changes.

Selection

PEER LEADERS. The best suited peer leaders for this type of program are strong, independent, student government types, or team captains. Their personality profile should be low-keyed, and they should exhibit high frustration tolerance to the potential resistance of passive-aggressive students in this population. They should exhibit good communication skills, organizational skills, reliability, and endurance.

They should have sufficient time in their schedules to allow them to attend group meetings before and after school and during lunch. Their lunch schedules must be coordinated with the lunchtime meetings of PIN groups.

Occasionally, they may have to be released from additional classes to attend emergency sessions focused on particular problem behaviors such as intractability of particular group members.

RECEIVING STUDENTS. Distribute Teacher Referral Forms (See Appendix A, Model 23) to teachers and other appropriate referral sources.

After you have met with all professional personnel and received referrals from teachers and guidance counselors, go through the student files, study the permanent records, report cards, and standardized achievement tests as well as behavioral profiles described by those who made referrals. The entry criteria should include the following qualifications:

• A prolonged period of underachievement.

• Reading and math levels not more than one year below average.

• Mild disciplinary problems.

• Potential passive or withdrawn behavior.

• Occasional acting-out such as name-calling, talking in class, etc.

• Poor homework production.

• Alliance with negative peer subculture.

After reviewing candidates for above criteria, select a group of six to eight students, interview them, describe the proposed intervention, and check schedules for matching lunch periods, study periods, physical education periods, and availability before and after school.

Meet with administrators who are in charge of scheduling to assemble a preliminary meeting schedule which insures weekly conferences. Some options include lunchtime meetings, early morning meetings before the official start of school, sessions in lieu of physical education classes, or after school meetings.

Training

Peer leaders should be trained in basic communication guidelines and barriers. They should be well versed in the behavioral warning signals and referral procedures.

The most viable training model for this program is to include one peer leader as an assistant group facilitator who enters the group process, observes your leadership, and then becomes a coleader after the completion of one PIN cycle.

Distribute a Group Leadership Checklist to your trainee and request periodic feedback related to the goals of the group. (See Section 2, Session 42.)

Parental Permission

Parental awareness and support are essential to the successful implementation of PIN. Thus, your contact with parents must include a program description. This is perhaps the most important step in the planning procedure. There are several informal ways to make contact with parents:

1. Phone them. Describe the program and how their children fit the criteria.

2. Write informal notes describing the program. Use Goals listed on pp.225-226, and the PIN Fact Sheet as a guide. Distribute your program descriptions to parents.

3. Call an informal meeting to outline the program.

Regardless of how you make contact, the first part of your presentation should focus on the parents' experience with their children who appear to be underachieving or poorly motivated. Once it is agreed that your perceptions of their children's academic and social problems are congruent with theirs, you will have a high potential for securing their support.

Explain that group sessions will be mandatory parts of each student's schedule, and that they will be required to attend these sessions in order to develop goals, action plans, and partnerships.

Explain that students will be receiving phone calls from their shadows who serve as guides to help them implement their plans of action. Describe the incremental aspect of the program which includes each participant's right to discharge his or her shadow whenever his/her stated goals are complete. For example, if a youngster is receiving D's in pre-algebra, and sets his/her goal as a C by the mid-marking period, that outcome becomes a necessary criteria for discharging his or her shadow. When a person has reached his/her goal, he/she remains available as an expert to assist other members in making personal changes.

Once you have fielded questions from parents, distribute the parent consent forms which request authorization and support at home. Explain to parents that if they succumb to their children's manipulation and pressure to remove them from the group, it would undercut the entire program and destroy its integrity. After you receive signed Receiving Student Parent Consent Form from all parents, you are ready to begin. (See Appendix A, Model 11.)

Implementation

Arrange your first month to include at least two meetings per week at different times. Arrange a schedule and notify all guidance counselors of the target population to make necessary adjustments. Essentially, you are creating PIN as a part of each student's schedule which is written and sent home to the parents.

Arrange transportation for your peer leader trainee. Write and distribute schedules to all peripheral personnel and begin your program.

GROUP FUNCTIONING. A PIN group begins as a somewhat coercive experience with leaders serving as containers for much resistance and passive-aggressive behavior. This is the type of behavior which manifests itself as abdication of responsibility, lack of homework production, and alliance with negative peer subculture. Underlying authority problems usually contribute to this underachievement profile.

Groups of six to eight students are assembled to meet regularly before, during, and after school (i.e. lunch conferences). Each student in the group chooses a shadow. The shadow is responsible to assist his/her partner in identifying major problem areas and setting goals.

For example, if a student experiences morning gridlock and is frequently late for school, on-time arrival may become a legitimate goal, assisted by the shadow's involvement. After the goals are identified, an Action Plan is developed mutually between the shadow and the partner.

In the case of the oversleeper, as one part of the Action Plan, a shadow might agree to stop by the partner's house on the way to school and help him/her get there on time.

Once the goals and Action Plans have been established, the shadow and partner mutually agree upon other resources to call upon for backup and assistance. For example, a group member competent in pre-algebra may be called upon to assist another partner who is experiencing difficulty. Specific tutoring arrangements, like times and places of meetings, can be built into the Action Plan. Each member is assigned a shadow, but must also serve as a shadow to another student. No reciprocal arrangements are allowed because of the potential of collusion.

As part of the group process, each person's skills and competencies are identified, listed, and shared as areas of expertise. A Resource Network Sheet is produced so that names,

phone numbers, and skills may be shared as necessary. This process creates mutual consultants who can assist each other.

In addition to internal group consultants, the process also identifies specific teachers, adults, and community members who may be sought to assist group members in their areas of weakness.

After initial group building, partner assignments, Self-Evaluations, and Action Plans have been accomplished, the group should focus on individual progress reports presented by each partner's shadow during each session. A typical session might review four out of six members' progress on their particular goals. Shadows introduce each partner's goals, Action Plans, and steps taken to attain the goals.

Feedback is provided for each student and where intractability occurs, the group must come up with alternate suggestions which are recorded on the particular partner's Follow-up Plan. Shadows are requested to make phone calls and interventions throughout the week between sessions. These interventions are strategies targeted to assist each student in his/her goal accomplishment.

Once a member has completed his or her goals, he or she may "fire" her or his shadow and then serve as an "expert" in behavior change. This expert status is frequently sought after by members of the group through time, as more and more members become experts and shed their shadows. They remain in the group as prestigious, high status role models.

Usually a PIN program unfolds in three distinctive stages: resistance, polarity, and unity. During all stages it is important that both coordinator and peer leader carefully monitor the group for behavioral warning signals. Any member who exhibits high risk behavior should be referred to an appropriate practitioner immediately.

Paper Trail

1. Receiving Student Parent Consent Form. *(See Appendix A, Model 11.)*

2. Peer Leader ID Card Prototype. *(See Appendix A, Model 17.)*

3. Peer Leader Pass. *(See Appendix A, Model 15.)*

4. Receiving Student Pass. *(See Appendix A, Model 16.)*

5. Teacher Referral Form. *(See Appendix A, Model 23.)*

6. Group Leadership Checklist. *(See Section 2, Session 42.)*

7. PIN Fact Sheet. *(See p. 240.)*

8. Self-Evaluation Sheet. *(See p. 241.)*

9. Action Plan Sheet. *(See p. 242.)*

10. Resource Network Sheet. *(See Section 3, Session 1, Part 6.)*

11. Teacher Feedback Sheet. *(See p. 243.)*

12. Follow-Up Action Plan Sheet. *(See p. 244.)*

13. PIN Evaluation Sheet. *(See p. 246.)*

Trainees' Observation of All Sessions

Time
Approximately fifteen sessions, one per week, forty-five minutes per session.

Goal
• To prepare one experienced peer leader to function as coleader in a Peer Intervention Network (PIN) group.

Materials
All PIN student materials, Group Leadership Checklists (see Section 2, Session 42), and pencils.

Process
Peer program coordinator discusses the three stages of the PIN group, while an experienced peer leader observes the process and assists. Peer leader receives copies of Leader's Guide for this section, follows procedures, and meets with group leader after each session to assess progress, plan future sessions, and decide upon intervention strategies for weaker members. Students who exhibit warning signal behaviors are identified and referred to appropriate professionals.

Periodically, peer leader rates coordinator on a checklist and reviews feedback which should generate improved management techniques.

After one cycle is complete, the peer leader assumes responsibility for major group coleadership, while being observed by an adult supervisor and a new, inexperienced peer leader trainee. Thus the cycle repeats.

Outcome Indicators
1. Peer leader assistant should identify at least 50% of the skills listed in the Group Leadership Checklists.

2. At stage three (Unity) peer leader assistant should play an active leadership role and demonstrate competence in 75% of skills on checklists.

Orientation

Stage 1: Resistance

During the first six weeks, it is not uncommon for the group to express resistance and anger about the membership requirements, coercive assumptions in the group, and negative behaviors which precipitated each person's membership. You, the leader, will be the target of such resistance to a series of clearly defined routines, expectations, and requirements. You may have to deal with complaints, requests to parents for withdrawal, excuses for not participating, and absenteeism.

At this stage, where one or two particular members become extremely resistant, and perhaps miss two group meetings, stricter rules must be made to deal with these problems.

Frequently, the group is put on "red alert" which means that it must meet daily until its resistant members respond to the group efforts to address their goals. If the shadows' efforts break down, it is not uncommon for members to swap shadows and partners until the right match is found.

A parent may phone the coordinator to protest the program's effects on his/her child's attitudes. Coordinators should remind parents that if children withdraw, it may undercut the group's effect and cause possible disruption to the program.

If shadows and partners continue to struggle to find successful approaches to attain their goals, it is likely that the goals are too difficult and should be renegotiated with the help of a general brainstorming session. Essentially, in this stage, it is critical to select goals which will bring some small but verifiable progress.

Frustration often mounts when goals are too difficult. It is also essential that the group's resources be used effectively. Careful monitoring by shadows is another essential activity at this stage of group development.

Stage 2: Polarity

After four to six weeks, the group usually enters a stage of polarity, which is signaled by a divergence in members' progress. The group splits into two extremes, showing different levels of functioning on Teacher Feedback Sheets, compliancy with rules, attendance, goal completion, and problem-solving abilities.

The cooperative students offer a stark contrast to the seemingly intractable members who refuse to complete their homework. Toward the end of the marking period, some of the more responsive members begin to receive higher grades on report cards and fire their shadows. They release the stigmas of custodial supervision and become consultants to the more needy group members.

Thus, the focus of the group shifts to the more resistant group members. Frequently, the group must reinitiate its "red alert" status, zeroing in on one or two members who are having trouble with a given subject area or are refusing to study for their tests.

It is at this stage of development where the peer pressure makes a considerable difference in productivity. More anger is usually vented but is now directed towards the maverick members. It is often helpful to contact parents of more resistant members to encourage their feedback, input, and support.

LEADER'S GUIDE
Orientation continued

Stage 3: Unity

The final phase of PIN usually begins the third or fourth month and continues until the group has disbanded. During this stage, called Unity, coleaders must decide when to terminate the group. Not all of its members can succeed in attaining their desired outcomes before the group comes to a close.

Coleaders often solicit the advice of group members to redefine and reduce the difficulty of weaker members' goal definitions until some progress is shown. It is during this period of time that most members have finally released their shadows and are focusing upon the weaker members to assist them in gaining more competence.

Much applause is received by the prestigious success stories of those who set the standard for compliance for other members. Essentially, the students have learned to monitor themselves, request feedback from those less active students, and offer suggestions and assistance in difficult homework assignments, test preparation, and conceptual explanations.

Parents are often contacted during this phase to become more actively involved with the weaker members within the home environment. The complaints usually subside at this time, while attendance improves, and group cohesiveness develops.

LEADER'S GUIDE

Session 1: Introduction

Time
Forty-five minutes

Goal
• To introduce group members, describe the ground rules of the group, and make partner-shadow assignments.

Materials
PIN Fact Sheets and meeting schedules.

Process
Coleaders initiate self-disclosure exercises as icebreakers. Beginning with leaders, each person introduces himself/herself, describes his/her background, and identifies essential goals to be addressed in this group.

Coleaders distribute PIN Fact Sheet which outlines all the rules and procedures in the group. Members take turns reading aloud the various items on the fact sheet. Question and answer period follows.

Coleaders ask group members to form pairs, interview each other, and determine who they would like to choose as their "personal shadows." Pairs are encouraged to regroup every three minutes until all decisions are made.

Before dismissing the group, leaders encourage further decision-making around activities which should occur before the next session. Next meeting's day and time is announced and the group is released.

Outcome Indicators
1. All members' names should have been identified through icebreaker exercise.

2. Questions and answers should have clarified all procedures and routines written on the PIN Fact Sheet.

3. At least two sets of paired interviews should have produced a high number of shadow-partner arrangements.

Session 2: Self-Evaluation

Time
Forty-five minutes

Goal
• To complete Self-Evaluation Sheet, identifying name of shadow, academic difficulties, and reasons for underachievement.

Materials
Self-Evaluation Sheets and pencils.

Process
Coleaders begin the group promptly, requesting each member to write down the names of his/her shadow on a piece of paper. The partners are then asked to join with their shadows in two sessions, twenty minutes each. After twenty minutes, request members to shift pairs so that each member takes the role of partner or shadow for one cycle.

During each session, the group is instructed to form partnerships to identify academic problems, reasons for failure, and "stuck spots" in reversing negative trends. Leaders serve as consultants, visiting pairs upon request for input and assistance as members fill out Self-Evaluation Sheets.

After Self-Evaluation sheets are filled out by each member, coleaders should make two photocopies, returning original to the partner, giving a copy to the partner's shadow, and maintaining one for the group files. The next meeting day and time is set and the group is released.

Outcome Indicators
1. All shadows should be chosen during this group. They should be recorded on a single sheet of paper with names and phone numbers.

2. Each member should have a completed Self-Evaluation Sheet by the end of the session.

Session 3: Action Plan

Time
Forty-five minutes

Goal
• To develop Action Plan as method of addressing academic and social problems.

Materials
Action Plan Sheets and pencils.

Process
Coleaders distribute Action Plan Sheets and instruct the group to break up into partner-shadow pairs for twenty minutes, and then shift roles, reforming pairs accordingly. Coleaders instruct each pair to come up with a plan of action responding to the problem which was identified during Session 2.

Shadows and partners must collaborate to develop and describe specific steps to be taken to make improvements. Furthermore, daily contacts and shadow assistance strategies should be elicited.

At the end of the second pairing cycle, coleaders should collect Action Plans, make photocopies, distribute the original to partner, give a copy to shadow, and retain a copy on file for the group.

Outcome Indicators
1. All members should have completed Action Plans.

2. Action Plans should include desired outcome, steps, resources, and verifiable actions.

LEADER'S GUIDE

Session 4: Resource Network

Time
Fifteen minutes

Materials
Paper and pencils.

Goal
• To develop an extended network to assist members in achieving their outcomes.

Process
Note to user: Please see Section 3, Session 1, Part 6. Follow the same procedure.

Sessions 5-6: Processing

Time
Forty-five minutes per session

Goals
• To assess members' abilities to reach their desired outcomes.

• To assess the use of shadows and resources in the goal completion process.

• To encourage each shadow to introduce his/her partner's progress and barriers in achieving goals.

Materials
Self-Evaluation Sheets, Action Plan Sheets, Resource Network Sheets (see Section 3, Session 1, Part 6), Teacher Feedback Sheets, Follow-Up Action Plan Sheets, and pencils.

Process
Coleaders read and share results of Teacher Feedback Sheets received since last PIN session. Improvements in homework and classwork should be highlighted and applauded publicly, with receiving students sharing their reactions to the new trends in their functioning.

Negative feedback such as overdue assignments, poor classwork, or any conduct disorders should be openly discussed and counterbalanced with improvement strategies. Group members should be encouraged to suggest alternate resources and techniques to interrupt negative patterns.

After reviewing Teacher Feedback Sheets, coleaders should select one partner's shadow and ask him/her to review the newly formed Self-Evaluation and Action Plan. Specific emphasis should be placed on the desired outcomes selected and their appropriateness. After identifying the plan, the shadow is instructed to describe what efforts he or she has made to assist the partner in attaining his or her goals.

Specific resources should be identified, activities discussed, and any resistance to improvement openly addressed. The group is asked to share its comments and make any suggestions as to how this person might advance his/her goal attainment efforts. This information should be recorded on Follow-up Action Plan Sheets.

Usually, at this stage of the program, group members offer some resistance by complaining about the group, its requirements, and the rules. It is not uncommon to spend the first six weeks fielding these complaints, briefly addressing them through discussions of each member's own objectives, and then continuing on with the task at hand.

Outcome Indicators
1. At least two shadows should present their partners' current status in the group.

2. For each member discussed, at least two improvement strategies should be formulated by the group.

Sessions 7-10: Support

Time
Forty-five minutes

Goals
• To assist unresponsive members in developing desired outcomes and reorganizing strategies to attain these goals.

• To continue to support productive behavior, reassess participants' status, and formulate new goals.

Materials
Self-Evaluation Sheets, Follow-Up Action Plan Sheets, Resource Network Sheets (see Section 3, Session 1, Part 6), Teacher Feedback Sheets, and pencils.

Process
Coleaders adopt a more task oriented posture, making alliances with both responsive and unresponsive members. Coleaders should offer praise and encourage input from the newly established "experts" who have released their shadows. On the other hand, they must enlist support for the weaker, frustrated, or more withdrawn members who have yet to achieve their goals.

In choosing two members per session to profile, coleaders must be mindful of selecting one "success story" and one weaker member. Thus, a leader might first focus upon the weaker member's shadow and enlist support of the group in redefining goals or reorganizing strategies to achieve current goals. Resources must be called into action as necessary.

The sessions might end more appropriately with presentations from the shadows of a positive, responsive member who has made some strides. This person then shares his/her positive approaches with the weaker members.

Outcome Indicators
1. This stage of polarized status usually continues for a few weeks until progress reports or marking period grades improve in more members.

2. About one half the group should attain their desired outcomes and lose their shadows.

Sessions 11-18: Closure

Time
Forty-five minutes

Goal
• To monitor and support weaker students while acknowledging the strengths and successes of new "experts" who have become prestigious independently functioning participants.

Materials
Self-Evaluation Sheets, Follow-up Action Plan Sheets, Resource Network Sheets (see Section 3 Session 1, Part 6), Teacher Feedback Sheets, PIN Evaluation Sheets, and pencils.

Process
Coleaders continue to operate in the same fashion as during the Resistance and Polarity phases, introducing the group with feedback from teachers, and moving from recognition of successes to remediation of more resistant students.

At this stage, the majority of members who have positive experiences and status can turn their attention towards sharing skills and providing more support to others. Frequently guest appearances by teachers at these meetings shed new light on strategies for improvement of weaker members.

At this time the group decides when to hold its final session. Criteria for this decision usually includes some marginal success for each student or modification of goals until such improvements are registered by the entire group. When all members have shown at least some improvement, a final

session date is arranged by the group. The group plans some festivities and refreshments for the celebration of closure.

During the last session, a PIN Evaluation Sheet is distributed and filled out by each student. The group is encouraged to continue its support network and assist each other.

Outcome Indicator
1. At least two-thirds of the students in the group should reach their goals by the fourth month of operation.

Evaluation
Ongoing evaluation is built into the PIN program through its process and the use of shadow reports, teacher feedback, parent feedback, and the forms used during sessions. The Student Evaluation is a solid reflection of the program's impact on students. As a follow-up, coordinator might check report cards for two marking periods after PIN formally disbands.

Follow-Up
Coleaders should use all data to review the program for the next cycle. Occasional reunion sessions of the original group to rekindle the network spirit are often valuable.

During the next cycle, the peer leader assistant usually takes a more active leadership role while supervised by the coordinator. A new trainee enters the group as an assistant observer as the program perpetuates itself.

PIN Fact Sheet

Name_____   Date_____

PIN stands for Peer Intervention Network

1. Who is in this group?

This group is made up of kids who are bright, normal, not disturbed, and capable of succeeding in school. For various reasons its members have not succeeded in passing all subjects. Before this group ends, you will overcome your barriers to achievement.

2. The group's purpose is to assist one other in improving schoolwork, social relationships, and time management.

3. The way PIN operates:

• Meets once or twice a week.

• Listens and reacts to progress reports.

• Explains what is blocking you and what you will do to unblock.

• Sets up times of shadow and teacher contacts.

4. You are required to attend all sessions.

5. You must serve as a shadow to another group member. Keep a record of all assignments and do anything legal and ethical to help your partner improve her/his work. Your own partner cannot be your shadow. You must have a different shadow, not the one you supervise.

6. If, at the end of the marking period, you raise your grades and reach your goals, you will no longer need supervision and can drop your shadow. But, as an expert, you remain in the group and continue as someone's shadow.

7. If your shadow is not helping you, he/she must suffer the consequences and can be fired, provided he/she can find another member who will accept his/her supervision (an even exchange).

8. You are in this together until school ends.

9. Each week you must report on how your Action Plan is going and supply evidence of progress (grades on tests, assignments, etc.) If things are not going well, the group must meet until a new plan has been developed and your goals are reached.

Good Luck,

_____
Program Coordinator

Self-Evaluation Sheet

Name_____ Date_____

Class_____ Grade _____

Directions
Use this form to evaluate your current functioning in school and decide what you want to improve.

1. Who is your shadow? _____

2. Warning notices

_____

_____

_____

3. What problems do you have in these areas?

a. Homework _____

b. Understanding materials _____

c. Teacher(s) _____

d. Class notes _____

e. Tests _____

4. Why are you doing poorly? _____

_____

_____

5. What has kept you from putting more effort into your studies?

_____

_____

_____

Action Plan Sheet

Name_____   Date_____

Shadow's name _____

Directions
Use this form to plan an approach to setting goals and accomplishing them.

1. Desired outcome:_____

_____

2. Steps to be taken to improve your work:

a._____

b._____

c._____

3. Planned contacts with shadow (times and places): _____

_____

_____

4. Steps to be taken by shadow to assist you:

a._____

b._____

c._____

5. Subjects to be worked on:_____

_____

_____

6. Other resources to be used: _____

_____

Teacher Feedback Sheet

Student's Name _____

Teacher _____

Date _____

Directions
Please fill out the information below on the above named student to assist our program in upgrading his/her functioning.

	Homework			Classwork			Behavior			Teacher's Signature and Comments
	Complete	Unfinished	Not done	Excellent	Needs Improv.	Poor	Involved	Bothers Others	Uninvolved	
Language Arts										
Math										
Social Studies										
Science										
Physical Education										
Other										
Other										

_____ Parents Signature

_____ Peer Leader's Signature

_____ Coordinator's Signature

Follow-Up Action Plan Sheet

Name_____   Date_____

Shadow's name _____

Directions
Use this form to reevaluate your previous outcomes, and create new goals and strategies to accomplish them.

1. Previous desired outcome: _____

2. Steps taken to improve your work:

a._____

b._____

c._____

3. Daily contacts with shadow (times and places):_____

_____

_____

4. Steps taken by shadow to assist you:

a._____

b._____

c._____

5. Subjects worked on: _____

_____

_____

_____

Page 2 - Follow-Up Action Plan Sheet

6. Changes for next week:

Desired outcome _____

New strategies _____

_____

Other resources _____

_____

_____

PIN Evaluation Sheet

School _____ Class _____ Grade _____

Leader(s)_____ Date_____

Directions
You have just completed a support network to assist you in improving your grades, problem-solving abilities, and quality of life.

Please take a few minutes to fill out this questionnaire so that we may gain valuable information about your experience and make any changes necessary.

Please read the statements and write the number 1, 2 or 3 on each line below.

1. Excellent   **2. Adequate**   **3. Needs Improvement**

1.____Group leaders were involved, active, and skillful in managing this group.

2.____Leaders encouraged my participation and helped me to improve.

3.____Group members helped me to select the desired outcomes and make positive changes.

4.____My shadow was helpful to me in making improvements.

5. Read the statements below and check yes or no.

I think groups like this should be available to more students. ____Yes ____No

When I get to high school, I would like to be trained as a group leader. ____Yes ____No

6. The advantages of this group were:

_____

_____

_____

7. This group needs to make the following improvements:

_____

_____

_____

SECTION 7 —
PLANNING LEISURE ACTIVITIES NOW (PLAN)

SECTION 7 — PLANNING LEISURE ACTIVITIES NOW (PLAN)

Description

A significant population of students at the middle school level are faced with unsupervised time after school. Their parents often work and do not arrive home until dinner hour. These students are sometimes left to supervise younger siblings or remain alone.

PLAN is intended to respond to the needs of these students in such a way as to promote more productive use of their after school time when they are not under direct supervision of adults. It makes a distinction between the concepts of loneliness versus solitude, the first being designated as a negative state and the second as a productive, creative, positive state. PLAN promotes productive solitude as well as socialization.

The program develops an ongoing support group intended for sixth through ninth grade students. Optimum size for such a PLAN group is eight to ten members. Sessions are conducted by at least one trained peer leader who has overcome the dilemma of how to use unsupervised after school time.

The group should be supervised by a certified adult staff member who may remain nearby for support or back up. Sessions are structured to include introductory activities, assessment of members' current leisure time activities, and problem-solving and decision-making strategies to overcome the barriers of changing unproductive use of time.

A ten session cycle is an adequate format for such a group which may be held during lunch periods, before school, or after school, depending on the leader's high school schedule constraints.

Goals

• To assess current use of leisure time in a target population.

• To investigate the group's satisfaction levels and quality of their after school time.

• To generate alternative activity options more fulfilling than current activities.

• To explore ways of making decisions about new activities, create support systems, and collaborate to develop new interests and skills.

Planning

The usual program approval method should be used to gain endorsement and support from the chain of command in any given school district or agency. The Superintendent, principal, teacher assigned to designated group room, and secretarial personnel who record scheduling should all be involved in this preliminary planning process.

Selection

PEER LEADERS. Either one or two male or female peer leaders with strong leadership skills are suitable to lead this group. They should have at least three free periods per week to devote to the project.

RECEIVING STUDENTS. The peer leaders and program coordinator describe the program to a wide variety of students in physical education classes. The students are presented with the goals of the program (for unsupervised after school activity improvement). They sign up if they are interested and willing to give up either a morning, afternoon, or lunch period.

Candidates are then screened by the program coordinator and professional staff of that particular setting to determine their interest level, unsupervised status, and single parent or two parent background. Ten students should be selected to comprise a heterogeneous population of mixed gender and mixed background. All of them should have unsupervised after school time.

Training

A high school peer leader who has overcome the obstacles of unsupervised time should be trained through the usual format described in Section 2, Preliminary Training Guide. This person should be sensitive, strong, flexible, and able to command the respect of a younger, middle school population.

In addition to the regular sensitivity training and communication skills provided as part of a peer support program, the peer leader should undergo a preliminary run-through of the various structured experiences. Once a peer leader has been trained to run PLAN, a new potential group leader may observe the process and ready himself/herself for the next program cycle. (See Group Leadership Checklist, Section 2, Session 42.)

Parental Permission

Distribute a program description and Receiving Student Parent Consent Form (see Appendix A, Model 11,) to ten receiving students who will then take them to their parents for written approval. Once all signed parent consent forms have been returned by the students, PLAN begins.

Implementation

The group meets weekly for ten sessions with an option of extending the time period. The decision to continue is made during the tenth session. The sessions unfold within a format of group dynamics exercises, brainstorming techniques, and other structured experiences.

Interwoven within these structured experiences should be discussions and feedback which build on participants' experiences and generate new alternatives for productive activities. Supervisors meet regularly with peer leaders to review group activities, check progress, and make any necessary referrals activated by warning signals.

Evaluation

At the end of the final session, a PLAN Evaluation Sheet is distributed to the members of the group to offer feedback on their experience, learning, and suggestions for improvement. (See PLAN Evaluation Sheet.) Coordinator or supervisor should collect these unsigned documents, process them, note program weaknesses, and make modifications accordingly. In addition, program coordinator should confer with the peer leader and elicit suggestions for modification and improvements. Trainees who observe the program cycle and peer leader also review checklists and completed PLAN Evaluations and make necessary revisions at the last supervisory session.

Follow-Up

After evaluations are processed, revise program as needed and begin new cycle the following year. As part of the follow-up, coordinator may elect to send a written report to supervisors including participant feedback and changes.

Paper Trail

1. Receiving Student Parent Consent Form. *(See Appendix A, Model 11.)*

2. Peer Leader ID Card Prototype. *(See Appendix A, Model 17.)*

3. Peer Leader Pass. *(See Appendix A, Model 15.)*

4. Receiving Student Pass. *(See Appendix A, Model 16.)*

5. Group Leadership Checklist. *(See Section 2, Session 42.)*

6. Resource Network Sheet. *(See Section 3, Session 1, Part 6.)*

7. Weekly Reaction Sheet. *(See p. 263.)*

8. The Concerned Teacher Story Sheet. *(See p. 265.)*

9. PLAN Evaluation Sheet. *See p. 266.)*

Trainees' Observation of All Sessions

Time
At least ten forty-five minute group sessions plus additional supervising conference time.

Goals
• To familiarize new trainees with the new program through observation of experienced group leaders in action.

• To provide opportunity for peer leaders to improve group leadership skills.

Materials
All those used in sessions, Group Leadership Checklists (see Section 2, Session 42), and pencils.

Process
Peer leader trainee observes and completes a checklist for each session conducted by the experienced peer leader. During each supervisory session, trainee participates in progress review and provides feedback to the peer leader. Any students who show behavioral warning signals should be identified and referred to appropriate professionals.

At the end of the program, trainee and peer leader meet with program supervisor to review student evaluations and revise the program. At that time trainee clarifies any concerns before leading the next program cycle.

Outcome Indicators
1. Peer leader trainees should observe sessions and complete Group Leadership Checklists.

2. Trainees should offer feedback to experienced leaders during supervisory sessions.

3. All should review program evaluations and participate in program revision.

4. Trainees should rehearse the program and make necessary adjustments in leadership style.

5. Experienced leaders and supervisor should rate trainees as competent before they lead a new program cycle.

LEADER'S GUIDE

Sessions 1-3: Personal Collage

Time
Three forty-five minute periods

Goals
• To assist participants in gaining awareness of their interests, skills, hobbies, and feelings about themselves.

• To initiate a skills network of students based on shared interests and talents.

• To encourage the development of trust within the group.

Materials
Large construction paper, old newspapers and magazines, pens, magic markers, scissors, tape, and paste.

Process
Note to User: See Section 2, Session 2, for instructions. Follow the same format.

Outcome Indicators
1. Trainees should discuss their hobbies, interests, occupational goals, and thoughts about freedom, dating, parents, politics, or education.

2. Trainers should look for cues indicating interest. Examples include: alertness, eye contact, changes in voice inflection from high to low, or soft to loud, and contents of collages (sports, ideals, life goals).

Session 4: Resource Network

Time
Fifteen minutes

Goal
• To develop an extended resource network to assist members in achieving their goals.

Materials
Resource Network Sheet (see Section 3, Session 1, Part 6), and pencils.

Process
Note to User: Please see Section 3, Session 1, Part 6. Follow the same directions and format for this session.

Outcome Indicators
1. All group members should fill out the Resource Network sheets.

2. Network sheets should be photocopied and distributed to the entire group for use during the summer.

Session 5: Leisure Time Brainstorm

Time
Forty-five minutes

Goal
• To explore one's use of leisure time and to generate new outlets.

Materials
Chalk and chalkboard.

Process
Peer leader encourages the group to engage in a twenty minute brainstorm activity eliciting ways to use open time. Encourage unconventional uses that spur new hobbies and learning experiences. Help the students identify the activities, their limitations, potential, and rewards. Record all the activities, photocopy them on one sheet, and distribute them to the group during the following session. Continue over the weeks to encourage students to report on their new activities. Catalogue all activities on index cards and place them in a leisure time file to which students may refer.

Outcome Indicators
1. All group members should participate in the brainstorm.

2. No put-downs or negative responses should be allowed.

3. The group should report on follow-up activities.

Session 6: Resisting Peer Pressure

Time
Forty-five minutes

Goal
• To sensitize students to ways in which peer pressure can influence one's activities and behavior, both negatively and positively.

Materials
Popular magazines and other books.

Process
Peer leader instructs students to collect popular magazines and bring them into the group. Leader then instructs the group to look through the magazines and select the pictures which show people influencing or manipulating others.

Peer leader holds a discussion about the various situations, potential reasons, and methods people use to change the behavior of others. Elicit students' reactions to the manipulation by peers. Hold a brainstorming activity to generate alternative ways to resist others' manipulation.

Outcome Indicators
1. Each student should describe at least one situation involving peer pressure or manipulation.

2. The group should identify at least one adaptive response to each situation.

Sessions 7: Recognizing a Problem

Time
Forty-five minutes

Goal
• To heighten awareness of everyday conflicts in life.

Materials
None.

Process
Leader asks students to imagine themselves in bed on a Monday morning. Present the following passage:

The alarm rings and you are faced with a decision. One part of you says, "If I get up immediately I can have a nice shower, a leisurely breakfast, and arrive at school on time. But, I'm tired." The other part of you says, "I don't really need a shower. I just had one yesterday. If I skip it, I can sleep for ten more minutes."

Leader asks the students to rehearse their personal, unspoken debates about waking up in the morning. Request reactions to other conflicts and hold a general discussion to identify and recognize the dilemmas posed by the wake-up conflict.

Outcome Indicators
1. Group should describe one personal conflict.

2. Group should express pros and cons of getting up or staying in bed.

3. Group should identify ways to prevent the conflict.

Session 8: Information Gathering

Time
Forty-five minutes

Goal
• To use additional information in making decisions to engage in leisure time activities.

Materials
Paper and pencils.

Process
Peer leader calls the group together to pose and solve manageable problems that are interrupting ways of generating new, alternative activities during unsupervised time. Ask each student to bring in a list of his or her persistent problems. Encourage the group to exchange problems and enlist the support of the group to prioritize and address each problem.

Once the group prioritizes the problems, leader selects the first one and ask each student to list the major forces which keep the problem from being solved. Then ask students to list the resources that might help them to solve the problem. Call the group together to reach a consensus on the major forces and ways that the resources of the group could be used to solve the particular problem.

Leader encourages the group to establish a plan to resolve the problem. Focus on this potential plan and the student who has offered it. List the action to be taken and monitor the problem-solving plan as it progresses from week to week.

Outcome Indicators
1. The group should have focused on a problem presented by one member. The barriers and resources needed to overcome them should be addressed.

2. The group should have come up with some potential solution to this problem and offer to monitor the potential actions throughout the remainder of the group sessions.

Session 9: Personal Preferences

Time
Forty-five minutes (ten minutes per group for all remaining groups to review one member's reactions to his or her week).

Goal
• To enable students to express preferences in their personal choices of activities.

Material
Weekly Reaction Sheets and pencils.

Process
Peer leader asks each student to fill out a Weekly Reaction Sheet. Introduce the Weekly Reaction Sheet by describing its usefulness in developing personal goals and assisting the students to take responsibility for their own self-improvement.

Leader explains that the sheet monitors personal development, use of leisure time, energy, and resources. It clarifies each student's sense of direction. Suggest that each member fill out a sheet.

Leader distributes the Weekly Reaction Sheets to the group and requests that they fill them out. Hold general discussion of one member's Sheet.

Outcome Indicators
1. All students should fill out a Weekly Reaction Sheet.

2. A lively discussion should occur describing some of the activities, high points, etc. of one person's week. Group shares some alternatives which may be more productive.

Session 10: Evaluation of Consequences

Time
Forty-five minutes

Goal
• To evaluate the risks and consequences of decision-making.

Materials
Concerned Teacher Story Sheets and pencils.

Process
Leader distributes copies of the Concerned Teacher Story Sheets to the group members. Leader asks them to read the story quietly and write down two or three alternative responses Mrs. Rogers could have applied to John's problem.

After about ten minutes of silent work, encourage the group to brainstorm optional ways for Mrs. Rogers to deal with this problem. Ask them to describe the potential risks and outcomes of each possible reaction.

Outcome Indicators
1. All members should list at least two alternative responses to John's problem.

2. Group discussion should identify at least three of the following responses to the situation:

• Phone John's parents immediately and tell them what he intends to do.

• Ask the guidance counselor to persuade John to work things out with his parents.

• Explain the situation to John's friends and ask them to convince him to change his mind.

• Wait until John phones Mrs. Rogers. Then encourage him to get in touch with his parents.

Session 11: Progress Review

Time
Forty-five minutes

Goals
• To review the last nine weeks of group sessions, describe the process, and continue the Resource Network (see Section 3, Session 1, Part 6).

• To describe learning about potential new interests and leisure time activities.

• To determine whether to continue the group.

Materials
PLAN Evaluation Sheets (if group decides to disband) and pencils.

Process
Leader reviews the skills, ideas, and interests shared on the Skills Network Sheet and engages the group in a discussion about how students shared and promoted their leisure time interests with each other.

The leader requests each group member to complete the sentence, "I learned..." Hold a discussion describing the common learning and divergent discoveries generated by the group.

Finally, leader asks the group for reasons to either continue or terminate the group. A group decision should be made as to whether to continue the group throughout the rest of the academic year.

Outcome Indicators
1. Several of the skills, ideas, and interests elicited on the original Resource Network Sheet should have been shared throughout the existence of this group.

2. At least ten new activities or insights should emerge through the "I learned..." sentence completion exercise.

3. The group should make a decision whether to continue or disband, based on their needs.

4. If the group decides to disband, all members should fill out PLAN Evaluation Sheets anonymously.

LEADER'S GUIDE

Subsequent Sessions

Time
A set number of forty-five minute sessions to be determined by group.

Goal
• To continue generating new activities which are productive and positive.

Materials
As needed.

Process
Peer leader should continue in the same format and structure as practiced throughout the past ten sessions, encouraging spontaneous discussions of members' progress and their more productive use of leisure time

activities. Troubleshooting, solving problems, and monitoring should all be part of this follow-up experience. The group should become a support network for its membership.

Outcome Indicators
1. Continued discovery of new activities and continuation of newly learned positive actions should be discussed throughout the remainder of this group.

2. The final session should use same format as Session 10 with the exception of continuing the group. PLAN Evaluation Sheets should be filled out.

Weekly Reaction Sheet

Name_____   Date_____

Directions
Write your responses below to clarify how you spend your time and plan your goals.

1. What was the high point of the week?

_____

_____

_____

_____

2. Did you make any major changes in your life this week?

_____

_____

_____

_____

3. What kinds of activities did you do after school?

_____

_____

_____

_____

4. How satisfying were these activities?

_____

_____

_____

Page 2 - Weekly Reaction Sheet

5. Were these activities done alone or with other people?

_____

_____

_____

6. Can you think of any other activities for the following week which might be more useful?

_____

_____

_____

The Concerned Teacher Story Sheet

Name_____   Date_____

Goal
• To evaluate the risks and consequences of decision-making.

Directions
Read the story and decide how you might respond to the situation if you were Mrs. Rogers. Discuss your responses with each other.

Mrs. Rogers, a high school teacher, is well liked by her students because she relates to them honestly and treats them with great respect. John is an outstanding student in Mrs. Rogers' class. He often confides in her.

One day after class, John speaks to Mrs. Rogers about some problems he has with his parents. He tells her that he plans to run away from home tonight. He assures Mrs. Rogers that he will be safe and will phone her after he has found a place to stay.

PLAN Evaluation Sheet

School _____   Class _____ Grade _____

Leader(s)_____   Date_____

Directions
You have just completed a group experience to make you more aware of how to deal with your open time after school. We want to thank you for being a part of this learning experience and hope that you have gained some support from each other.

Please read each statement and write the number 1, 2, or 3 on the lines below.

1. Often   2. Sometimes   3. Never

1._____The experiences were interesting and held my attention.

2._____The leader(s) encouraged me to express my opinions in a friendly atmosphere.

3._____The program made me more aware of some of the feelings I have about the time I spend alone after school.

4._____I found the sessions to be helpful in developing and sharing ideas about other ways to spend this time.

5. Please read the statements below and check yes or no.

I found it easy to be more supportive to others. Yes_____No_____

I think other students should have this program. Yes_____No_____

6. I discovered: _____

_____

_____

7. Please give any suggestions or comments which might improve the PLAN program in the future.

_____

_____

_____

_____

SECTION 8 —
HUMAN RELATIONS

SECTION 8 —
HUMAN RELATIONS

Description

This program enlists a trained high school peer leader to provide structured experiences to special education classes at a middle school. The sessions help to promote self-awareness, self-esteem and positive social interaction skills. During the sessions, the students learn about the high school milieu from a high school peer leader, who prepares them for their forthcoming high school transitional adjustment.

The peer leader is introduced to the special education students, develops rapport, and then later serves as a guide to the entering high school students the following academic year.

Goals

• To provide experiential examples of human relations exercises for middle school special education students.

• To create a peer support network to assist the students in their adjustment to the high school milieu.

• To provide opportunities for the receiving students to learn about high school.

• To provide special education students with a

positive high school special education student role model who made a successful high school adjustment.

Planning

Convene a conference with a school administrator in charge of curriculum.

It is assumed that the administrator will have full knowledge of an approved ongoing peer support program within the school system. Arrange to discuss the goals and process of the Human Relations program. This program includes two sessions to orient and provide interpersonal skills for special needs students.

Set up a second conference with the teachers of the target classes. Develop a designated time frame of one week in May or June of the current academic year.

Arrange either taxi or other transportation and coordinate schedules so that the designated peer leader can be released and transported with his/her teacher's permission for one hour of class time on a two days of the same week.

Spend two periods with the leader prior to the human relations events. Use this time to review the procedures and rehearse for the two sessions.

Selection

PEER LEADERS. The peer leaders should be competent, compassionate, special education, high school, upper grade students who have shown progress and attained integration into the mainstream.

He/she should be open and honest about their disability and should be adept at communicating their feelings about its impact on personal functioning. He/she should be clear on the steps needed to accept and compensate for a disability. His/her schedule availability should match the time frames of the group sessions.

RECEIVING STUDENTS. Target population should include upper grade students in a middle school special education class. It is important to remember that for each special education class, you will need two Human Relations sessions. Special education classes should have a population of students who are about to exit the school.

Lower grade students should not participate, unless they are entering the high school the following year. These students should be high enough in their academic functioning to sustain some mainstreaming at the high school level. They should not be targeted for alternate special placements in a self-contained setting.

Training

The special education peer leader should have been trained in the standard program presented in this book. In addition, the trainee should observe the sessions led by a competent leader and provide feedback using the Group Leadership Checklist (see Session 42, Section 2.)

Each session should be reviewed with the supervisor. Then, trainee should rehearse the program with the observation of an experienced facilitator or supervisor who will rate his/her competency to conduct the program.

Parental Permission

A program description and consent form should be distributed and completed by parents of all student participants. This Human Relations program is not always part of the routine educational planning for special education students.

Implementation

Coordinator should be present while a high school leader facilitates one awareness session and two Human Relations sessions, assisting the middle school students in high school orientation and human relations skills.

SESSION 1, PART 1. A forty-five minute session unfolds to pose Facts and Myths about high school. Receiving students respond to some of the rumors which offer misconceptions. The purpose of this session is to clarify such misconceptions and allay any anxiety which is unfounded by fact.

SESSION 1, PART 2. Leader follows with a Human Relations session intended to discover how positive support and negative feedback effects learning and performance of the group.

SESSION 2, PART 1. Leader facilitates a session on needs assessment, belief systems, and valuable resources already present within the class.

SESSION 2, PART 2. Leader facilitates a session that stresses the importance of developing and sharing personal skills and resources. The group creates a class directory of names, phone numbers and skills they are willing to share with others.

After each session, a follow-up meeting should process the experience, provide feedback on leader's skills and assist the new trainee with any questions. Students who display behavior warning signals should be identified and referred to appropriate professionals.

Evaluation

Receiving students fill out the Human Relations Evaluation Sheet to provide information about the peer leader's skills in facilitating the sessions. Program content, relevancy, and suggested improvements are also requested on these sheets. These sheets should be reviewed with advisors at the end of the final session, and revisions should be written and applied in the forthcoming cycle.

Follow-Up

In the fall, a special education student leader should be available as part of a resource network to the incoming ninth grade group, should any of the students have questions or emergent needs regarding their transition to the high school. Essentially, this special education student leader serves as guide to special education students entering high school. Additional professional support should be available to these students as needed.

After evaluations are processed, revise program as needed and begin new cycle the following year. As part of the follow-up, coordinator may elect to send a written report to supervisors including participant feedback and changes.

Paper Trail

1. Receiving Student Parent Consent Form. *(See Appendix A, Model 11.)*

2. Peer Leader ID Card Prototype. *(See Appendix A, Model 17.)*

3. Peer Leader Pass. *(See Appendix A, Model 15.)*

4. Group Leadership Checklist. *(See Section 2, Session 42.)*

5. Facts and Myths about High School Sheet. *(See Section 3, Session 1, Part 3.)*

6. String Maze Question Sheet. *(See p. 277.)*

7. Needs Auction Question Sheet. *(See p. 278.)*

8. Resource Network Sheet. *(See Section 3, Session 1, Part 6.)*

9. Human Relations Evaluation Sheet. *(See p. 280.)*

Trainees' Observation of All Sessions

Time

Two forty-five minute sessions (for observation), two forty five-minute sessions (for rehearsal), and four supervisory sessions.

Goals

• To familiarize new trainees with the Human Relations program through observation of experienced group leader in action.

• To provide opportunity for peer leader to gain group leadership competence.

Materials

Group Leadership Checklists (see Section 2, Session 42) and pencils.

Process

Trained special education peer leader observes two Human Relations sessions from the back of the room. He/she completes Group Leadership Checklists during each session and attends follow-up supervision sessions designed to process the activity's impact and offer feedback to the leader.

After the end of the program cycle, leader attends a follow-up session to review completed evaluations, make necessary program revisions, clarify concerns, and refer students who exhibit warning signal behaviors.

The peer leader rehearses the two sessions as the experienced leader and supervisor rate his/her leadership abilities and offer constructive suggestions.

Outcome Indicators

1. Peer leader trainee should observe sessions and complete Group Leadership Checklists.

2. Trainee should offer feedback to experienced leader during supervisory sessions.

3. All should review program evaluations and participate in program revision.

4. Trainee should rehearse the program and make necessary adjustments in leadership style.

5. Experienced leaders and supervisor should rate trainee as competent before he/she leads a new program cycle.

LEADER'S GUIDE

Session 1, Part 1: Facts and Myths about High School

Time
Twenty minutes (part one of a forty-five minute class period).

Goals
• To enable special education students to identify and clarify their concerns about high school, demystify the myths, and distinguish between rumor and truth.

• To assist special education students in overcoming fears about what might happen to them at high school.

Materials
Facts and Myths about High School Sheets (see Section 3, Session 1, Part 3).

Process
Note to User: Please see Section 3, Session 1, Part 3. Follow the same format for this session.

Outcome Indicators
1. All students should complete the forms.

2. Students should ask several questions about high school.

3. Group discussion should focus on the continuum ranging from truth to exaggeration to falsehood.

Session 1, Part 2: String Maze

Time
Twenty-five minutes (part two of a forty-five minute class period)

Goal
• To discover how positive and negative feedback affects learning and performance.

Materials
Blindfold, chalk or magic marker, String Maze Question Sheets, tape or string, and pencils.

Process
Leader tells the group that they are to participate in an experiment to see how they can influence each other's performance. Leader asks one person to volunteer as the performer.

With a long piece of string or tape laid straight on the floor, extending from one wall to the opposite wall, leader instructs the performer as follows:

Your task is to keep your feet on the line as you walk from one side to the other. You will be wearing a blindfold. The group will guide you.

Peer leader asks other students to assemble on each side of the line, leaving sufficient space for the "performer" to walk without colliding with observers. Leader puts blindfold on performer.

TRIAL 1: Leader instructs group to give negatively toned verbal feedback (i.e.,"You're way off." "Come on, can't you do better than that?" "You're off the mark"). As performer walks the line, negative reactions are given by observers. Leader instructs one participant to count the number of times the performer's foot touches the line during the first trial. A tally should be kept on the board.

TRIAL 2: As performer walks the line, observers are instructed to give positive verbal feedback (i.e., "You are getting close." "You're on it." "You're doing great.") Again throughout this process, assigned participant counts the number of times each foot touches the line and records the number of touches on the board.

Scores are tallied. Repeat the process with different performers walking the line. Leader distributes Question Sheets and allows five minutes for performers and observers to respond in writing.

Then leader holds a five minute discussion on the different conditions and how they affect performers' behavior as well as that of observers. The discussion should focus on how positive and negative feedback affects students' performance in other areas of their lives.

Outcome Indicators
1. Performer should walk the line while observers give appropriate feedback.

2. Students should notice differences in performers' physical and facial expressions during positive and negative trials.

3. Usually performers should score higher during the positive feedback trials.

LEADER'S GUIDE

Session 2, Part 1: Needs Auction

Time
Thirty-minutes

Goals
• To learn about student's values, needs, and resources already present within their lives.

• To assist students in setting goals and discovering their positive talents and qualities.

Materials
Play money, chalk, Needs Auction Question Sheets, and pencils.

Process
Before entering the class, leader checks the number of students in the class and divides up unequal amounts of play money.

Leader requests the group to brainstorm a few talents, possessions, traits, and qualities most sought after by the participants. These are listed on the board and the group is asked to select ten of the most popular needs and attributes.

Play money is distributed to the students, and they hold a mock auction during which participants establish which needs are important and how much money to spend. They then bid for these desirable things and talents. The process will show the group what qualities are of high and low value. Keep a record of the selling price of each need and the name of each person who bought it. Make a chart with which to generate discussion at the end of the auction.

Needs Auction Question Sheets are passed out and students are requested to write their responses. A general discussion is held to emphasize how needs are satisfied and what positive qualities students already have.

Outcome Indicators
1. Auction should produce lively reactions among the group.

2. Discussion of questions should identify needs that are already met as well as talents and attributes they would like to develop.

LEADER'S GUIDE

Session 2, Part 2: Resource Network and Evaluation

Time
Fifteen minutes

Goal
• To set up a support network based on abilities and talents that students are willing to share with each other.

Materials
Resource Network Sheets (see Section 3, Session 1, Part 6), Human Relations Evaluation Sheet, and pencils.

Process
Please see Section 3, Session 1, Part 6. Follow the same directions and format for this session.

Then leader asks group members to fill out Human Relations Evaluation Sheets anonymously.

Outcome Indicators
1. Support network should be filled with at least ten different skills that members are willing to share with others.

2. Human Relations Evaluation Sheet should be filled out by each member.

String Maze Question Sheet

Name_____   Date_____

Directions
Please write your answers below to clarify your experience during this exercise.

1. What was it like to put down the person walking the line?

_____

_____

_____

_____

2. How do you feel and react when others put you down?

_____

_____

_____

_____

3. What kinds of tasks do you perform better with praise?

_____

_____

_____

_____

4. List some things you do better under pressure or criticism from others.

_____

_____

_____

Needs Auction Question Sheet

Name_____   Date_____

Directions
Please answer the questions below to clarify your needs and priorities.

1. What needs, qualities, or skills were most important to you? List them below.

_____

_____

_____

2. What was it like to bid for what you wanted?

_____

_____

_____

_____

3. If you were outbid, what was your reaction (inside) to those who received the skill, value, or quality you wanted?

_____

_____

_____

_____

4. Which needs or qualities do you think your parents would want to have?

_____

_____

_____

_____

Page 2 - Needs Auction Question Sheet

5. What are some of the things on the board that money cannot buy?

_____

_____

_____

_____

6. Which of the skills, values, or qualities on the list do you already have?

_____

_____

_____

_____

7. Which talents, skills, values, or qualities are you willing to teach or share with others?

_____

_____

_____

_____

Human Relations Evaluation Sheet

School _____ Class _____ Grade _____

Leader(s)_____ Date_____

Directions

You have just completed a series of group experiences to help you become more aware of your-selves, your needs, and how you relate to others. Thank you for being part of this learning experience. As you know, you will be able to seek advice from the peer leaders next year at the high school.

Please read each statement and write the number 1, 2, or 3 on the lines below.

1. Always   **2. Sometimes**   **3. Never**

1._____The experiences were interesting and held my attention.

2._____The leader helped me to express my opinions.

3._____The sessions made me aware of my own needs and goals, and of how I relate to others.

4._____The sessions made me more aware of who I am.

Read each statement and check yes or no.

5. The high school student did a good job of leading the Facts and Myths session.

Yes_____ No_____

6. The high school student did a good job of leading the String Maze exercise.

Yes_____ No_____

7. The String Maze helped me to learn about how I react to support and harassment.

Yes_____ No_____

8. The Needs Auction was helpful in learning about myself and others.

Yes_____ No_____

9. I think that other students should have this program.

Yes_____ No_____

Page 2 - Human Relations Evaluation Sheet

10. I discovered:

_____

_____

_____

11. Please add any comments or suggestions about the program.

_____

_____

_____

_____

SECTION 9 —
KIDS 'R SAFE

SECTION 9 —
KIDS 'R SAFE

Description

Kids 'R Safe is a program which responds to the recent surge in child abduction and abuse by strangers. We have all witnessed the increase of missing children caused by kidnapping throughout the nation. The program is intended to educate students in grades K through 2 about different ways of remaining safe when unsupervised by adults.

This program uses two or three positive high school role models who enter an elementary school class one session a week for three weeks. These trained peer leaders are supervised by an adult advisor. The peer leaders instruct the students to draw pictures of some of the places they go and to discuss their activities.

This activity is then followed by puppet shows which illustrate some potentially harmful situations and then provide strategies to avoid these situations. The final session features a game to reinforce some of the concepts stressing safety tactics. After each student has named a safety strategy, he/she receives a balloon and a button which states, "I am a Kids 'R Safe member."

The approach is entertaining and lively. Experiential sessions are designed to allay anxiety and produce positive effects.

Goals

• To make students aware of potentially dangerous situations which might occur while they are unsupervised.

• To teach and reinforce strategies to protect their safety.

• To teach the students safe procedures to follow if they get lost.

• To create a pupil support system which encourages mutual appeals for cooperation and communication about safety tactics.

Planning

Administrative approval should be obtained before this program begins. Planning stages should include consultations with building administrators, appropriate supervisors, and teachers in the host setting designed to identify needs and enlist support. Parents may also be involved in preliminary planning stages.

After professionals and parents accept the program design, Board of Education approval should be finalized. Teachers of the selected classes should be available to remain in the classes as observers during the three sessions.

Appropriate classes are selected through the voluntary efforts of building administrators and cooperating teachers of grades K-2.

Selected classes receive announcements which are transferred to the parents to make them aware of the program before it begins. (See Kids 'R Safe Sample Announcement, Appendix A, Model 24.) Administrators, teachers, program coordinator, and peer leaders meet to set convenient times and dates which include one forty-five minute period per week for three weeks.

Review the Kids 'R Safe Game (see pp. 295-298.) with peer leaders.

Coordinator contacts appropriate manufacturers to order balloons and buttons. The buttons should be approximately 2 1/2 inches in diameter and can be designed by one of the peer leaders. Each button should read "Kids 'R Safe Club Member" (and the student's name). This preparation should take place at least a six weeks before the program begins. Be sure to order sufficient quantities of buttons. Names of students should be received from the teachers well in advance.

Program coordinator arranges for transportation for high school students to attend the elementary school classes. Release time from high school classes is also coordinated by administrators and program coordinator.

Selection

PEER LEADERS. Peer leaders should be chosen on the basis of maturity, experience, interest in younger pupil populations, and leadership skills. They should also meet the regular selection criteria. It is advisable to choose one boy and one girl to work together as peer leaders in these elementary classrooms. Schedule availability and grade performance are also factors influencing selection of peer leaders.

RECEIVING STUDENTS. Since Kids 'R Safe is purely an educational prevention program, any or all classes at the K-2 grade level are an appropriate population.

It may not be possible to cycle this program through all K-2 classes in a given school system because of time and resource restrictions. Therefore, it is best to request interested K-2

teachers to sign up voluntarily, and then select randomly from a list of volunteer teachers.

Training

Peer leader training should follow the usual group program format which emphasizes:

• Recognizing and attending to students exhibiting behavioral warning signals.

• Seeking back-up as necessary.

• Always working with a supervising teacher present.

The training follows a three session observation/rehearsal format. Trainees observe coordinator or another trainer conduct the program. As a follow-up, trainees rehearse three sessions taking leadership roles and receiving verbal and written feedback from trainees.

The Group Leadership Checklist (see Section 2, Session 42) is used as an evaluation instrument. Each session with the students is preceded by a forty-five minute preparation conference where troubleshooting and planning occur under coordinator's direction.

Parental Permission

The announcement below should be distributed and signed by the parents of the receiving population prior to the first session.

Description

Kids 'R Safe is a program which responds to the recent surge in child abduction and abuse by strangers. We have all witnessed the increase of missing children caused by kidnapping throughout the nation. The program is intended to educate students in grades K through 2 about different ways of remaining safe when unsupervised by adults.

This program uses two or three positive high school role models who enter an elementary school class one session a week for three weeks. These trained peer leaders are supervised by an adult advisor. The peer leaders instruct the students to draw pictures of some of the places they go and to discuss their activities.

This activity is then followed by puppet shows illustrating some potentially harmful situations and strategies to avoid them. The final session features a game to reinforce some of the concepts stressing safety tactics. After each student has named a safety strategy, he/she receives a balloon and a button which states, "I am a Kids 'R Safe member."

The approach is entertaining and lively. Experiential sessions are designed to allay anxiety and produce positive effects.

Implementation

The following sequence of sessions should unfold as the program is implemented.

SESSION 1: PICTURE DRAWING. Peer leaders enter a classroom, introduce themselves, and distribute paper and crayons to the class. Then they request students to draw pictures of their favorite place to go, their methods of transportation, with whom they go, the time of day, and the activities that take place at the particular location.

After the students have completed their drawings, the peer leaders seek volunteers from the class to introduce their drawings to the group.

Leaders then collect, review, and discuss them with the program coordinator after the session is completed. The drawings usually portray universal locations such as public places, restaurants, park scenes, baseball fields, urban centers, and friends' houses.

In order to generate effective safety strategies, the peer leaders use the drawings to trigger possible scenarios illustrating safety measures. Two different vignettes using puppets and role playing procedures unfold in the next session.

SESSION 2: PUPPET SHOWS. Leaders select two three possible story lines from the following:

1. The Public Place
This is a story of a boy who gets lost in a toy store and is reunited with his father.

2. The Park
This is a story about a young child who is accosted by a stranger and seeks help to return

home safely.

3. The Zoo
In this story two children have a close encounter with Bad Man Bob at the zoo. They are rescued by their mother.

SESSION 3: KIDS 'R SAFE GAME. This session reinforces and reviews some of the concepts which have unfolded throughout the first two sessions. The format includes a game called "The Kids 'R Safe Game," which is a board game set up in a step by step format. The students must help Ann, the main character in the game, arrive home safely from a park through a pathway with several steps along the way.

Use the gameboard art on pages 295-298. The four pages can be photocopied and enlarged. Trim along the borders, color the art, and then mount the four sections on a large piece of poster board.

Peer leaders divide the class into two small groups, approximately six to eight members each. Each peer leader facilitates one group with a game board and a pawn. The students are asked questions referring to safety measures. Each correct response moves the pawn closer to the safety of home.

After the Kids 'R Safe Game is complete and the characters are home safe, the class is reassembled as a total group. The peer leaders then ask each class member to state one concept they have learned throughout the last three sessions. When all class members have shared their new learning, the peer leaders pass out Kids 'R Safe balloons and member buttons.

Evaluation

The following evaluation measures may be used as appropriate:

1. Sample interviews: teachers, peer leaders, and/or coordinator meet with small, random samples of target groups, issuing standardized questions to glean data regarding impact of Kids 'R Safe program. Included in the questionnaires will be some suggestions for improvement generated by the student recipient, as well as peer leaders.

2. A parent assessment group may be polled through a questionnaire or a meeting to gather impressions of the project's strengths, weaknesses, and impacts on the student recipients. (See Kids 'R Safe Evaluation Sheet.)

3. A PTA representative may be asked to observe peer led sessions and to record specific reactions to the program.

Follow-Up

Teachers may construct a bulletin board including the student made pictures of their favorite places and appropriate protective defense strategies that can be used in each setting. They can list the strategies under each picture. Peer leaders may revisit the class periodically to review the concepts.

Peer leaders, new trainees, and the supervisor convene a meeting to review the Kids 'R Safe Evaluation Sheets and revise the program.

Paper Trail

1. Receiving Student Parent Consent Form. *(See Appendix A, Model 11.)*

2. Peer Leader ID Card Prototype. *(See Appendix A, Model 17.)*

3. Peer Leader Pass. *(See Appendix A, Model 15.)*

4. Receiving Student Pass. *(See Appendix A, Model 16.)*

5. Group Leadership Checklist. *(See Section 2, Session 42.)*

6. Kids 'R Safe Sample Announcement. *(See Appendix A, Model 24.)*

7. Kids 'R Safe Gameboard. *(See pp 295-298.)*

8. Kids 'R Safe Questions. *(See p. 299.)*

9. Kids 'R Safe Evaluation Sheet. *(See p. 300.)*

Trainees' Observation of All Sessions

Time
Three forty-five minute group sessions plus additional supervising conference time.

Goals
• To familiarize new trainees with the new program through observation of experienced group leaders in action.

• To provide opportunity for peer leaders to improve group leadership skills.

Materials
Group Leadership Checklists (see Section 2, Session 42) and pencils.

Process
Two or three trained peer leaders observe three Kids 'R Safe sessions from the back of the room. They complete Group Leadership Checklists during each session and attend follow-up supervisory sessions, during which they process the activity's impact and offer feedback to the leader. Students who show behavioral warning signals should be referred to appropriate profes-sionals.

After the end of the program cycle, peer leaders attend a follow-up session to review completed evaluations, make necessary program changes, and clarify their concerns.

Then peer leaders rehearse the four sessions as the experienced leaders and the supervisor rate their leadership abilities and offer constructive suggestions.

Outcome Indicators
1. Peer leader trainees should observe sessions and complete Group Leadership Checklists.

2. Trainees should offer feedback to experienced leaders during supervisory sessions.

3. All should review program evaluations and participate in program revision.

4. Trainees should rehearse the program and make necessary adjustments in leadership style.

5. Experienced leaders and supervisor should rate trainees as competent before they lead a new program cycle.

Session 1: Picture Drawing

Time
Forty-five minutes

Goals
• To identify some of the places that students in the class frequently visit.

• To identify some popular activities.

Materials
White construction paper, crayons, and magic markers.

Process
Peer leaders introduce themselves to the class, explaining who they are, the name of the program (Kids 'R Safe), and some of the activities that will occur. The activities include picture drawing, puppet shows, and a game.

Peer leaders ask students to imagine their favorite place, what they like to do there, who they are with, and how they will get home. Then leaders distribute materials and ask students to draw pictures of what they just imagined. Peer leaders also participate in this activity.

When students complete their drawings, peer leaders ask them to introduce themselves and explain their pictures to the group. If a particular pupil is having difficulty describing his or her picture or identifying its location, peer leader should offer assistance by making up a game whereby the rest of the class must guess what the picture shows. Then the student who drew the picture can react to each guess.

The pictures are then collected by the peer leaders who explain that the class members will receive them at the third session of the program. Peer leaders say good-bye to the students and tell them that they will be back the following week.

Outcome Indicator
1. Each student should draw a picture of his/her favorite place. The picture should be complete with a portrayal of the student in the setting as well as a method of transportation to and from home.

Follow-Up
After Session 1, the peer leaders should locate some simple hand puppets with which to create the stories about the pictures. Peer leaders should create stories which are somewhat reflective of the pictures drawn by the class members. Peer leaders can make their own stage by using a large cardboard box.

LEADER'S GUIDE ==

Session 2: Puppet Shows

Time
Forty-five minutes

Goal
• To illustrate the various safety tactics and possible errors that a child can make in a given situation.

Material
Hand puppets, piano, and cardboard stage.

Process
Peer leaders may spend ten minutes before class setting up the puppet show. Then they return to the classroom, introduce themselves again, and tell the students:

Today we are going to have two puppet shows based on the pictures which you drew last week. During the skits you will notice wrong decisions are made by the boys and girls. Each time you see someone make a wrong decision, raise your hand and give the right way of acting. Remember, you must pay close attention and be sure to raise your hand before calling out the right thing the character should do. You will be questioned about this story at the end.

The puppet shows should illustrate the following principles which will be phrased as questions to use after the scenarios are complete:

1. Always say "no" to a stranger who approaches and offers you a ride or candy.

2. Always call home when it gets dark. Never walk home alone.

3. Never take a shortcut home through the woods or in dark areas.

4. If a stranger comes up to you, be careful not to believe him/her even if he mentions that your parent has told him to help you.

5. If you are ever lost or a stranger is following you, find a public phone or a safe adult, such as a policeman or shopkeeper, who can help you.

6. If a stranger is following you in a car, run in the opposite direction.

7. When using the phone, dial "0" or "911" if you have no money to call home. Be sure to tell the operator your name, address, and where you are.

8. You may want to think up a secret password with your parents in case of an emergency or if you are bothered by a stranger. The stranger won't know the password, but your parents will, and they will know you are in danger.

9. If there are no familiar people nearby, it is best for you to stay where you are.

Leaders choose two from the story lines below, or make up a new script if necessary.

1. THE PUBLIC PLACE
Johnny and his Dad are in a toy store shopping for his little sister's birthday present. While Johnny's father is looking for the present in the doll section, Johnny is preoccupied with some of the other attractions. One of these attractions, an elaborate train set, catches his eye.

Quickly, he tugs at his father's shirt asking him to accompany him to the section. After getting no response from his father, he wanders off by himself going from one section to another taking shear delight in all the exciting things to see.

Johnny has drifted through several sections by this time and realizes that he is lost. A few more minutes pass, and then Johnny is confronted by a shopper, a total stranger, who asks if he needs help. He is now faced with a decision: whether to go with this lady or find an appropriate person to help him.

He politely refuses the help from the female shopper and proceeds to find the main cashier who seeks assistance from the manager of the store. After some announcements are made on the PA, Johnny and his father are reunited.

2. THE PARK
Sue and Ann, two first grade students, are having a great time swinging in the park as twilight approaches. Sue realizes that darkness is approaching and tells Ann that she is going to phone her mother to get a ride home.

Sue invites Ann to accompany her to the phone. Ann declines the invitation, stating, "I know a shortcut which could get me home real soon. I am going home now. See you later, Sue."

As Ann is walking home alone, she is confronted by a stranger, a man in a car who offers her a lift home. The man tells Ann that her mother has sent him to pick her up. Ann asks the stranger his name. The stranger replies, "Forget it, kid" and drives off.

Realizing that she has had a close encounter with danger, Ann becomes upset and immediately rushes to the nearest pay phone to call her mother for a lift home. She realizes that her pockets are empty.

Suddenly she remembers that she can reach her mother by dialing zero. She dials zero, asks for assistance and reaches her mother collect. Five minutes later her mother picks her up, and the story ends safely.

3. THE ZOO
Peer leaders introduce the characters and describe the setting. Sally and Jeffrey, two children aged 7 and 5, are with their mother at the zoo on a sunny Saturday afternoon. They have an encounter with Bad Man Bob.

Peer leaders continue: While admiring the monkeys, Mom spots a refreshment stand and informs the children that she is going to get some drinks and sternly tells the children that they must remain where they are until she returns.

Mom: Remember kids, stay right here by the monkeys while I get some lemonade. Stay put! I'll be right back.

Sally: Okay Mom. We'll be right here. (Mom exits.) Wow Jeff, look at the monkeys swinging through the trees!

Jeff: Aw, that's no fun. Let's go check out the lions. They're scary and more exciting than this stuff. GRRR!

Sally: No Jeffrey, Mom told us to wait here.

Jeff: No way. I'm going to have some fun. Are you coming or not?

Sally: But Jeff, Mom said, "Stay put."

Jeff: Sally, let's just go for one minute.

LEADER'S GUIDE
Session 2: Puppet Shows continued

Sally: But Jeff!

Jeff: Let's go! (Jeffrey slowly moves away.)

Sally: Alright, I'm coming but only for a minute. (Sally moves towards Jeff.)

Jeff: (approaching the lion's cage) Gee, look at them! Look at the teeth on that animal!

Sally: Yeah, they're scary. Now let's go. (Sally starts to walk away. Bad Man Bob approaches her.)

Bad Man Bob: Why hello, kids! (Sally grabs Jeff to hold him back from Bad Man Bob.)

Jeff: Hi!

Bad Man Bob: So little boy, what's your name?

Jeff: Jeff.

Bad Man Bob: Jeff, do you want to see some tigers now?

Jeff: Wow, yeah!

Sally: No, Jeff. No, sir, we have to go now.

Bad Man Bob: Come on, you two, we'll just be gone for a few minutes. You'll love to see the tigers. They're great!

Jeff: (Turns to Sally.) Come on, Sally, we'll be quick.

Sally: Okay, I guess its alright for a little while.

Mom: (off stage.) Sally? Jeff? Sally? Where are you kids?

Sally: Mom's calling us. We've got to go, Jeff.

Jeff: Yeh mister, we've got to go, now!

Bad Man Bob: (He reaches towards them as they run away.) Oh, no you don't. You're not going anywhere!

(If piano or other instrument is available, a loud, chord should punctuate the climax.)

After the stories are complete, peer leaders ask the class members to identify some correct responses made by the characters in the scenarios. If time permits, the dramas should be played with the incorrect responses replaced by correct reactions stated by class members.

Outcome Indicators
1. Students should be raising hands and interrupting the stories when errors are made by characters.

2. Class members should identify the correct and incorrect responses by characters in these stories with at least 75% accuracy.

3. Peer leaders should correct any misunderstandings by class members by stating the proper procedures.

LEADER'S GUIDE

Session 3: Kids 'R Safe Game

Time
Forty-five minutes

Goal
• To review and reinforce the principles of safety tactics which were introduced in Sessions 1 and 2.

Materials
Kids 'R Safe Game, a pawn, Kids 'R Safe Question Sheets, Kids 'R Safe balloons or Kids 'R Safe membership buttons, Kids 'R Safe Evaluation Sheets, and student drawn pictures to be used as components of a bulletin board.

Process
Peer leaders divide the group into two sections, each conducting the Kids 'R Safe game. Peer leaders should explain the rules and sequence of the game. Each peer leader has a list of questions based on the principles in the puppet shows. The object of the game is to get Ann, the pawn, home safely.

Peer leader explains that the students must raise their hand in order to answer each question, one at a time. As the question is asked, and each student responds, the peer leader asks the rest of the group to either accept or correct the response to the question given by the particular student. When each response is understood, peer leader moves pawn one space closer to home on Kids 'R Safe gameboard. This continues until the pawn arrives home safely.

After all the students have responded to the questions in each separate group, peer leaders should request each member, round robin style, to offer a statement about what they have learned. When all of the students have responded, peer leaders should distribute Kids 'R Safe balloons and buttons with the inscription "Kids 'R Safe Clubmember" and each student's name.

Peer leaders distribute Kids 'R Safe Evaluation Sheets to the children and instruct them to bring them home and ask their parents to complete them. Make sure to collect them from the teachers to review the results.

Outcome Indicator
1. Students should be active participants, exhibiting supportive comments to each other, and responding to the game's questions with 75% accuracy.

Follow-Up
Teachers may construct a bulletin board including the student-made pictures of their favorite places and appropriate protective defense strategies that can be used in each setting. They can list the strategies under each picture. Peer leaders may revisit the class periodically to review the concepts.

Peer leaders, trainees, and the supervisor convene a meeting to review the Kids 'R Safe Evaluation Sheets and revise the program.

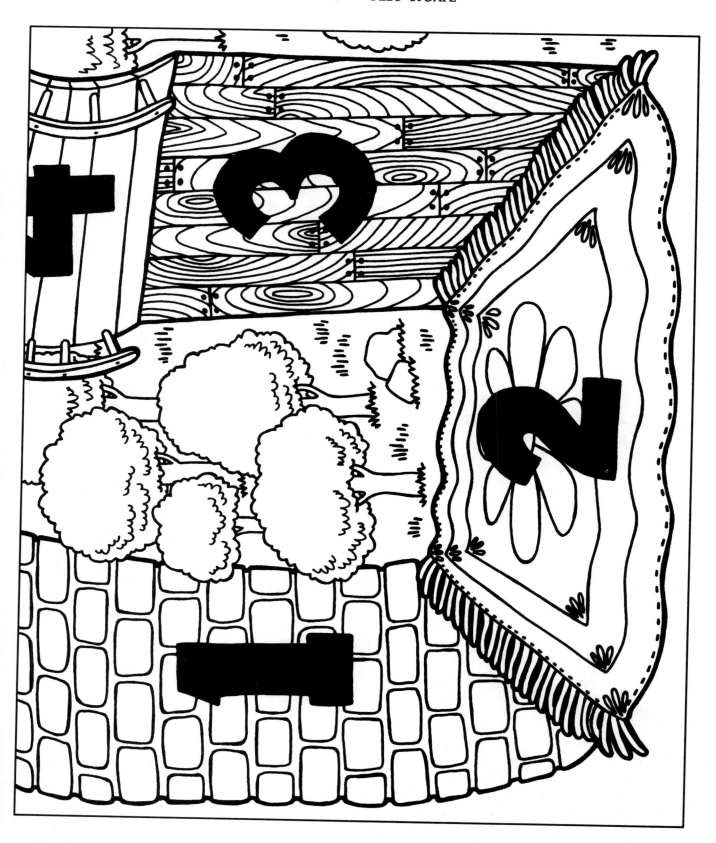

Kids 'R Safe Questions

Name_____   Date_____

Directions
Use these questions to play the Kids 'R Safe Game. Ask the students to raise their hands if they have an answer. Score each correct response with a move of the pawn on the board. The game is complete when the pawn reaches home.

1. After the little league game, a woman in the park asks Ann if she needs a ride home and offers her some candy. What should she say and do?

2. It is ten minutes to five in the evening. Ann starts to walk home.

She has ten minutes to get home. What should she do?

3. It's getting darker out. Should she take the shortcut home through the woods, or stay on the lighted sidewalk?

4. A stranger stops Ann and asks her the time and then some personal questions. What should she do?

5. The stranger seems to be following her. What should she do? Where should she go?

6. The stranger is no longer following her. Since Ann was so nervous, she now has become lost. There is a pay phone, but she has no change. What should Ann do?

7. What number or numbers should Ann dial?

8. What kind of information should she know to tell the operator or person she speaks with on the phone?

9. Should Ann tell anyone about the stranger? If so what kind of information should she try to remember.

10. Which safety rules should Ann and her parents set up so that she will arrive home unharmed?

Kids 'R Safe Evaluation Sheet

Name (Optional) _____ Date_____

School _____

Class _____ Grade _____

Leader(s) _____

_____

Dear Parent:

Your child has just participated in a three session educational pilot program led by trained Peer Leaders from _____ High School, supervised by _____.

The sessions focused on ways for your child to distinguish between helpful and harmful strangers and to develop strategies to promote safety in public places.

We would appreciate your filling out the following questionnaire to assist us in our program improvements. Please chek yes or no on the lines below.

1. My child told me about the Kids 'R Safe Program. Yes___ No___

2. Based on the information my child gave me, some positive strategies were presented. Yes___ No ___

3. I think Kids 'R Safe should be extended to other classes in our district. Yes___ No___

Comments about the program_____

_____

_____

_____

_____

_____

Please return to your child's teacher.

SECTION 10 —
CLOSE ENCOUNTERS

SECTION 10 —
CLOSE ENCOUNTERS

Description

Trained high school peer leaders conduct four sessions stressing facts and myths about chemical dependency, peer pressure, refusal skills, and naturally generated breakthrough experiences. The sessions are supervised by an adult but facilitated by the peer leaders and delivered to middle school students in grades five through seven. Each session lasts forty-five minutes.

Goals

• To prevent early patterns of chemical dependency in students in grades five through seven by enlisting older peer role models to run sessions promoting refusal skills and alternative behaviors to substance and alcohol abuse.

• To review the facts, myths, and information about chemical dependency and its effects.

• To assist students in learning the consequences of embarking upon chemical dependency oriented lifestyles.

• To increase awareness of cultural heritage and family customs which build a foundation for personal pride.

• To educate students in refusal skills and effec-

tive ways of saying no to peer pressure situations which may precipitate experimentation or chemical dependency.

• To identify experiences from the past which develop self-esteem.

• To encourage students to retrieve and share previous, naturally induced positive experiences and access these inner states through trigger mechanisms. Such trigger mechanisms can then be used in situations where a positive state is desired through natural sources other than drugs and alcohol.

Planning

The coordinator should secure permission from appropriate administrators to initiate such a preventive program. Review the family life curricula and locate preventive measures against chemical dependency. Invariably, these curricula call for consultants to present and reinforce preventive techniques and interventions.

A written statement describing the program and its goals should be prepared in advance and distributed to the principal, Superintendent, and Board of Education or any other agency hierarchy for approval.

After attaining approval, meet with the school principal or site administrator who may assist in providing staff resource backup. For example, if you wish to initiate this program in a family life class, the family life teacher may need to be involved in the preparation process. Further, the classroom teacher will need to select appropriate receiving students and assist in supervision of peer leaders as they conduct their four sessions.

Selection

PEER LEADERS. Select experienced, trained peer leaders who have been in your program for a long enough time period to have operated in one-to-one relationships and groups. It is best to select one male and one female peer leader to serve as a partnership.

These leaders should be energetic and reflective. They must also demonstrate good rapport skills and sufficiently high academic performance to afford the four hours of missed class time to lead this project.

These students should be selected by peers, responsible staff members, and the program coordinator. They should be interviewed and make a verbal or written commitment to act responsibly and live a lifestyle free of chemical use. They should also agree to maintain confidentiality of information regarding this program with the exception of chemical use or dependency problems which may become obvious through the sessions. In such cases, they should be aware of the referral procedures and activate them immediately.

RECEIVING STUDENTS. The most appropriate grade levels to receive Close Encounters are five through seven. These students have heard about chemical dependency issues through friends, parents, older siblings, and media, but have most likely not embarked on a self-destructive chemical dependency lifestyle.

The facts and figures have been presented in awareness sessions in many of their health classes, but they have not had the opportunity to review these facts with trained, positive role models. It is best to select one target class as a pilot program upon which to embark and then reevaluate. Designate one staff member (perhaps health education or family life teacher) to select the most appropriate class to receive the

first cycle.

Training

Peer leaders should be trained in the skills taught in Section 2. Their specific preparation for Close Encounters should begin with an observation of the Close Encounters Program, conducted by the coordinator. They should provide observational feedback for the coordinator by using the Group Leadership Checklist (see Section 2, Session 42).

Then peer leaders facilitate the four sessions, while coordinator and staff members critique their communication skills and group management skills using Group Leadership Checklists. After processing the four sessions and reviewing necessary improvements, peer leaders are then ready to lead their own groups.

Peer leaders should be taught the warning signals displayed by high risk receiving students. Furthermore, they should be directed to refer any potential at-risk students to appropriate staff members. The referrals should be made in writing.

Parental Permission

Parent consent forms should be completed for peer leaders and their receiving populations before the program begins.

Implementation

Identify dates, times, and locations with peer leaders and all support staff. Classroom teachers of receiving students should provide advance notice to the class to prepare them for the program. Transportation should be arranged in advance.

Coordinator should secure permission from teachers of nonessential classes who may allow peer leaders release time. Makeup arrangements should also be made in advance and Leader Passes should be issued. Plan to supervise peer leaders and provide professional advice and backup on a weekly basis after each of their Core Awareness sessions. Such supervisory arrangements can be made in the mornings before classes begin.

An alternate time for such meetings may be during lunch. Constant monitoring and feedback should be encouraged, and problem-solving techniques developed through the natural support group process of the high school peer leaders. Use these sessions to gather feedback from peer leader trainees about students who exhibit behavioral warning signals. Review and revise program format as necessary.

SESSION 1. Peer leaders present a twenty-five point checklist of different facts and myths about substance abuse and then discuss some of the factual information with the receiving students. Hold follow-up supervisory sessions.

SESSION 2. Peer leaders read "The Word Is No," a scenario which pressures young people to take drugs or drink alcohol. In the session, students are requested to identify some of the consequences of chemical experimentation. These consequences are then listed on the board and discussed. Follow-up supervisory session processes the exercise, offers feedback to leaders from the trainees, and identifies students who show warning signal behaviors.

SESSION 3. Peer leaders elicit from the group their own battery of refusal skills and then ask them to select those most responsive to "The Word is No." Leaders then suggest ways to refuse drugs and alcohol in the future. Follow-up supervisory session processes and checks levels of skills in the group.

SESSION 4. Peer leaders ask students to bring up previous positive internal states. They search through their minds for successful breakthroughs or exhilarating experiences that came through their own natural initiative.

Then peer leaders are asked to take their experiences, anchor them, and store them so that these experiences may be resurrected to prevent potential escapist types of behaviors brought on by peer pressure. Particular attention is paid to the ways of using positive states to counteract temptations of substance abuse.

Evaluation

The assessment process should include feedback on the effectiveness of peer leaders, group facilitators, and communicators as well as peer leaders' own personal benefits. During the training process, the Group Leadership Checklists (see Section 2, Session 42) should be used as instruments to assess group management skills.

After the program, Close Encounters Evaluation Sheets should be filled out by receiving students to evaluate their peer leaders' management skills, credibility, and effectiveness.

Follow-Up

At the end of the program cycle, conferences should be held with participating administrators, classroom teachers of receiving students, peer leaders, and program coordinator to determine assets and liabilities of the previous cycle and to suggest changes, additions, or deletions as necessary. Any students exhibiting behavioral warning signals should be discussed and referred to appropriate professionals.

As a training follow-up, new peer leaders may enter future Core Awareness sessions as observers so that they may be trained in the group leadership roles.

Paper Trail

1. Peer Leader ID Card Prototype.   *(See Appendix A, Model 17)*

2. Peer Leader Pass.   *(See Appendix A, Model 15.)*

3. Group Leadership Checklist.   *(See Section 2, Session 42.)*

4. Facts and Myths about Chemical Dependency   *(See p. 317.)*

5. The Word Is No Story Sheet.   *(See p. 318.)*

6. Close Encounters Program Evaluation Sheet.   *(See p. 319.)*

Trainees' Observation of All Sessions

Time
Four forty-five minute sessions for observation; four forty-five minute sessions for rehearsal; and four follow-up supervisory sessions.

Goals
• To familiarize new trainees with the Close Encounters program through observation of experienced group leaders in action.

• To provide opportunity for peer leaders to improve group leadership skills.

Materials
Group Leadership Checklists (see Section 2, Session 42), and pencils.

Process
Trained peer leaders observe four Close Encounters sessions from the back of the room. They complete Group Leadership Checklists during each session and attend follow-up supervisory sessions, during which they process the activity's impact and offer feedback to the leader. Students who show behavioral warning signals should be referred to appropriate professionals.

After the end of the program cycle peer leaders attend a follow-up session to review completed evaluations, make necessary program sessions, and clarify their concerns.

Then peer leaders rehearse the four sessions as the experienced leaders and supervisor rate their leadership abilities and offer constructive suggestions.

Outcome Indicators
1. Peer leader trainees should observe sessions and complete Group Leadership Checklists.

2. Trainees should offer feedback to experienced leaders during supervisory sessions.

3. All should review program evaluations and participate in program revision.

4. Trainees should rehearse the program and make necessary adjustments in leadership style.

5. Experienced leaders and supervisor should rate trainees as competent before they lead a new program cycle.

Session 1: Facts and Myths about Chemical Dependency

Time
Forty-five minutes

Goal
• To provide students with a review of facts and myths regarding chemical dependency and its effects.

Materials
Facts and Myths about Chemical Dependency Sheets and pencils

Process
Peer leaders introduce the session by explaining the purpose of their visit, namely, to discuss the facts and myths about chemical dependency.

Peer leader introduces the Facts and Myths Sheet as follows:

We are giving you a list of 18 physical and mental effects of chemical and alcohol abuse. Some of the information deals with ways to become addicted, patterns of use, and reasons for chemical dependency or experimentation. There are also some consequences of chemically dependent behavior. Many of you have learned some of this information through parents, teachers, or your friends.

Please indicate true or false for each of the twenty-five items. Then we will discuss them. Raise your hands when you are finished.

After the students have completed their Facts and Myths Sheets, go over each statement, identify false statements, and discuss the statements. Try some of the following formats:

• Ask for a show of hands for each answer.

• Ask students to read their answers to the questions and justify them.

• Read the statements and answers with explanation for each.

• Ask for counter-examples for each statement from the group.

Once all twenty statements have been reviewed, ask students to correct and review them with their teachers and parents.

Outcome Indicators
1. All students should complete the Facts and Myths Sheets.

2. Lively discussion should also include counter-examples and opposite opinions.

3. Peer Leaders should take time to carefully review each of the correct explanations.

Follow-Up
Review students' reactions and leadership skills with supervisor and observers. Be sure to discuss any students who exhibit warning signals or any potential substance abuse behaviors. Make necessary referrals.

Facts and Myths Answer Key

__T__ 1. It is a well-known fact that teens are influenced by peer pressure more than any other age group.

__T__ 2. Often people build up tolerances for drugs, resulting in the need to increase the amount taken to get the same effect. There are some exceptions to that general principle. For example, alcoholics frequently need less quantity to achieve the sensation of being drunk.

__F__ 3. If your friendship is worth anything, you need to attempt to be a positive influence and encourage your friend to seek help to stop using.

__F__ 4. Studies have shown that cocaine is extremely addictive. One study using rats showed that when given the choice of food, water, or cocaine, they excluded food and water, eating cocaine until they died of malnutrition.

__F__ 5. Beer contains the very same alcohol found in vodka, whiskey, rum, and all the other addictive beverages. It affects the body and causes addictions in the same way.

__T__ 6. There is a lot more tar in marijuana than is found in cigarettes. Marijuana also changes the structure of genes and can cause serious birth defects.

__T__ 7. Heavy drug use can cause erratic eating habits, and intensified or reduced appetites which can cause serious malnutrition.

__T__ 8. There are countless ways to enjoy natural highs without the assistance of artificial substances. Singing, hearing someone say "I love you," watching a sunset, winning a game, learning a new sport are but a few.

__F__ 9. Drinking has no positive impact on your overall popularity. It may contribute to your acceptance by other students who abuse drugs and alcohol, but it will most likely provide a negative reputation with the mainstream population of the school and community.

__F__ 10. There is an ever increasing population of students who are choosing drug and alcohol-free lifestyles. Latest statistics indicate that approximately 68 percent of high school students in America are living their lives without substance abuse.

__T__ 11. Prescription drugs are often helpful to relieve medical symptoms but only if you follow your doctor's directions.

__T__ 12. It takes more drugs to get high, because the body will frequently build up a tolerance to their effects. But the increased doses still cause major damage to the system.

__T__ 13. It is estimated that six out of every ten fatal auto accidents are alcohol related.

__T__ 14. The key to remaining sober after rehabilitation is after care support, making friends with drug-free peer group, and attending regular family counselling sessions. Otherwise, the chances are 75% that a person will go back to taking drugs or alcohol.

__F__ 15. Cocaine, alcohol, hallucinogens, barbituates, and even tobacco are highly addictive. They are taken without needles.

LEADER'S GUIDE
Session 1 continued

__F__16. Coffee does not neutralize the effects of alcohol. Time is the key factor to reduce the impaired functioning.

__F__17. Anebolic steroids have very dangerous side effects including shrinking genitals and impotence in males, and deformities and serious damage to reproductive system in females.

__F__18. Alcohol depresses the brain functions. In high doses it produces stupor, coma, and even death.

Session 2: The Word Is No

Time
Forty-five minutes

Goal
• To assist students in identifying the consequences of pursuing a chemically dependent lifestyle.

Materials
The Word Is No Story Sheets, paper, and pencils.

Process
Peer leaders read "The Word Is No" drug and alcohol party scenario to the members of the group and ask them to respond. After each member has had an opportunity to list some of the potential consequences of chemical use and abuse, lead a discussion which identifies and expands some of the potential consequences that could occur. They should include at least two of the following possibilities:

1. Somebody overdoses and has to be taken to the emergency ward of the local hospital.

2. You join in the fun and get so involved that you forget about your parents and are late to meet them when they come to pick you up.

3. The police search for you and find you at your parents' request. When they finally catch up to you, they also bust your friends for substance and alcohol abuse. You all go to the police station.

4. Your parents have to pay a lot of money to get you out of the police station. They are very angry with you and yell at you when you come home.

5. You have to go to court for substance abuse by minors.

Outcome Indicators
1. All students should list at least two consequences of two scenarios.

2. Group members should discuss their consequences without necessarily coming up with alternatives at this point.

3. Future consequences should also be discussed, including the potential hazards of pursuing a chemical dependency lifestyle.

Follow-up
Discuss student reactions and leadership skills with your supervisor. Review and revise format as necessary. Identify and refer students who show warning signal behaviors.

BRAINDEAD
Later for you.
Forget it!
No Way!
I DON'T NEED THAT!

Session 3: Responding to Peer Pressure

Time
Forty-five minutes

Goals
• To increase awareness of cultural heritage and family customs which build a foundation for personal pride.

• To develop and enhance effective refusal skills and practice using them appropriately to say no to peer pressure which may encourage chemical use or abuse.

Materials
The Word Is No Story Sheet from Session 2 and pencils.

Process
Peer leaders describe their backgrounds and some of the values promoted by their families and their culture. For example, in the Arabic heritage, it is a custom to give something to a friend that he admires, in the spirit of sharing. The Jewish tradition of commemorating deceased loved ones annually is designed to keep their good qualities alive as examples to follow.

Peer leaders ask class members to jot down some special family or ethnic traditions that are positive, natural, and have special meaning to them.

Encourage the class members to make a list of special values taught to them by their families. Ask the group members to identify certain behaviors that go against their cultural values and family rules and examples of how they have avoided these behaviors.

Peer leaders then ask students to recall past situations where they have used their own refusal skills quite effectively. This should be

followed by a review of "The Word Is No" described in Session 2. After the review of the scenario, peer leaders should lead a group discussion to generate alternate ways to practice refusal skills. Each strategy should be listed on a page to be photocopied and distributed. At the end of the exercise, the group should rank each refusal skill in order of effectiveness, from most to least.

Introduce the exercise as follows:

This is an exercise designed to help you identify some of the powerful ways you have used to avoid other peoples' influence and get out of doing things you don't want to do.

For example, all of us in this school have probably been asked to clean up our rooms. And probably every single one of us has found ways to avoid doing that. We also find ways to avoid taking out the garbage, caring for younger brothers or sisters, and doing other kinds of chores such as homework.

There are times when we have also refused to do things friends have asked us, especially when these things could bring down a lot of heat from adults. You may have also resisted taking a dangerous dare from friends or actions that go against the teachings of your family background. Maybe some of these would include stealing from your family or bad-mouthing your religion or a deceased loved one.

I'd like you to go through your past experience and think of some situations which you have seen, heard, and felt in your lives when you have successfully avoided doing things which others have asked you to do. Take a moment to go through your past and jot some of these responses down on a piece of paper.

LEADER'S GUIDE
Session 3 continued

After about five minutes, lead the group in a short discussion about their responses, trading similar incidents and reactions as well as alternate ways of resisting peer intimidation. Be sure to allow students to pass should they feel uncomfortable sharing their own life events.

Then re-read "The Word Is No" story as follows:

I'm going to reread last session's "The Word Is No" story. This time as I read through the party situation, I would like you to use your personal bank of refusal skills to identify which ones might apply to the particular situation you have to cope with. Pretend you are in the situation now.

Peer leader reads "The Word Is No" story and continues as follows:

Now that you have heard this story, I would like you to share some of the possible ways you might avoid some of the negative consequences.

Record responses on the board and encourage the students to discuss some of the alternate ways to avoid negative consequences. List them on a page which you photocopy and distribute to the group at the end of the session. Before the session ends, make sure to spend about three or four minutes asking the group to decide which of the refusal skills appear to be most and least effective. Rank them starting with #1 as the most effective. Then copy and distribute to the group.

Hold a general group discussion on refusal skills. Then say:

Now that you have listed ways to get out of dangerous situations, here is a chance to demonstrate how they work.

The peer leader calls up volunteer class members to role play responses to peer leaders who try to convince them to drink.

Outcome Indicators
1. Each member should list at least two customs that reflect family or cultural pride.

3. Each member should list at least one action they have refused because they know it goes against their family culture or heritage.

4. Each member should list at least two refusal skills from their past.

5. Each member should identify one effective response to this negative "The Word is No" story. The group should rank each of the refusal skills from most to least effective, starting with #1 as highest rank.

Follow-Up
Discuss students' reactions and leadership skills with supervisor. Review and revise as necessary. Identify and refer students as necessary.

Session 4: Positive States without Drugs

Time
Forty-five minutes

Goals
• To encourage students to identify, retrieve, and share positive early experiences with the group.

• To review consequences, refusal skills, and naturally-induced positive experiences with the group.

• To project ways of using natural, positive behaviors and positive internal states to resist temptations of peer pressured substance abuse.

Materials
Close Encounters Program Evaluation Sheets and pencils.

Process
Peer leaders help group members to go into themselves, review their past, and identify some exciting events, triumphs, and breakthroughs which were successfully produced without drugs or alcohol. Then ask members to make up codes and triggers which can be used as reminders of their own natural abilities to feel the personal power of self-esteem.

A code may be a special name, color, or symbol of the experience such as a baseball to represent a first home run. It may be a gateway to the experience such as a landmark or a door knob to represent entering a first successful party.

After students have discussed their potentials for accessing personal power, lead a discussion to review the consequences of chemical abuse, ways of using refusal skills, and potential future challenges which can be

met through the techniques they have just learned. Set up a support system through a phone network within the group in an effort to develop a positive support system.

Peer leaders introduce the exercise as follows:

We have just spent the last three sessions going over some facts and myths, consequences, and refusal skills that you can use to avoid getting involved in drug and alcohol abuse. Today we're going to ask you to use your own personal power as a reminder that you can run on your own fuel without any additives.

Take a few moments to close your eyes and drift backwards in order to find a time in your life when you really felt that you had it all together. It may been a time when you were very young or it may have been a time just two or three days ago. Some of these possible situations might include learning to do something new (like riding a bike), or giving your first successful speech, doing your favorite activity (like tennis or football), getting a high test grade, or attending a concert.

I'd like you to take a moment to enjoy the experience and relive it with all of its full color, sound, and feelings. Make up your own internal movie screen and run the experience in slow motion as large or small, loud or soft, as intense or as flat as you would like it to be. (Pause about one minute.)

Now I would like you to invent a code name or a symbol for that experience and write it down on a piece of paper. It can be a baseball to represent your first home run or a heart to symbolize your first kiss. (Pause for about one minute.) Raise your hand when you have gotten your code so that I know that we can continue.

LEADER'S GUIDE
Session 4 continued

After each student has successfully relived his or her positive experience and formulated a code or symbol (written or drawn), peer leaders should proceed as follows:

Any of you who wish to share this experience might want to describe your code first or show it to the group. As each member describes his/her code to the group, request the other members to guess what it might symbolize or what story might have occurred. Respect members' privacy by allowing them to pass if they wish. Request the students to reveal the true positive experience symbolized by their code names or symbols.

After some sharing has gone on, ask the group to brainstorm some ways in which they can use these experiences to ward off any possible chemical dependency in future challenges.

Ask them to remember their codes or symbols and use them the next time they are faced with a challenge which might tempt them to use alcohol or other drugs. They might also create a group collage out of the class's symbols.

Review some of the consequences of substance abuse, listing them on the board as the group responds. Use the same procedure to review the potential refusal skills, emphasizing most effective techniques.

Complete this final session with a round of statements from each member describing what they may have learned or their impression of this whole experience.

Before the group leaves, ask the members if they would be willing to offer support to each other to ward off any potential substance abuse. This support can take the form of sharing their strengths, breakthroughs, and refusal skills.

If the group consents, distribute blank sheets of paper and request members to write their names and phone numbers to create a support system. Peer leaders should also include their names and phone numbers on the support network. Photocopy the papers and distribute them to the group so that they have an ongoing network to rely upon.

Distribute Close Encounters Program Evaluation Sheets, allowing five minutes for them to be filled out. Collect the sheets, and say good-bye to the students.

Outcome Indicators
1. All members should have formulated a code or symbol for their previous positive experience.

2. At least 15% of the class should have shared some of their positive experiences and identified how to use their own personal power to relive these positive internal states.

3. Members should have been able to identify at least three consequences and three refusal skills applicable to "The Word is No" story.

4. At least 75% of the class should have listed their names and phone numbers on the support network.

5. All Close Encounters Evaluation Sheets should be returned to peer leaders (without names).

Follow-up
Discuss student reactions to this session and all previous sessions.

Review Group Leadership Checklists for all sessions and recommend changes in style and delivery as necessary.

LEADER'S GUIDE
Session 4 continued

Review student evaluation sheets, revise and amend program. Follow up on any students requiring referrals. Revisit the class periodically to reinforce learning and assess program impact.

Facts and Myths about Chemical Dependency Sheet

Name_____   Date_____

Directions
Place "T" for true and "F" for false by each statement.

_____1. Teenagers often drink because their friends tell them to do it.

_____2. Often people start taking a few drugs and then take more.

_____3. If a friend gets involved with drugs or alcohol, it is best to mind your own business and leave him or her alone.

_____4. Cocaine is not an addictive drug.

_____5. Drinking beer is safer than hard liquor and does not usually lead to alcoholism.

_____6. Two marijuana cigarettes cause about the same amount of lung damage as a pack of regular cigarettes.

_____7. Heavy drug and alcohol use affects eating behavior.

_____8. People can have positive experiences without alcohol and drugs.

_____9. Kids who drink are more popular than nondrinkers.

_____10. All young people smoke and drink a little bit.

_____11. Some drugs are OK to take.

_____12. Regular users of drugs and alcohol need to take more to get high.

_____13. Auto accidents, the leading cause of death among teenagers, are often caused by drunk or drugged drivers.

_____14. Most teenagers who return from rehabilitation programs go back to abusing substances.

_____15. Only people who use needles are drug addicts.

_____16. A cold shower or coffee will sober up a drunk person.

_____17. Anebolic steroids are safer than most other drugs and alcohol.

_____18. Alcohol usually increases your energy.

The Word Is No Story Sheet

Name_____   Date_____

Directions
Read the story below and write your responses.

You have just come to middle school and are attending your first school dance. You and some friends are walking around, feeling a little uncomfortable and not knowing what to do. So, you get some refreshments, listen to the music, and watch the others dance.

Then, you notice that your friend's older sister has arrived on the scene. She is a good looking cheerleader, popular and well-liked by many people at the high school. You are excited that she has stopped to talk with you. She tells your group about a really great party that's about to begin in an out of the way place nearby. She invites you all to join her (and some older kids) and share in the fun.

You are not sure what to do, but all of a sudden you notice a lot of your friends jump to the occasion and off you go with the group. You end up behind the school where you see a few older teenagers, most of whom are in couples, breaking out six-packs of beer and passing around marijuana cigarettes to each other.

Suddenly you remember that your parents will be waiting for you when the dance ends in about half an hour. As you're thinking of this, you find a full beer can thrust in your hands, closely followed by a marijuana joint which is being passed around the group. You hear instructions from your friends about how to inhale it, holding it deeply inside your lungs. You hear coughing from other members of the group. Then you hear lots of laughing and see silly behavior.

Now, make believe you have a giant movie screen in your head. Pretend you are there now, stop the action, and freeze the scene on your personal screen with all the sights and sounds and colors. Think of some of the negative results that could occur if you were to join in the fun and get involved in this drug and alcohol party.

Write your ideas below.

_____

_____

_____

_____

_____

_____

Close Encounters Program Evaluation Sheet

School _____ Class _____ Date _____

Leader(s)_____ Grade _____

Directions
You have just completed a program about substance abuse and ways to avoid drugs and alcohol. Please let us know your reactions to the program and the peer leaders by responding to the following statements.

Your reactions to this program can help us to improve it for others. Please read each statement and write the number 1, 2 or 3 on each line below.

1. Often   2. Sometimes   3. Never

1._____The sessions were interesting and held my attention.

2._____The sessions were clear and I understood what the peer leaders said.

3._____The peer leaders helped me to share my ideas with others in an open, nonthreatening way.

4._____The sessions were useful to me because they were based on my real experiences.

5._____The Facts and Myths Sheet helped me to review my knowledge about substance abuse.

6._____I am convinced that I will never abuse drugs and alcohol.

7._____I discovered new ways to react to negative peer pressure.

8._____Read each statement and check yes or no.

The sessions encouraged me to use earlier breakthroughs as reminders that I can have personal power without substance abuse.

Yes_____ No_____

I learned some of the problems that are caused by substance abuse.

Yes_____ No_____

I think other students should have this program.

Yes_____ No_____

Page 2 - Close Encounters Program Evaluation Sheet

9. I discovered _____

_____

_____

_____

_____

10. These are my comments and suggestions about the Close Encounters Program.

_____

_____

_____

_____

_____

_____

SECTION 11 —
PARTNERS AGAINST SCAPEGOATING (PAS)

SECTION 11 — PARTNERS AGAINST SCAPEGOATING (PAS)

Description

Partners Against Scapegoating (PAS) is a peer support program which uses positive peer role models as change agents who enter middle school health or family life classes and conduct four sessions. These eleventh or twelfth grade peer partners lead group sessions to heighten middle school students' awareness of the harmful effects of verbal harassment of and hostile behavior towards peers.

Although scapegoating and ridicule are almost universal phenomena at the middle school age level, this program recognizes that early intervention may have some preventive impact on the potential catastrophic results of aggressive behavior and scapegoating on a broader level.

Students entering the middle school find themselves enduring rigorous rites of passage, being criticized and harassed by older students. PAS responds to these younger middle school students' emotional needs by attempting to promote more humanistic attitudes and enlisting the support of their older peers.

PAS consists of four weekly sessions integrated into a family life education or health education curriculum at the middle school level. Two peer partners, one male and one female, make guest appearances in family life or health classes. They initiate five experiential exercises which include a test on "Planet 455," the Labeling Game, the Needs Auction, IALAC Story, and the "Wrong Kind of Laughter," a poem by Bill Sanders.

The process begins with a high-powered approach which sensitizes the aggressors to their impact upon others, and concludes with a supportive, collaborative atmosphere at the end of the fourth session.

Goals

• To raise awareness of scapegoating and harassment as phenomena at the middle school level.

• To explore some of the reasons for these behaviors.

• To explore the impact upon the victims and introduce coping strategies to deal with their aggressors.

• To pose alternate ways of managing destructive impulses.

• To create a natural peer support system which

---

embodies the values of mutual respect and concern for others.

Planning

Before embarking on such a high impact program, submit a brief but complete proposal including goals and specific curriculum to supervisory personnel. These may include the Superintendent of Schools, principal, and teachers. You may also want to include the health or family life coordinator, guidance coordinator, and any other human service support staff.

After explaining the intent of such a program and obtaining board or administrative approval, meet with the above professionals to clarify the program goals and process.

Logistics can be worked out through the building supervisors and teachers of family life or health classes. Typically, a particular health class can receive the program one class session per week for four weeks.

Transportation for high school students can be provided by the coordinator, bus, or taxi, depending on district resources. The class period should be chosen on the availability basis of high school peer leaders who serve as partners. Written communication about program design, dates of sessions, and times should be forwarded to appropriate high school personnel responsible for releasing the partners as well as the teachers of health or family life classroom teachers.

Selection

PEER LEADERS. Peer leaders should be selected on the basis of articulation skills, strength of character, self-confidence, ability to speak in groups, and maturity.

RECEIVING STUDENTS. Recipients should be selected randomly by choosing specific health or family life classes.

Training

The peer leaders (partners) should be trained by first observing the program and then running through the exercises. They should receive observational feedback from their peers and supervisor, using Group Leadership Checklist. These partners should explore their own leadership roles and dilemmas, interpersonal dynamics, group management abilities, and gender stereotypes.

They should be taught the warning signals of high risk receiving students and instructed to take preventive measures to protect the weaker students from undue stress throughout the program. Furthermore, they should be directed to refer any potential high risk students to appropriate staff members. The referrals should be made in writing.

Parental Permission

All partners should receive signed parental consent slips, authorizing their participation in the program.

The eighth grade receiving students are not required to gain written parental consent because PAS should be a part of the middle school family life or health curriculum presented to all students.

Implementation

All subject teachers releasing these students to attend middle school PAS sessions should also receive written notice and give their approval. Arrange transportation through proper channels. The logistics of the program require the peer partners to be released from two successive classes in the high school, preferably nonacademic, one session per week for four weeks.

The peer partners receive on-site coaching by the program coordinator or licensed designee, who remains within eye contact of the classroom throughout each session. The coordinator should set up weekly, forty-five minute supervision sessions with peer partners.

If subject curriculum includes sections on peer pressure or student harassment, then provisions for guest speaker consultation on this subject should afford necessary approval for peer partners to lead the sessions. After all pertinent staff members have been made aware of dates and times for four sessions, the program may begin.

SESSION 1. High school partners use this first session to arouse anxiety and produce a high stress atmosphere, using intimidation to simulate an atmosphere of beratement and devaluation.

Students are given a reading comprehension test on the strict time limits are used. The test is difficult to read because of the reduced size of print. Titled "Planet 455," the story serves as a metaphor for some of the wider ramifications produced by global conflict, unbridled hostility, competition, and world tension. Students are asked to read the paragraph, write their answers to the questions, and then read them aloud in front of the class and the peer partners. The partners should renounce inaccurate replies disparagingly. Peer leaders serve as harsh reminders of the effects of criticism and degradation in the lives of their younger peers.

Follow-Up
After Session 1, partners meet with program coordinator to process the session, identify any students exhibiting behavioral warning signals, and make tags with labels on them. Based on their observation of students during the first session, peer leaders make up labels which differ from the students' real qualities.

SESSION 2. The object of this session is to sensitize the group to the effects of being labeled by others. Partners print the stereotypes on self-adhesive labels. The exercise unfolds as each youngster is treated as though his/her personality reflects the characteristic of his/her label. Class members must come to the front of the room, tell stories, receive feedback from the group, and attempt to guess their labels. A general discussion about the effects of labeling wraps up the session.

Follow-Up
As a follow-up to Session 2, a forty-five minute supervision conference is held, during which partners discuss the reactions of the group to the Labeling Game. The personality profiles which emerged in Sessions 1 and 2 generate more detailed characteristics of group members. Vulnerable students are identified and receive more support and praise during Session 3. Students who show warning signals are also identified.

SESSION 3. This session uses a simulated auction to elicit members' needs from the group. They must identify them and then go on to bid for each with different allocations of play money distributed to each class member. The exercise spurs a lively debate and sensitizes the group to some of their desirable trappings, separating those that can be bought from those that must be developed naturally.

As a follow-up to the Needs Auction, the partners develop a list of attributes that students actually possess. The group creates a written support network, based on skills and attributes they would be willing to share with each other. The network is then passed to each member of the group for future support in new endeavors.

Follow-Up
During this session, partners and supervisors process the Needs Auction session noting the needs of individuals and the skills and attributes offered by students. Potential matches are formulated to initiate helping relationships.

SESSION 4. The goals in this session are to engender compassion for the scapegoat and to elicit appropriate responses to verbal attacks from others. The partners lead an exercise based on the IALAC Story concept, portraying a youngster who starts out his day with a feeling that he is lovable and capable, and then begins to witness the erosion of his self-esteem as the day unfolds.

Class members are asked to create the remainder of the story by adding negative episodes in round-robin style until the youngster's day finally culminates. As each negative event unfolds, a peer partner rips a piece of the IALAC sign until it is almost destroyed.

After hearing the negative IALAC story, the group is asked to recreate another scenario in which the positive events in a youngster's day unfold to rebuild his self-confidence. The peer leaders are careful to guide the class members in developing positive scenarios which are feasible.

Peer partners then read "The Wrong Kind of Laughter," a poem by Bill Sanders, which illustrates some of the merciless beratement often perpetrated upon students by their peers. The session culminates with the group sharing impressions and reactions to the first three sessions.

Peer partners assist members in forming their own helping alliances to share skills. After explaining the dynamics of scapegoating, the group develops alternatives to prevent pranks, abuse, and harassment of others. An evaluation form is distributed to the class and collected after it is complete.

Evaluation

A written program evaluation completed by recipients offers reactions to the program, comments on its effectiveness, rates the peer leaders, and suggests improvements.

Follow-Up

After evaluations are complete, peer leaders and program coordinator review the comments and adjust the program accordingly, offering modifications or deletions which improve its mission. Any participants who exhibited behavioral warning signals are referred to professionals. Peer leaders may revisit the classroom periodically to reinforce concepts and reassess impact.

Paper Trail

1. Peer Leader ID Card Prototype.   *(See Appendix A, Model 17)*

2. Peer Leader Pass.   *(See Appendix A, Model 15.)*

3. Group Leadership Checklist.   *(See Section 2, Session 42.)*

4. Planet 455 Story Sheet.   *(See p. 336.)*

5. Loveisnowhere.   *(See p. 337.)*

6. Would you rather have an elephant eat you or a gorilla?   *(See p. 338.)*

7. Labeling Game Question Sheet.   *(See p. 339.)*

8. Needs Auction Question Sheet.   *(See Section 8, Session 2, Part 1.)*

9. Resource Network Sheet.   *(See Section 3, Session 1, Part 6.)*

10. The Wrong Kind of Laughter   *(See p. 341.)*

11. PAS Evaluation Sheet.   *(See p. 343.)*

Trainees' Observation of All Sessions

Time
Four forty-five minute sessions for observation, four forty-five minute sessions for rehearsal, and three supervisory sessions.

Goals
• To familiarize new trainees with PAS program through observation of experienced peer leaders in action.

• To provide opportunity for peer leaders to gain group leadership competence.

Materials
Group Leadership Checklists (see Section 2, Session 42) and pencils.

Process
Two trained peer leaders observe all four PAS sessions from the back of the room. They complete Group Leadership Checklists during each session and attend follow-up supervisory sessions, during which they process the activity's impact and offer feedback to the leader.

Students who show behavioral warning signals should be referred to appropriate professionals.

After the end of the program cycle, peer leaders attend a follow-up session to review completed evaluations, make necessary program revisions, and clarify their concerns.

Then peer leaders rehearse the four sessions as the experienced leaders and supervisor rate their leadership abilities and offer constructive suggestions.

Outcome Indicators
1. Peer leader trainees should observe sessions and complete Group Leadership Checklists.

2. Trainees should offer feedback to experienced leaders during supervisory sessions.

3. All should review program evaluations and participate in program revision.

4. Trainees should rehearse the program and make necessary adjustments in leadership style.

5. Experienced leaders and supervisor should rate trainees as competent before they lead a new program cycle.

LEADER'S GUIDE

Session 1: Planet 455

Time
Forty-five minutes

Goal
• To arouse anxiety, produce a high stress atmosphere, and sensitize students to the effects of intimidation which trigger feelings of incompetency.

Materials
Two signs: Loveisnowhere and Would you rather have an elephant eat you or a gorilla?, Planet 455 Story Sheets, and pencils.

Process
Peer partners enter the classroom somberly, posing as designated teachers. Your posture should be austere and stern. Dim the lights, separate the students' desks, and administer reading comprehension test. The test is produced in small type, making it very difficult to read.

Partners instruct the students that they will have a five minute time limit to complete the test. Then instruct the class that this test will count heavily in their grade averages. One partner calls out the time every minute.

At the end of five minutes, the tests are collected and questions regarding this story are read aloud by the peer partners who solicit answers from various members of the group. As each member of the class answers, those inaccurate replies should be treated disparagingly, with such responses as:

"This is ridiculous."
"Where did you learn to read?"
"I can't believe this is an eighth grade group."

Use your Planet 455 Answer Sheet on page

330 to guide you in reviewing the test with the class. After the correct answers are supplied, the partners rip up the test papers in disgust and announce that the entire class has failed.

Immediately following the test, partners should display two signs:

• Loveisnowhere

• Would you rather have an elephant eat you or a gorilla?

These signs are intended to indicate whether the majority of the group is experiencing a negative or positive learning set. It is important to request the class members to read the signs aloud in unison. In response to the loveisnowhere sign, most of the class members should be reading it as: "love is nowhere" as opposed to "love is now here."

It is likely that most answers to the question "Would you rather have an elephant eat you or a gorilla?" will be: an elephant (or a gorilla). The connotation suggests that the only choice is to be eaten by either the elephant or the gorilla. In actuality, a third choice is to have the elephant eat the gorilla.

While one partner displays each sign, the other should record the group's reaction. It is important that a show of hands for each response or each interpretation of the sign indicate the number of positive versus negative responses. One partner should record this on the board and keep a record for future reference.

Draw parallels between Earth and Planet 455, explaining that competition, aggression, and the effects of thwarted peace keeping

---

agencies are the result of global hostilities that have gone out of control.

Question the group on its own experience of being harassed, reacting under stress, and being intimidated by older peers. Students should share how intimidation tactics are used within their own group in the school setting. Specific examples of verbal harassment at the middle school level should be identified by the group, and reactions should be discussed.

Peer partners should be particularly sensitive to any youngsters who are exhibiting signs of anxiety or emotional distress. If this occurs, the particular student in distress should be called out of the room and comforted by one of the peer partners while the other continues the session.

It is very important to clarify to any emotionally upset youngsters that this session is only a demonstration and not a real harassment situation.

At the end of the class, the group should be told that it was the intent of this session to arouse anxiety and to produce a high stress atmosphere in order to sensitize the students to the effects of harassment, stress, and intimidation which result in feelings of incompetence.

The group should be told that this is not a real test and that the entire experience only exemplifies some of the conditions of harassment which they have already experienced.

Outcome Indicators
1. During the test, students should be com-

pliant and ask questions about the seriousness of the exercise.

2. Any protesting class members should be strongly redressed by the peer partners.

3. By the end of the exercise, all class members should be made aware that the exercise was only a simulation.

4. Most student responses to the signs at this stage of the program should be negatively toned. Approximately 70% of the students should have indicated Love is Nowhere and that they would rather be eaten by either an elephant or a gorilla. This trend would suggest that the harassment in the first session has yielded a negative reaction.

Follow-Up
Peer leaders should discuss the class members' profiles during a forty-five minute supervisory session with the program coordinator. They should focus on different roles and personality types within the group.

Peer leaders should devise twelve descriptive labels to be printed on self-adhesive paper strips which will be used in an upcoming exercise, The Labeling Game.

Based on the information gleaned from the first session, the partners should develop labels which are different from each member's true characteristics. For example, an athletic boy in the group would be labeled clumsy or an attractive female would be labeled plain.

Planet 455 Answer Sheet

Story
Life on Planet 455 was a series of never-ending conflicts. The Mulkro Desert People weakened the Nogoozoon fortress by syphoning their fuel supply and depleting their main food source, Pushkin mushrooms. The Yoohoo warriors, situated in temporary space stations, bombarded the planet's wildlife with laser guns in hopes of clearing the land for more permanent settlements. Xion and Rheon tribespeople were driven to surpass one another in armaments while the Rootex continued to bury their radioactive dead near the planet's largest water supply.

Because of rising unemployment in Corporate Galactica Bases, unrest among red buttoned workers persisted. But the Zephers, who lived quietly beneath the land's middle core, struggled with a more peaceful task: writing a new constitution that would restore harmony to deteriorating Planet 455.

Questions
1. Describe the quality of life on Planet 455.

2. Which two tribespeople were involved in an arms race?

3. Is the water on Planet 455 safe to drink? Why or Why not?

4. Which inhabitants seem to be the most peace-loving?

5. Compare life in Planet 455 with life on Earth. How is life similar? How is life different?

Answers
1. It was a series of never-ending conflicts.

2. Xion and Rheon were the tribes involved in an arms race.

3. The water supply was not safe for drinking because radioactive dead were buried near the main water supply.

4. The Zephers were the most peace-loving people.

5. This is how life on Planet 455 can be compared with life on Earth.

Similarities
a. The inhabitants of Earth are having difficulty with their water supply and management of radioactive and toxic waste.

b. Constant conflicts in the Middle East, in Central America, and the Far East have been breaking out for the past twenty years.

c. The United Nations attempts to initiate peace-keeping activities.

d. The US and other countries continue to manufacture lethal weapons.

Differences
a. We have not yet invented such sophisticated weapons.

b. We have not buried our radioactive dead, but instead have buried our radioactive waste.

c. We are not traveling between planets.

LEADER'S GUIDE

Session 2: The Labeling Game

Time
Forty-five minutes

Goal
• To sensitize the group to the effects of being labeled or berated by others.

Materials
Labeling Game Question Sheets, 1-1/2 x 3 inch self-adhesive labels, and magic markers.

Typical Labels:
• unattractive
• fearful
• overweight
• silly
• clumsy
• foolish
• athletic
• brain
• handsome
• popular
• lazy

Process
Before the session begins, partners should write labels on the self-adhesive strips. Partners enter the session in a cool, calm, dispassionate, business-like fashion and give instructions for the labeling game to the group.

Each class member should be called up to the front of the room, and one of the partners should give him/her a label with a random characteristic on it, one which may or may not be different from the true profile of that particular student. The label should be placed on the student's forehead to prevent him/her from seeing it.

Peer partners instruct each person to go to the front of the room and tell a little story about their weekend, or school day experience, while the group responds to each individual as though the label actually reflected their true personality.

Members of the group must not repeat the actual label when questioning or responding to each participant. At the end of about one minute, the participant in the front of the room is asked to guess his/her label.

At the conclusion of the class, after each student has gone to the front of the room, partners ask the group to discuss the feelings aroused by ridicule, being labeled, and their overall reactions to the exercise.

It should be explained that the actual labels do not reflect the true personality characteristics of each person who participated. Partners may wish to use the Labeling Game Question Sheets by actually distributing them to the class after the simulation has been completed.

Partners request each member to either write or respond verbally to questions to initiate a discussion of such issues as criticism, judgments, stereotyping behavior, and inaccuracies.

Outcome Indicators
1. Each student should have the opportunity to tell his/her story while others react to his/her label.

2. During the discussion period, students should express their reactions to the exercise and how harassment occurs in the school setting.

3. Class members should give examples of other qualities which often go unnoticed as a

LEADER'S GUIDE
Session 2 continued

result of stereotyping and labeling.

Follow-Up
During a forty-five minute supervision session, partners should discuss the reactions of the group to the labeling game with their program coordinator and note the differences in each class member.

Various individuals' reactions should reflect their own personalities, many of which are

like the labels used to describe others.

It is important to identify any vulnerable or upset students who should be singled out to receive support and praise during Session 3.

Students who acted like positive leaders during Session 2 should be given more active roles, while the more negative students should be confronted during Session 3.

Session 3: Needs Auction

Time
Forty-five minutes

Goals
• To assess students' needs, talents, and skills already present within their lives.

• To assist students in deciding the importance of their needs and resources and sharing them with the rest of the group.

• To establish a support network based on abilities and talents that students are willing to share with each other.

Materials
Play Money, chalk, Needs Auction Question Sheets (see Section 8, Session 2, Part 1), Resource Network Sheet (see Section 3, Session 1, Part 6), and pencils.

Process
The Partners enter with a more understanding, sympathetic attitude to develop a more supportive atmosphere. This activity marks the turning point of a PAS program. It is intended to help the group to develop a more supportive atmosphere: partners identifying members' resources, sharing them, and promoting mutual support as an alternative to scapegoating.

Please see Section 8, Session 2, Part 1. Follow the same directions and format for this session.

Please see Section 3, Session 1, Part 6. Follow the same directions and format for this session.

Outcome Indicators
1. The auction should produce lively discussion among the group.

2. Discussion of questions should identify needs that they have already met as well as the talents and qualities the group wants.

3. Resource Network Sheets should be filled out with a total of at least ten different skills which members are willing to share with others.

Follow-Up
Before the final session, the partners and supervisor review some of the steps of the problem-solving approach. In general, the purpose of the final session is to identify some of the conditions which create negative self-esteem and to replace them with experiences to create positive self-esteem.

In addition, the process of how people project their own unwanted feelings upon others should also be explored. The final session should create a support system based on positive qualities which students are willing to share with others.

Session 4: The IALAC Story

Time
Forty-five minutes

Goals
• To use IALAC to teach negative effects of put-downs.

• To use IALAC in reverse to teach support building, self-esteem enhancement skills.

• To use "The Wrong Kind of Laughter" to reinforce the negative effects of verbal denigration and the need for kindness.

Materials
IALAC sign, copies of "The Wrong Kind of Laughter", and two signs: "Loveisnowhere" and "Would you rather have an elephant eat you or a gorilla?", and PAS Evaluation Sheets.

Process
Partners enter this session with a supportive attitude, practicing active listening skills and promoting cooperation among the student. Participants are encouraged to share stories from their own experiences of scapegoating and harassment.

Peer partners begin by explaining briefly the IALAC story. IALAC stands for I am likeable and capable. Most of us start our day with the potential to feel that way. We carry an imaginary IALAC sign that can be destroyed by a day of ridicule or failure experiences. The first story describes a typical bad day in the life of a student. Each student is asked to make up a negative event in the boy's day and contribute one sentence to the story.

In this variation, use a standard 8-1/2 x 11 sheet of paper with the word IALAC

inscribed in large letters on the face. As the story progresses with each negative event, the paper should be folded in halves and quarters, finally ending with a piece of approximately 3 x 3.

Partners then lead off with a story about a youngster going to the middle school in the morning on the bus. He arrives at school facing the prospect of taking a difficult math test. He has just stayed up all night to study. Partners should then turn the story over to the class, with each student adding one sentence to support the main character and improve his/her day.

The support should be based on gestures of kindness, not magical occurrences. As each student describe his/her part of the sequence, partners should unfold the paper one fold at a time until, after about eight students have participated, the entire IALAC sign should merge in full view of the class.

As a review of all the previous sessions, one partner reads "The Wrong Kind of Laughter" by Bill Sanders. After the poem has been read, lead a discussion on some negative aspects of scapegoating, ways to react when victimized by others, and some methods of cooperating and supporting others. Distribute copies of the poem to all students.

Now one partner displays the sign, "Loveisnowhere," and elicits two types of responses from the group:

1. Those who saw "love is nowhere."

2. Those who saw "love is now here."

The second partner records responses by students. Partners should then switch roles

LEADER'S GUIDE
Session 4 continued

with one partner explaining the sign "Would you rather have an elephant eat you or a gorilla?" The other partner records two types of responses by the students:

1. Those that indicate being devoured by either elephant or gorilla.

2. Those that indicate that the elephant eats the gorilla.

As a follow-up discussion, partners indicate any pattern between previous and present negative and positive interpretations. Partners hold a general discussion about positive and negative attitudes.

During the discussion, participants should be sharing anecdotes from their own experiences regarding incidents of scapegoating and harassment. Using problem-solving and brainstorming techniques, encourage students to generate different alternatives to scapegoating.

Distribute PAS Evaluation Sheets to students. Then distribute completed copies of Resource Network Sheets to all group members. Encourage the group to use them.

Outcome Indicators
1. At least seven students should contribute to the positive IALAC story with productive, realistic support by peers.

2. A significant number of positive responses to the signs should be noted after the partners have read, "The Wrong Kind of Laughter" by Bill Sanders.

Follow-Up
Partners should arrange to copy and distribute Resource Network Sheets and copies of Bill Sanders' poem to each member of the group.

Any members of the group who show warning signals of distress should immediately be reported to the program coordinator, classroom teacher, and any other relevant staff member. Follow-up contacts with these students may be initiated with the assistance of appropriate staff members.

Partners should review all completed PAS Evaluation Sheets and write a short report on the program's impact. This report should be submitted to the program coordinator and shared in a general discussion which should produce additions, changes, and deletions as necessary. These new modifications should be incorporated in subsequent program cycles.

It is possible to train new partners during subsequent cycles. For example, experienced partners serving as session leaders may be observed by less experienced peer leaders during the four sessions.

After these sessions are complete, trainees may rehearse the program using the experienced peer leaders and program coordinator as an audience. Group Leadership Sheets can be used to identify and correct any weaknesses in the trainees' leadership abilities.

Classroom teachers should be encouraged to continue follow-up discussions on the issue of peer pressure and scapegoating. They should also continue to foster a spirit of harmony by asking class members to describe any positive changes in their behavior as a result of the sessions. Monitoring the support system and skill sharing activities may also be facilitated by the regular classroom teacher.

Planet 455 Story Sheet

Name_____   Date _____

Directions
Read the story and answer the questions below.

Planet 455™

Life on Planet 455 was a series of never-ending conflicts. The Mulkro Desert People weakened the Nogoozoon fortress by syphoning their fuel supply and depleting their main food source, Pushkin mushrooms. The Yoohoo warriors, situated in temporary space stations, bombarded the planet's wildlife with laser guns in hopes of clearing the land for more permanent settlements. Xion and Rheon tribespeople were driven to surpass one another in armaments while the Rootex continued to bury their radioactive dead near the planet's largest water supply. Because of rising unemployment of Corporate Galactica Bases, unrest among red buttoned workers persisted. But the Zephers, who lived quietly beneath the land's middle core, struggled with a more peaceful task: writing a new constitution that would restore harmony to deteriorating Planet 455.

Comprehension Questions
1. Describe the quality of life on Planet 455.
2. Which two tribespeople were involved in an arms race?
3. Is the water on Planet 455 safe to drink? Why or Why not?
4. Which inhabitants seem to be the most peace-loving?
5. Compare life on Planet 455 with life on Earth. How is life similar? How is life different?

Loveisnowhere

Would you rather have an elephant eat you or a gorilla?

Labeling Game Question Sheet

Name_____   Date_____

Directions
Please react to the labeling game by writing your responses below.

1. What was your label?

_____

2. How easy or difficult was it to discuss your label?

_____

_____

3. Do you see it as a positive or negative label?   Why?

_____

_____

_____

4. Can you remember one or two statements others made about you during the labeling game?
Write them below.

_____

_____

_____

_____

5. How did it feel to be labeled?

_____

_____

_____

_____

Page 2 - Labeling Game Question Sheet

6. Did the label really reflect your personality or qualities?

_____

_____

_____

If "no" is your answer, then how would you correct the label to reflect the real you?

_____

_____

_____

7. How do you think others see you? Write down what you believe to be your reputations or the word others use to describe you.

_____

_____

_____

_____

8. What are the other qualities you have that you would like people to notice?

_____

_____

_____

_____

The Wrong Kind of Laughter

Name_____   Date_____

Directions
Read the poem below to the class with even pacing and feeling.

It's wrong to put down
The new student, the poor student,
The one who walks funny and talks funny,
Let's call him skinny and call her fat,
And "What kind of shirt do you even call that?"
"Hey, giraffe, how'd ya get no place to fall?"
"Check out buckteeth, and look at those ears."
"Hey elephant nose, why all the tears?"

And the one with no friends, she eats all alone,
Bet we could make her cry all the way home.
Let's laugh at that guy, he got cut from the team,
"You're the worst player we've ever seen!"
And "She was too chicken to stay with the play,
It's cause she talks funny and forgot what to say."

I heard his parents both left home.
"If you weren't adopted, you'd be all alone."
"Hey her mother's real sick. Oh that's too bad."
Don't wait around for us to be sad.

"Look who's coming, it's crater face,
I'm glad I don't have zits all over the place."
"You're just a loser, you'll never win,"
And "How dare you come to our school,
with the wrong color skin!"

Yes, we're the populars, we have to be cool,
And as you've seen, we can sure be cruel.
But as long as you do all the things that we say,
You too can be privileged with our group to play.
But there's no security being part of our team,
We even turn on our own, as you've probably seen.
But if you're cute and handsome and really smart,
Why you'll fit in right from the start.

But you must never disagree,
And for heaven's sake, don't turn ugly,
Or we'll kick you out, right into the street.
For us to be popular, we'd even cheat.

Page 2 - The Wrong Kind of Laughter

We don't believe in the things from above,
Like honesty, integrity, and brotherly love.
Society's taught us to be number one.
Who cares if you're hurt, we're having fun.

It's not just students we pick on each day,
But anyone who's different and gets in our way.
Society has taught us, don't worry what you say,
and forget the consequences past today.

We also pick on teachers who are old and shy,
And we love to make the bus driver cry.
And the cooks, last week we threw food
Right in their face, and the counselors
And subs we love to disgrace.

And of course the principal we always boo.
It's nothing personal, just the thing to do.

And there's Mom who we're mad at,
And Dad who's unfair,
Of all the nerve, yesterday he even
asked me to move a chair.

I've covered them all so I'm ready
To stop, but wait, there's one more,
I almost forgot.
It's my dear, charming brother,
Who puts chips in the pop.

— by Bill Sanders

PAS Evaluation Sheet

School_____ Class_____ Grade _____

Leader(s) _____ Date_____

Directions
You have just completed a group experience to help make you more aware of how you treat others and how you are treated by others. Thank you for being part of this learning experience. Please take a couple of minutes to answer the following questions.

Please read each statement and write the number 1, 2, or 3 on each line below.

1. Often   **2. Sometimes**   **3. Never**

1._____The exercises were interesting and held my attention.

2._____The leader(s) encouraged me to express my opinions.

3._____The program made me aware of how it feels to be put down and labeled by others.

Read the statements below and check Yes or No.

4._____I found it easy to be more supportive to others. Yes_____ No_____

5._____I think other students should have this program. Yes_____ No_____

6. I discovered _____

_____

_____

7. Please add any comments about the experience below.

_____

_____

_____

_____

_____

SECTION 12 —
PEER ASSISTANTS TO INTERPERSONAL RELATIONS (PAIRS)

SECTION 12 — PEER ASSISTANTS TO INTERPERSONAL RELATIONS (PAIRS)

Description

This program enlists the aid of four trained high school peer leaders (two boys and two girls) to hold six sessions on friendship and dating awareness for students in health or family life classes in grades seven through nine.

The sessions are designed to be upbeat, active, and student-centered, using group exercises and role playing to illustrate the principles. All assumptions and beliefs about the nature of friendship and cross-gender relationships are explored in nonbiased, impartial formats.

The program begins with students defining their existing relationships, identifying what they need from each type, and thinking about what they are getting. Then, same and cross-gender relationships are compared and contrasted in terms of similar and different needs and behaviors.

A Friendship Needs Auction highlights the most desirable characteristics of same and cross-gender relationships by instituting a forced-choice game format. The program continues by exploring what causes conflicts in cross-gender relationships. Typical reactions to put-downs, inauthentic, or stereotypical behaviors are introduced through open-ended, interactive role plays. Students make up an inventory of positive profiles of potential friendships and develop strategies to attain positive relationships.

The program then focuses on situations in friendships that require setting limits. Refusal skills are introduced with attendant attitudes necessary to say no. Conflicts in relationships are addressed with a social problem-solving model.

Finally, class members are asked to review the qualities of ideal relationships, delineate individual priorities, identify killer statements to avoid in relationships, and describe the criteria and procedures to use refusal skills and problem-solving techniques.

Goals

• To identify the qualities of an ideal relationship.

• To explore the differences between boy-girl and same sex relationships.

• To set priorities of desirable qualities in same and cross-gender relationships.

• To evaluate the qualities of one's existing relationships.

• To identify interpersonal situations that create conflict and stress.

• To explore how to detect deceitful behavior and form authentic relationships based on honest self-disclosure.

• To identify some ways to avoid conflicts by using refusal skills.

• To identify some ways to resolve conflicts by using problem-solving techniques.

• To identify some ways to develop relationships with people who can meet individual expectations.

Planning

Before embarking on such a high impact program, submit a brief but complete proposal, including goals, objectives, and specific curriculum to supervisory personnel. These may include the Superintendent of Schools, principal, and teachers.

You may also want to include health or family life coordinator, guidance coordinator, and any other human service support staff. After explaining the intent of such a program and obtaining board or administrative approval, meet with the above professionals to clarify the program goals and process.

Logistics can be worked out through the building supervisors and teachers of family life or health classes. Typically, a particular health class can receive the program, one class session per week, for six weeks.

Transportation for high school students can be provided by the coordinator's car, bus, or taxi, depending on district resources. The class period should be chosen upon the basis of availability of high school peer leaders who serve as partners. Written communication about program design, dates of sessions, and times should be forwarded to appropriate high school personnel responsible for releasing the partners as well as the teachers of health or family life classroom teachers.

Selection

PEER LEADERS. Peer leaders should be

selected on the basis of articulation skills, rapport with others, strength of character, self-confidence, ability to speak in groups, ability to form lasting friendships, maturity, and availability.

RECEIVING STUDENTS. Recipients should be selected randomly by choosing specific health or family life classes.

Training

The peer leaders should be trained by first observing the PAIRS program and then running through the exercises. They should receive observational feedback from their peers and supervisor using the Group Leadership Checklist.

These leaders should explore their own leadership roles and dilemmas, interpersonal dynamics, assumptions about friendship, group management abilities, and gender stereotypes. They should be taught the warning signals of high risk receiving students and instructed to take preventive measures to protect the weaker students from undue stress throughout the program.

Furthermore, they should be directed to refer any potential at-risk students to appropriate staff members. The referrals should be made in writing.

Parental Permission

All leaders should receive signed parental consent slips, authorizing their participation in the program.

The receiving students are not required to gain written parental consent because PAIRS should be a part of the middle school family life or health curriculum presented to the general student population.

Implementation

All subject teachers releasing these students to attend middle school PAIRS sessions should also receive written notice and give their approval. Arrange transportation through proper channels. The logistics of the program require the peer leaders to be released from two successive classes, preferably nonacademic, one session per week for six weeks.

The peer partners receive on-site coaching by the program coordinator or licensed designee, who remains within eye contact of the classroom throughout each session. The coordinator should set up weekly, forty-five minute, follow-up, supervision sessions with peer leaders.

If subject curriculum includes sections on peer relationships, then provisions for guest speaker consultation on this subject should afford necessary approval for peer partners to lead the sessions. After all pertinent staff members have been made aware of dates and times for four sessions, the program may begin.

SESSION 1. This session focuses on personal beliefs and attitudes about relationships. Small groups are formed to generate some individual ideas about the elements of ideal qualities in same and cross gender relationships. The class identifies the most common characteristics chosen for both types of relationships.

Follow-Up
After Session 1, partners meet with program coordinator to process the session, identify any students exhibiting behavioral warning signals, and list the major characteristics chosen for same and cross-gender relationships.

SESSION 2. This session begins with a Friendship Needs Auction to simulate the difficulty in meeting and attaining specific needs in relationships. Students then categorize the different needs of same and cross-gender relationships, as they exist for boys and girls. Class members are asked to prioritize qualities from most to least sought after. Four lists are created by the class: boys' and girls' priorities for same and cross-gender relationships.

Groups form to discuss what is working for them in relationships and what they need to add. Students then create individual ratings of their own friendships and cross-gender relationships.

Follow-Up
After Session 2, partners meet with program coordinator to process the session, identify any students exhibiting behavioral warning signals, and make any necessary referrals. The prioritized qualities of relationships should be listed and distributed at the beginning of Session 3.

SESSION 3. This session uses peer leader open-ended role plays to introduce conflict situations in interpersonal relationships. It continues with small group discussions about trust, authentic behavior, and how to recognize positive and negative behaviors in others.

Follow-Up
As a follow-up to Session 3, a forty-five minute supervision conference is held, during which partners discuss the reactions of the group to the exercises and identify the prevailing attitudes about authenticity and deceit. Behavioral warning signals are identified and followed up.

SESSION 4. Using a refusal skill model and role plays, students practice identifying potentially dangerous challenges and ways to deal with peer pressure.

Follow-Up
As a follow-up to Session 4, a forty-five minute supervision conference is held. At this time, partners discuss the reactions of the group to the exercises, list the most effective ways to predict high risk behaviors, and consider ways to confront peer pressure. Behavioral warning signals are identified and followed up.

SESSION 5. Students develop their own imaginary scenarios portraying problems that occur in relationships, learn to set realistic goals, develop desirable outcomes, anticipate potential consequences, and test out strategies to resolve conflicts.

Follow-Up
As a follow-up to Session 5, a forty-five minute supervision conference is held. At this time partners discuss the reactions of the group to the exercises, list the most desirable outcomes, and consider the most effective strategies to achieve them.

SESSION 6. Some of the common positive expectations, behaviors, and beliefs about relationships are reviewed. Peer leaders initiate activities to brainstorm the rules and behaviors that lead students to positive relationships.

Class members are asked to review the qualities of ideal relationships, delineate individual priorities, identify killer statements to avoid in relationships, and describe the criteria and procedures to use refusal skills and problem-solving techniques. Evaluation sheets are filled out by the class.

Follow-Up
During this final session, partners and supervisors process the five sessions and the evaluations and make the appropriate modifications for the next cycle.

Evaluation

A written program evaluation completed by recipients offers reactions to the program, comments on its effectiveness, ratings of the peer leaders, and suggestions for improvements.

Follow-Up

After evaluations are complete, peer leaders and program coordinator review the comments and adjust the program accordingly, offering modifications or deletions to improve its mission. Any participants who exhibited behavioral warning signals are referred to professionals. Peer leaders may revisit the classroom periodically to reinforce concepts and reassess impact.

Paper Trail

1. Peer Leader ID Card Prototype.   *(See Appendix A, Model 17)*

2. Peer Leader Pass.   *(See Appendix A, Model 15.)*

3. Group Leadership Checklist.   *(See Section 2, Session 42.)*

4. Friendship Needs Auction Question Sheet. *(See p. 359.)*

5. Refusal Skills Guidelines Sheet.   *(See Section 2, Session 37.)*

6. Pathways to Solutions Guidelines Sheet. *(See Section 2, Session 34.)*

7. PAIRS Questionnaire.   *(See p. 361.)*

8. PAIRS Evaluation Sheet.   *(See p. 363.)*

Trainees' Observation of All Sessions

Time
Six forty-five minute sessions for observation, five forty-five minute sessions for rehearsal, and three supervisory sessions.

Goals
• To familiarize new trainees with PAIRS program through observation of experienced peer leaders in action.

• To provide opportunity for peer leaders to gain group leadership competence.

Materials
Group Leadership Checklists (see Section 2, Session 42) and pencils.

Process
Two trained peer leaders observe all four PAIRS sessions from the back of the room. They complete Group Leadership Checklists during each session and attend follow-up supervisory sessions, during which they process the activity's impact and offer feedback to the leader. Students who show behavioral warning signals should be referred to appropriate professionals.

After the end of the program cycle, peer leaders attend a follow-up session to review completed evaluations, make necessary program sessions, and clarify their concerns.

Then peer leaders rehearse the four sessions as the experienced leaders and supervisor rate his/her leadership abilities and offer constructive suggestions.

Outcome Indicators
1. Peer leader trainees should observe sessions and complete Group Leadership Checklists.

2. Trainees should offer feedback to experienced leaders during supervisory sessions.

3. All should review program evaluations and participate in program revision.

4. Trainees should rehearse the program and make necessary adjustments in leadership style.

5. Experienced leaders and supervisor should rate trainees as competent before they lead a new program cycle.

LEADER'S GUIDE

Session 1: Ideal Relationships Brainstorm

Time
Forty-five minutes

Goals
• To identify the qualities of an ideal relationship.

• To explore the differences between boy-girl and same-sex relationships.

Materials
None.

Process
Four trained peer leaders, two boys and two girls, introduce the program as an opportunity to explore the various needs and beliefs about relationships and ways to improve friendships and boy-girl relationships. Leaders introduce Haves and Have-nots warm-up activity.

Leaders divide group into two sections. One section, the Haves, has everything they could possible want while the other group, the Have-nots, has nothing except themselves. Ask the Have-nots to think of some important physical, mental, material, and spiritual needs. Within a five minute time period the Have-nots must try to get as many needs as possible from the Haves without any verbal communication. The Haves may or may not decide to meet their demands. Total time: ten minutes.

Then the peer leaders divide the class into two mixed-gender groups, each led by peer partners (male and female). The groups are instructed to brainstorm desirable qualities of relationships, first same-sex and then boy-girl. Allow ten minutes for each brainstorm.

Each group appoints a recorder who makes four lists of ideal qualities:

• Boys' version-same gender; boy-girl

• Girls'version-same gender; boy-girl

Then groups are asked to discuss their reactions to the different ideal qualities chosen by girls and boys.

The class reassembles and leaders initiate an activity to create four lists from the entire class:

Ideal Qualities in Relationships

Boys	Girls
Same gender	Same gender
Boy-girl	Boy-girl

Common and different qualities for boys and girls are identified, listed and discussed.

Outcome Indicators
1. All class members should identify ideal qualities for both same-gender and cross-gender relationships.

2. Four lists should be developed by the group.

Follow-Up
After Session 1, partners meet with program coordinator to process the session, identify any students exhibiting behavioral warning signals, and list the major characteristics chosen for same and cross-gender relationships.

LEADER'S GUIDE

Session 2: Friendship Needs Auction

Time
Forty-five minutes

Goals
• To set priorities of desirable qualities in same and cross-gender relationships.

• To evaluate the qualities of one's existing relationships.

Materials
Play money, chalk, Friendship Needs Auction Question Sheets, and pencils.

Process
Leaders divide unequal amounts of play money to distribute to the class. Begin this event by putting the two lists from Session 1 on the board:

Same Sex Qualities   Boy-Girl Qualities

Leaders distribute play money to the students and hold a mock auction during which participants have to establish which qualities are important and how much money they want to spend to get each one. They then bid for these needs.

The process will show the group what qualities are of high and low value. Keep a record of the selling price of each quality and the name of each person who bought it. Make a chart with which to generate discussion at the end of the auction.

Peer Leaders distribute Friendship Needs Question Sheets, request group to write its responses, and hold a general discussion emphasizing how needs are satisfied and what positive qualities students already have as personal resources.

Then, sorting for gender differences, boys and girls are asked to prioritize their qualities from most to least desirable.

Outcome Indicators
1. Auction should produce lively reactions among the group.

2. Discussion of questions should identify needs that are already met as well as attributes the students would like to find in others.

3. Discussion of questions should identify attributes they would like to develop.

Follow-Up
After Session 2, partners meet with program coordinator to process the session, discuss the class members' reactions, and identify any students exhibiting behavioral warning signals. The major themes about relationships should be listed.

The missing elements of relationships should be identified to be introduced as additional needs during Session 3.

Permission to reprint for classroom use. Copyright © 1992. V. Alex Kehayan, *Partners for Change* (Program Guide). Jalmar Press: Rolling Hills Estates, CA.

LEADER'S GUIDE

Session 3: Positive and Negative Dialogues

Time
Forty-five minutes

Goals
• To identify interpersonal situations that create conflict and stress.

• To explore how to form authentic relationships based on honest self-disclosure and detect deceitful behaviors.

Materials
None.

Process
Peer leaders introduce the session by reviewing the male and female priorities listed from the Friendship Needs Auction. Leaders then state that they are about to role play a social situation which features a type of relationship. The peer leaders perform an open-ended role play. The drama enacts a typical, shallow, boy-girl relationship.

Peer leaders instruct the group to observe the role play and notice the negative responses, including put-downs, cheap shots, and sexist comments. Observers must prepare to replace negative comments with positive ones in their replays.

CHARACTERS:
John is good-looking, self-indulgent, egotistical, fast talking, well-dressed, macho, and used to exploiting girlfriends. He comes from a divorced home where his mother was totally dependent upon his father for her income and needs. He relies on glitz, cutting remarks, and hard line profile to hide his real feelings.

Debbie is a blonde, sexy, fashionable freshman, used to being indulged by boys,

actively teasing, and very provocative. She is idolized by her parents and gets whatever she wants.

SCENE:
A freshman is on the phone with his new girlfriend. This is their second date. It is Friday night around 6:00 P.M. and they are about to plan their evening: John: Hi Debbie! What are you doing?

Debbie: So. I hear you won the track meet. What were you on, steroids or speed?

John: Just my natural superhuman energy.

Debbie: Are you calling about tonight?

John: Yeh. So, what will it be for tonight?

Debbie: I'm ready for anything.

John: Well, in that case let's fast forward the evening, and go over to my place. My parents are out.

Debbie: What do you have in mind?

John: Let's have some fun.

Debbie: I think you have the wrong channel.

John: What do you mean? That's not what I've heard.

Debbie: Well, I've got news for you. What you hear from me now is what you get. And that's nothing.

John: Come on, don't play hard to get.

LEADER'S GUIDE
Session 3 continued

Debbie: By the way you're acting, there is no way I would do anything with you.

John: I think you really want to.

Debbie: Wrong again!

John: There's only one way to find out.

Debbie: You're not going to find out. Bye!

Peer leaders question the audience about the role play, asking the group to identify:

• Things in life most important to these characters.

• How they might feel about each other.

• Whether they know people like that.

• Whether they ever have dialogues like that sequence.

Then, the class forms subgroups with each peer leader facilitating one group and asking members to identify the negative remarks that are intended to attack each character. Each group must come up with a replay which replaces the negative remarks with positive dialogue. They are to create two new character profiles with less glitz and more human concern for each other as people, not objects.

After the groups replay the dramas with new responses, they are asked to pick out the one of the dramas they observed which best fits their model of a respectful relationship. They must give the type of relationship a name, describe how it fits their model, and explain how it provides respect and concern for both parties. This information is to remain private.

Outcome Indicators
1. All students should give alternate responses to the role play.

2. All students should write down a choice that fits their own model of genuine relationships.

Follow-Up
As a follow-up to Session 3, a forty-five minute supervision conference is held, during which partners discuss the reactions of the group to the exercises and identify the prevailing attitudes about authenticity and deceit. Behavioral warning signals are identified and followed up.

Session 4: Refusing High Risk Behavior

Time
Forty-five minutes

Goals
• To identify some ways to avoid conflicts by using refusal skills.

• To practice your refusal skills.

Materials
Refusal Skills Guidelines Sheets (see Section 2, Session 37) and pencils.

Process
Follow directions under Process, Section 2, Session 37.

Outcome Indicators
1. An example of each technique should be given.

2. A discussion should point out the reasons for using the refusal skills.

Follow-Up
After Session 4, partners meet with program coordinator to process the session, discuss the class members' reactions, and identify any students exhibiting behavioral warning signals. The major refusal skills developed by the group should be listed.

LEADER'S GUIDE

Session 5: Problem-Solving in Relationships

Time
Forty-five minutes

Goal
• To identify some ways to resolve conflicts by using problem-solving techniques.

Materials
Pathways to Solutions Guidelines Sheets (see Section 2, Session 34) and pencils.

Process
Peer leaders introduce the problem-solving model to the class by reviewing the seven steps to attaining a positive outcome. The peer leaders then lead a brainstorm activity with the group to determine the types of problems that occur in same and cross-gender relationships.

Then, leaders lead small groups which are asked to pose typical problems in relation-ships, and use the Pathways to Solutions model to set goals and resolve the conflicts. Peer leaders follow same directions listed in Section 2, Session 34.

Outcome Indicators
1. All class members should review the model.

2. Small groups should determine the problems, goals or changes, personal assumptions, roads to solve them, and behaviors that lead to positive outcomes.

Follow-Up
After Session 5, partners meet with program coordinator to process the session, discuss the class members' reactions, and identify any students exhibiting behavioral warning signals. The major conflict resolution strategies should be reviewed, listed and distributed to the group during Session 6.

LEADER'S GUIDE

Session 6: Review

Time
Forty-five minutes

Goal
• To identify some ways to develop positive relationships with people who can meet individual expectations.

Materials
PAIRS Questionnaires, PAIRS Evaluation Sheets, and pencils.

Process
Peer leaders ask class members to do some individual review work at their seats. Distribute the PAIRS Questionnaires. Then peer leaders review the responses, allowing members to pass if they chose.

Finally, the leaders distribute PAIRS Evaluation Sheets.

Outcome Indicators
1. All class members should respond to the PAIRS Questionnaires.

2. At least 60% of members should share answers to PAIRS Questionnaires.

3. All class members should fill out Evaluations.

Follow-Up
During this final session, partners and supervisors process the five sessions, review the evaluations, and make the appropriate modifications for the next cycle.

Friendship Needs Auction Question Sheet

Name_____   Date_____

Directions
Answer the following questions to review what you learned during the last five sessions. Be prepared to discuss your answers in the group.

1. What needs and qualities were most important to you? List below.

_____

_____

_____

_____

2. What was it like to bid for what you wanted?

_____

_____

_____

_____

3. If you were outbid, what was your reaction to those who received the quality or need you wanted?

_____

_____

_____

_____

4. Which needs or qualities do you think your parents would want to have?

_____

_____

_____

Page 2 - Friendship Needs Auction Question Sheet

5. What are some of the qualities on the board that money cannot buy?

_____

_____

_____

_____

6. How many of the qualities on the list have you found in others?

_____

_____

_____

_____

7. How many of the qualities on the list do you have?

_____

_____

_____

_____

PAIRS Questionnaire

Name_____   Date_____

Directions
Answer the following questions to review what you learned during the last five sessions. Be prepared to discuss your answers in the group.

1. What are three separate qualities of an ideal relationship?

_____

_____

_____

_____

2. Can you list the quality you find most important and tell why?

_____

_____

_____

_____

3. Can you give three types of reactions in relationships to avoid and tell why? Give examples.

_____

_____

_____

_____

Page 2 - PAIRS Questionnaire

4. What are three situations which would get a "no" response from you?
Tell why.

_____

_____

_____

_____

5. Can you describe three ways to say no to a negative or risky situation?

_____

_____

_____

_____

6. How can you use the Pathways to Solutions model to solve a specific problem?

_____

_____

_____

_____

PAIRS Evaluation Sheet

School _____   Class _____   Grade _____

Leader(s)_____   Date_____

Directions
You have just completed a group experience to help make you more aware of what you need from relationships, how you treat others, and how you are treated by others. Thank you for being part of this learning experience. Please take a couple of minutes to answer the following questions.

Please read each statement and write the number 1, 2, or 3 on each line below.

1. Often   **2. Sometimes**   **3. Never**

1._____The exercises were interesting and held my attention.

2._____The leader(s) encouraged me to express my opinions.

3._____The program made me aware of what I expect in relationships and what to avoid.

4._____The program gave me some ideas about how to treat others with respect.

5. Read each statement and check yes or no.

I found it easy to relate to the peer leaders. Yes_____ No_____

I think other students should have this program. Yes_____ No_____

6. I discovered _____

_____

_____

7. Please add any comments about the experience below.

_____

_____

_____

_____

SECTION 13 —
HIV AWARENESS PROGRAM (HAP)

Section 13 — HIV Awareness Program (HAP)

Description

This HIV awareness project operates under the assumption that peers can serve as useful adjuncts to professionals in helping to prevent the spread of AIDS. Peers often impact their contemporaries more effectively than adults because of their greater rapport, mutual respect, and influence. They also serve as powerful role models who promote positive behavior in younger students.

This program enables two to four peer leaders to conduct four sessions for health or family life classes to reinforce the school's HIV/AIDS prevention curriculum. Recommended grade levels are seventh through tenth. Facts and myths about HIV, potential risks and consequences, and reactions incurred by peers and family members are presented along with strategies to distinguish negative from positive responses to infected individuals and to provide support to others.

Goals

• To review the facts and myths about the HIV virus and clarify any misconceptions.

• To learn about the way in which the spread of the HIV virus may suddenly change one's life.

• To identify some feelings and behaviors that might emerge upon ones's awareness of HIV infection.

• To learn about the ways in which the spread of the HIV virus may impact friends and relatives of infected.

• To identify the potential stigmas, labels, and emotional traumas experienced by HIV infected individuals and their close friends and relatives.

• To encourage others to be more sensitive to friends and family members of HIV infected individuals.

• To demonstrate and practice positive responses to HIV infected individuals.

• To review and evaluate the program.

Planning

Before embarking on such a high impact program, submit a brief but complete proposal, including goals, objectives, and specific curriculum to supervisory personnel. This may include the Superintendent of Schools, principal, and teachers. You may also want to include health or family life coordinator, guidance coordinator, and any other human service support staff.

Frequently, curricula include sections on peer pressure and personal reflection. They often provide for guest speakers and consultants. Trained peer leaders usually qualify to lead sessions in these roles without further approval. The lessons in this program are designed to match most accepted HIV prevention programs.

After explaining the intent of such a program and obtaining board or administrative approval, meet with the above professionals to clarify the program goals and process.

Logistics can be worked out through the building supervisors and teachers of family life or health classes. Typically, a particular health class can receive the program, one class session per week, for four weeks. Transportation for high school students can be provided by the coordinator, bus, or taxi, depending on district resources. The class period should be chosen upon the basis of high school peer leaders' availablilty.

Written communication about program design, dates of sessions, and times should be forwarded to appropriate high school personnel responsible for releasing the partners as well as health or family life classroom teachers.

Selection

PEER LEADERS. Peer leaders should be selected on the basis of articulation skills, strength of character, self-confidence, ability to speak in groups, and maturity. They should be sensitive to others' needs and skilled in non-judgemental communication skills.

RECEIVING STUDENTS. Recipients should be selected randomly by choosing specific health or family life classes.

Training

All peer leaders should receive the basic training in conscious and transformative communication as well as personal care.

They should receive additional training by the health teacher in the facts about HIV and the far-reaching impact of this disease.

The peer leaders (partners) should be trained by first observing the program and then running

through the exercises. They should receive observational feedback from their peers, using Group Leadership Checklist. These partners should explore their own leadership roles and dilemmas, interpersonal dynamics, group management abilities, and gender stereotypes.

They should be taught the warning signals of high risk receiving students and instructed to take preventive measures to protect the weaker students from undue stress throughout the program. Furthermore, they should be directed to refer any potential high risk students to appropriate staff members. The referrals should be made in writing.

Parental Permission

All peer leaders should receive signed parental consent slips, authorizing their participation in the program.

The receiving students are not required to gain written parental consent, because HAP should be a part of the district's family life or health curriculum presented to all students.

Implementation

All subject teachers releasing these students to attend HAP awareness sessions should also receive written notice and give their approval. Arrange transportation through proper channels. The logistics of the program require the peer leaders to be released from two successive classes, preferably nonacademic, one session per week for four weeks.

The peer leaders receive on-site coaching by the program coordinator or licensed designee, who remains within eye contact of the classroom throughout each session. The coordinator should set up weekly, forty-five minute, supervision sessions with peer leaders.

After all pertinent staff members have been made aware of dates and times for four sessions, the program may begin.

SESSION 1. Peer leaders distribute a fifteen item questionnaire to distinguish the facts from the myths about HIV. They hold a discussion with the group to provide an opportunity for review, clarification and additional learning.

Follow-Up
After Session 1, leaders meet with program coordinator to process the session and identify any students exhibiting behavioral warning signals. They should be referred to professionals and prevention experts.

Divide the class into two groups. Prepare enough envelopes for the entire class. Load half the envelopes with red stickers, and the other half with white stickers. Arrange sets of two envelopes, each containing the same color stickers. Staple the sets together so that there are two equal numbers of stapled envelopes.

SESSION 2. Peer leaders welcome the group to the class as they enter the room by handing half the class members stapled sets of envelopes selected randomly. The session begins with the Envelope Game, an exercise designed to highlight how the spread of HIV might impact the student's lives.

Follow-Up
As a follow-up to Session 2, a forty-five minute supervision conference is held, during which leaders discuss the reactions of the group to the Envelope Game, discussion, and the entire session.

SESSION 3. Peer leaders initiate a discussion about student' imagined reactions to their hypothetical awareness of HIV infections. Then, leader enacts a role play which presents the plight of an eighth grade girl whose brother has just been diagnosed HIV positive. She tells her friends and suffers the reactions. The drama presents the girl's reactions as well as her friend's difficulty accepting the reality of this horrible news.

The class is asked to identify the feelings and consequences suffered by friends and family members of HIV positive individuals. The group is asked how they might support HIV positive individuals in positive ways.

Follow-Up
During this session, leaders and supervisors review the lists of positive and negative responses and process the session, noting the students' reactions and listing some of the ways that victims are impacted socially.

SESSION 4. Leaders instruct the groups to develop three skits and enact them in order to demonstrate and practice positive reactions to AIDS victims.

Follow-Up
During this session, leaders and supervisors process the session noting the students' reactions and creating a list of high risk students who should be followed up with professional prevention initiatives such as counseling groups or periodic peer reviews. These should be submitted to the building principal.

Evaluation

A written program evaluation completed by recipients offers reactions to the program, comments on its effectiveness, rates the peer leaders, and suggests improvements.

Follow-Up

After evaluations are complete, peer leaders and program coordinator review the comments and adjust the program accordingly, offering modifications or deletions which improve its mission. Any participants who exhibited behavioral warning signals are referred to professionals. Peer leaders may revisit the classroom periodically to reinforce concepts and reassess impact.

Paper Trail

1. Peer Leader ID Card Prototype.　　*(See Appendix A, Model 17.)*

2. Peer Leader Pass.　　*(See Appendix A, Model 15.)*

3. Group Leadership Checklist.　　*(See Section 2, Session 42.)*

4. Facts and Myths about HIV Sheet.　　*(See p. 379.)*

5. Reaction Sheet for Infected Students.　　*(See p. 380.)*

6. Reaction Sheet for Noninfected Students.　　*(See p. 381.)*

7. HIV Response Sheet.　　*(See p. 382.)*

8. Scenario Sheet.　　*(See p. 384.)*

9. HAP Evaluation Sheet.　　*(See p. 385.)*

Trainees' Observation of All Sessions

Time
Four forty-five minute sessions for observation; four forty-five minute sessions for rehearsal; and four fifteen minute follow-up sessions.

Goals
• To familiarize new trainees with the HIV Awareness Program through observation of experienced group leaders in action.

• To provide opportunity for peer leaders to improve group leadership skills.

Materials
Group Leadership Checklists (see Section 2, Session 42) and pencils.

Process
Two to four trained peer leaders observe four HIV Awareness sessions from the back of the room. They complete Group Leadership Checklists during each session and attend follow-up supervisory sessions, during which they process the activity's impact and offer feedback to the leader. Students who show behavioral warning signals should be referred to appropriate professionals.

After the end of the program cycle, peer leaders attend a follow-up session to review completed evaluations, make necessary program sessions, and clarify their concerns.

Then peer leaders rehearse the four sessions as the experienced leaders and supervisor rate her/his leadership abilities and offer constructive suggestions.

Trainer should reinforce the need for peer leaders to be unbiased in their presentations. Personal values should not be discussed during sessions.

Review and practice nonjudgemental communication skills before allowing peer leaders to proceed.

Outcome Indicators
1. Peer leader trainees should observe sessions and complete Group Leadership Checklists.

2. Trainees should offer feedback to experienced leaders during supervisory sessions.

3. All should review program evaluations and participate in program revision.

4. Trainees should rehearse the program and make necessary adjustments in leadership style.

5. Experienced leaders and supervisor should rate trainees as competent before they lead a new program cycle.

Session 1: Facts and Myths about HIV

Time
Forty-five minutes

Goal
• To review the facts and myths about the HIV virus and clarify any misconceptions.

Materials
Facts and Myths about HIV Sheets and pencils.

Process
Peer leaders introduce themselves to the class, give a brief description of the goals and activities of the four upcoming sessions, and begin by distributing the Facts and Myths about HIV Sheets to the class.

Allow ten minutes time for the class to respond to the questionnaire, then peer leaders should review each question, solicit the correct answer from the group, and lead a discussion to identify the latest knowledge on AIDS. The discussion should provide an opportunity to clarify any misconceptions about the virus.

Peer leaders should state that although their responses are based on the latest evidence, new research results are constantly providing additional findings which sometimes change the original conclusions.

Outcome Indicators
1. All class members should respond to the questionnaire.

2. Class members should ask questions during the review.

3. Peer leader discussion should clarify any misconceptions.

Follow-Up
After Session 1, leaders meet with program coordinator to process the session and identify any students exhibiting behavioral warning signals. They should be referred to professionals and prevention experts.

Prepare for next session's exercise by dividing the class into two groups. Make enough envelopes for the entire class. Load half the envelopes with red stickers, and the other half with white stickers. Arrange sets of two envelopes, each containing the same color stickers. Staple each set into pairs, each having the same color stickers.

Facts and Myths about HIV Answer Sheet

Directions

Please use these answer sheets to review the class members' answers and supplement their knowledge base.

__F__ 1. A person may be a carrier without having visible symptoms. You cannot tell by looking at a person whether he/she is infected.

__T__ 2. The process of immune system breakdown leads to emaciation and susceptibility to a variety of debilitating diseases.

__F__ 3. The disease may be in an early stage before the symptoms have surfaced. Or the person may simply be a carrier.

__T__ 4. The virus is present in the largest amounts in semen and vaginal fluids.

__T__ 5. The blood from the used needle enters the receiver's system and transfers the virus.

__T__ 6. The virus can enter small cuts in the vaginal wall that cannot be detected by the female.

__T__ 7. Thin walls of the rectum break and cause bleeding of its lining which allows the virus to enter the bloodstream from the partner's penis.

__T__ 8. Abstinence, using rubber condoms, and knowing the sexual history of your partner are some ways to protect yourself. When you sleep with someone, it is as though you are sleeping with all their previous partners. A condom is more effective when combined with Noxinal, a vaginal contraceptive gel which kills the HIV virus.

__F__ 9. One out of every 3 persons with HIV is heterosexual. Teenagers have the highest of newly diagnosed cases of HIV. One out of every 200 teenagers is HIV positive. One out of every five teenagers has a sexually transmitted disease.

__F__ 10. The latest research shows that the risk is minimal, but one should take precautions anyway.

__T__ 11. Blood samples are routinely screened to avoid transmission of the HIV virus.

__F__ 12. The only ways to get it are through exchange of body fluids or transmission from mother to unborn fetus.

__T__ 13. The mother transmits the disease through the bloodstream into the placenta.

__T__ 14. Latest figures are that 2 in 1000 college age students will contract the HIV virus. There is an increase of heterosexual teenagers getting HIV. A recent study out of Rutgers University estimates that 5% of teens, age 12 to 17, are HIV positive.

__F__ 15. If you do not have genital or oral sex with someone, share needles, or exchange blood, it is very difficult to get the virus.

Session 2: The Envelope Game

Time
Forty-five minutes

Goals
• To learn about the ways in which the spread of the HIV virus may suddenly change one's life.

• To identify some feelings and behaviors that might emerge upon one's awareness of HIV infection.

Materials
Enough envelopes for the entire class, an equal number of white and red stickers, Reaction Sheets for Infected Students, Reaction Sheets for Noninfected Students, and pencils.

Process
Peer leaders welcome the group to the class as they enter the room by handing half the class members stapled sets of envelopes selected randomly. Peer leaders instruct the group to detach their envelopes and hand one to another student who is without one.

Then the peer leaders inform the group that they have just had unprotected sex with those who received their envelopes. The class is instructed to open their envelopes in unison. Leaders instruct the group as follows:

Imagine that those of you who have just received the red stickers have been infected with HIV and tested positive. Those of you fortunate enough to have received white stickers are noninfected. Remove your stickers and fasten them to your chests.

We want all of the infected students to move to the left side of the room and all noninfected stu-

dents to occupy seats on the right side.

By show of hands, show how many of you gave envelopes to people who you know well? How many passed them to friends? How many pass envelopes to members of the opposite sex? Same sex?

Peer leaders distribute two sets of reaction sheets to each group, HIV Reaction Sheets to those with red stickers and Reaction Sheets for Noninfected Students to those with white stickers, and instruct the class members to respond in writing.

Then, after about ten minutes, peer leaders divide the class into groups of six students and review the answers, noting differences for each group and allowing members to pass if they choose. As a follow-up, class members are told to imagine they have contracted HIV virus and that the principal and nurse would be the only ones in the school to be told.

Their assignment for the coming week is to make a mental note of how this knowledge would effect their daily lives and activities with peers, family, and other adults for the week that follows this session. They are told that they will discuss their detailed observations of activities during the next session.

Outcome Indicators
1. Peer leader questions should generate at least ten different reactions from peers towards infected HIV positive individuals.

2. Class members should identify the distinctions between how HIV victims react to others and how they are treated by others who know of their conditions.

LEADER'S GUIDE
Session 2 continued

3. Class members should discuss how they **imagine their lives might change if they tested HIV positive.**

Follow-Up
As a follow-up to Session 2, a forty-five minute supervision conference is held, during which leaders discuss the reactions of the group to the Envelope Game, discussion, and the entire session.

Session 3: The Secret Is Out

Time
Forty-five minutes

Goals
• To learn about the ways in which the spread of the HIV virus may impact friends and relatives of infected.

• To identify the potential stigmas, labels, and emotional traumas experienced by HIV infected individuals and their close friends and relatives.

• To encourage others to be more sensitive to friends and family members of HIV infected individuals.

Materials
HIV Response Sheets and pencils.

Process
Peer leaders initiate a discussion about students' imagined reactions to their hypothetical awareness of HIV infections. Then, leader enacts a role play which presents the plight of an eighth grade girl whose brother has just been diagnosed with HIV. She tells her friends and suffers the reactions. The drama presents the girl's reactions as well as her friend's difficulty accepting the reality of this horrible news.

Leaders ask the class to identify the feelings and consequences suffered by family members of HIV positive individuals. The group is asked how they might support AIDS victims in positive ways. Leaders enact the following role play.

CHARACTER PROFILES:
1. Kim. She is a good student who is friendly and popular with her peers. Her brother has been infected with HIV and shows symp-

toms of AIDS. She cannot accept it. Her best friend is Lara. Kim has been hiding the fact that her brother has AIDS for a month.

2. Lara. She is a cheerleader and a good student. She is Kim's best friend.

SCENE:
The action takes place in the library, while the two students are studying. Kim is helping Lara with an algebra assignment.

Lara: Kim, can you help me with my algebra homework? (a minute later) A couple of weeks ago you told me your brother was in the hospital. How's he doing?

Kim: He is still in the same condition.

Lara: Have you visited him lately?

Kim: I haven't had time. I've been real busy.

Lara: You don't have time for your own brother?

Kim: (with tears) My brother has AIDS.

Leaders divide the class into four equal-sized groups. Each group member is asked to give a example of how he or she might respond positively to Kim. Then members are asked to give examples of negative responses. Leader asks one member of group to record both positive and negative responses. Make a list combining positives and negatives from each group.

Leaders distribute HIV Response Sheets to each member and instruct the students to record their answers. Then, leaders review the groups' responses to the questions in a large group discussion. Peer leaders record the most prevalent positive and negative responses on two separate lists.

Outcome Indicators

1. Class members should demonstrate attentiveness to role play sequence.

2. Leaders should observe members of small groups discussing negative and positive responses to AIDS victims.

3. Each student should fill out Response Sheets, indicating his or her personal responses to HIV infected people.

Follow-Up

During this session, leaders and supervisors review the lists of positive and negative responses and process the session, noting the students' reactions and listing some of the ways that victims are impacted socially.

Peer leaders should discuss the class members' reactions and list them to review during the next session.

Session 4: Compassionate Responses

Time
Forty-five minutes

Goals
• To demonstrate and practice positive responses to HIV positive individuals.

• To review and evaluate the program.

Materials
Scenario Sheets, HAP Evaluation Sheets, and pencils.

Process
Leaders should distribute a list of reactions generated from the previous session and review the alternatives. Leaders divide the class into three small groups of approximately five to seven members each. Instruct the groups to develop three skits and enact them in order to demonstrate and practice positive reactions to HIV positive individuals.

Leaders distribute one Scenario Sheet to each group and inform members that they will have ten minutes to develop a skit around each of the scenarios. Leaders should assist each group in their skit development. After ten minutes preparation time instruct each group to act out the skit to demonstrate compassionate responses to HIV positive individuals.

Leaders hold a discussion to elicit more reactions from the entire group. Finally, leaders distribute HAP Evaluation Sheets and allow ten minutes for students to complete them.

Outcome Indicators
1. Each group should role play a particular skit demonstrating positive responses to a social situation interacting with infected individuals.

2. Discussion should elicit at least ten positive reactions.

Follow-Up
During this session, leaders and supervisors process the session noting the students' reactions and creating a list of high risk students who should be followed up with professional prevention initiatives such as counseling groups or periodic peer reviews. These should be submitted to the principal.

Facts and Myths about HIV Sheet

Name_____   Date_____

Directions
Decide whether the following statements are true or false. Write T for True and F for False before each statement.

_____ 1.When a person is infected with human immunodeficiency (HIV), he/she will always have symptoms.

_____ 2. ARC (also known as AIDS Related Complex) is a wasting away syndrome that some times precedes AIDS.

_____ 3. A person who does not have symptoms of AIDS cannot transmit the virus to anothe person.

_____ 4. HIV is present in large amounts in semen and vaginal fluids.

_____ 5. Sharing contaminated intravenous needles is a way in which HIV is transmitted from one person to another.

_____ 6. During vaginal intercourse an infected male can transmit virus to the female.

_____ 7. During anal intercourse an infected male can infect either a male or female.

_____ 8. There are things individuals can do to protect themselves from being infected with HIV.

_____ 9. HIV virus affects primarily the adult, gay population.

_____ 10. Open-mouth deep kissing can spread HIV.

_____ 11. There is little or no risk of HIV virus exposure through blood transfusions after March of 1985.

_____ 12. You can get HIV from contact with doorknobs, toilet seats, telephones, towels, and dishes.

_____ 13. A mother infected with HIV can pass it on to her newborn baby.

_____ 14. It is unlikely that school-aged persons will be exposed to the HIV.

_____ 15. A person should avoid being anywhere near another person infected with the HIV virus.

Reaction Sheet for Infected Students

Name_____   Date_____

Directions
Imagine you were found to be HIV positive. Please write your responses below.

1. List three feelings you might possibly have about being infected with HIV.

_____

_____

_____

2. Describe below the ways in which you might act differently towards family members, friends, and boyfriends/girlfriends.

_____

_____

_____

3. Describe some of the ways you imagine that your family, friends, and boyfriend/girlfriend might treat you differently:

a. Family _____

b. Friends _____

c. Girlfriend/boyfriend_____

4. Describe the ways in which you might react differently to school activities and responsibilities.

_____

_____

_____

Reaction Sheet for Noninfected Students

Name_____   Date_____

Directions
This is an attitude survey. Please write your responses below.

1. List three feelings and attitudes you have about people who are seriously ill.

a. Feelings: _____

_____

_____

b. Attitudes: _____

_____

_____

2. Describe your attitude towards those who have HIV or AIDS.

_____

_____

_____

3. Describe some concerns you would have if you got HIV and how your boyfriend/girlfriend might treat you differently.

_____

_____

_____

4. Describe the ways in which you might react differently to school activities and responsibilities if you had HIV.

_____

_____

_____

HIV Response Sheet

Name_____   Date_____

Directions
Please write your responses below.

1. If a close family member had HIV, whom would you tell?

_____

_____

_____

2. How might you tell them?

_____

_____

_____

3. How would you expect them to react?

_____

_____

_____

4. How would you handle the rumors?

_____

_____

_____

Page 2 - HIV Response Sheet

5. How would you react if someone told you were HIV positive?

_____

_____

_____

_____

_____

6. If you had HIV or AIDS, how would you want people to react to you?

_____

_____

Scenario Sheet

Name_____   Date_____

Directions
Use these scenarios to make up role plays demonstrating how to respond positively to these HIV infected individuals.

GROUP 1: The Dance. You are at a school dance and someone known to have AIDS asks you to dance. How would you react? What conversation might you initiate?

GROUP 2: Spotting on the Parallel Bars. You are in P.E. class and five of your squad must spot a student known to have HIV or AIDS as he climbs and uses the parallel bars. You notice that he is wincing in pain. How would you respond to his/her pain in a helpful way?

GROUP 3: The Put-Down. Your closest friend was stabbed by a needle and contracted HIV. You are walking outside the school building and notice a few of your own friends taunting him and telling him that he is soon to become history. How do you respond?

HAP Evaluation Sheet

School _____ Class _____ Grade_____

Leader(s)_____ Date_____

Directions

You have just completed a group experience to help make you more aware of HIV or AIDS and how getting it may change your lives and the lives of others close to you. Thank you for being part of this learning experience. Please take a couple of minutes to rate the program which best describes your experience.

Please read each statement and write the number 1, 2 or 3 on each line below.

1. Often   **2. Sometimes**   **3. Never**

1._____ The exercises were interesting and held my attention.

2._____ The leader(s) encouraged me to express my opinions.

3._____ The program made me aware of how it feels to have HIV and be labeled by others.

4._____ The program made me aware of how it might feel to have a brother or sister with HIV.

5. Two ways to relate to people infected with AIDS with compassion are:

a._____

b._____

6. Read the statement below and check Yes or No.

I think other students should have this program. Yes_____ No_____

7. I discovered _____

_____

8. Add any comments about the experience below.

_____

_____

_____

APPENDICES

APPENDIX A —
MODEL FORMS

Model 1:
Peer Leader Staff Nomination Form

Date _____

Dear _____ :

Within the next four weeks we will be selecting our peer leaders to reach out to younger students in a variety of ways individually or in groups.

Please give us the names of any students in grades 10-12 who fit the following profile:

- Wellness oriented

- Caring

- Trustworthy

- Academically above average

- Good communicator and listener

- Responsible

- Well-rounded

- Available for ____ periods per week

Students recommended:

_____

_____

_____

_____

Please return this form to our mailbox. Thanks for your help.

Sincerely,

_____
Program Coordinator(s)

Model 2:
Peer Leader Student Nomination Form

Date _____

Dear _____:

We are requesting your help in selecting a group of upper grade students who have some special qualities. They will be selected for a peer leadership program using positive students to reach out to younger students in a variety of programs.

Please give us the names of any students in grades 10-12 who fit the following profile:

- Wellness oriented
- Caring
- Trustworthy
- Academically above average
- Good communicators and listeners
- Responsible
- Well-rounded
- Available for ___ periods per week.

Students recommended:

_____

_____

_____

_____

Please return this form to our mailbox. Thanks for your help.

Sincerely,

_____
Program Coordinator(s)

Model 3:
Peer Leader Application

Date _____

Dear Student:

Within the next four weeks, we will be starting a peer helping program which will enable upper grade high school students to lend support to younger students in their academic and social functioning.

If you would like to be involved in this program as a high school peer leader and can afford three periods a week of released time, we urge you to apply. We will choose the students who have the following profile:

• Responsible and attaining a C+ average or above in all subject areas.

• Trusted by peers and able to keep confidences.

• Interested in helping others.

• Free period in schedule.

• Rounded personality with various hobbies and extracurricular activities.

• Consent from parents and the teachers of classes which helpers must miss.

• Ability to relate, communicate, and show concern for others.

• Drug and alcohol-free life-style.

If you are interested, please fill out the form on the next page and place it in our mailbox.

Very truly yours,

_____
Program Coordinator(s)

Page 2 - Model 3: Peer Leader Application

Name_____ Date_____

Homeroom_____ Grade _____

Subjects willing to tutor _____

Present academic average _____

Periods you can afford to miss _____

Your Schedule

Period	**Subject**	**Teacher**	**Room**
_____	_____	_____	_____
_____	_____	_____	_____
_____	_____	_____	_____
_____	_____	_____	_____
_____	_____	_____	_____
_____	_____	_____	_____
_____	_____	_____	_____

Model 4:
Pre and Post-Training Peer Leader Competency Assessment
(Index of Perception)

Directions
In the following exercise you will be given Conversation Sheets with twenty leader responses to rate. Rate them according to their level of helpfulness by putting in the best fitting number next to each response on the line (1.0, 1.5, 2.0, 2.5, 3.0, or 4.0).

Use the rating scale on the next page to determine which numbers to use to rate the helpfulness of each response.

Modified from *Human Relations Development: A Manual for Educators* by G. Gazda, F. Asbury, and F. Balzar, Boston: Allyn and Bacon, Inc. (1973)

Page 2 - Model 4: Pre and Post-Training Peer Leader Competency Assessment (Index of Perception)

Rating Scale

Leader:

1. Does not listen.

2. Ridicules.

3. Ignores difference between what receiver says and does.

4. Shows lack of concern.

5. Does not show involvement.

Leader:

1. Partially listens or distorts message.

2. Does not respond to emotions.

3. Gives cheap advice.

4. Does not reveal feelings.

5. Accepts differences in behavior but does not discuss them.

Leader:

1. Reflects receiver's feelings.

2. Is open.

3. Recognizes receiver as important person.

4. Shows interest and caring.

5. Reveals feelings.

Leader:

1. Relates what is happening now with past experiences.

2. Identifies deeper feelings of receiver.

3. Really cares.

4. Talks about what he/she feels and does.

5. Uses feelings to enhance helpee's self-esteem.

NO HELP		SOME HELP		MORE HELP		GOOD HELP
1.0	1.5	2.0	2.5	3.0	3.5	4.0

Modified from *Human Relations Development: A Manual for Educators* by G. Gazda, F. Asbury, and F. Balzar, Boston: Allyn and Bacon, Inc. (1973)

Page 3 - Model 4: Pre and Post-Training Peer Leader Competency Assessment (Index of Perception)

Conversation Sheet

Name_____   Date_____

Conversation 1 (RECEIVER TO LEADER)

Receiver: "I spent a few minutes working on my fractions, but I could not understand them. So I said, 'Forget it' and I watched some television."

_____1. LEADER: "If you spent more time on it, you'd find that math isn't so bad."

Receiver: "Well, it doesn't matter how much time I spend, it's really boring and I'll never get it."

_____2. LEADER: "Who are you kidding? You really don't care anyway. Five minutes doesn't show very much effort to me. I really want you to do well, but I can't help you unless you try to help yourself."

Receiver: "It's easy for you to say that I should work. You're not the one who really has to do it."

_____3. LEADER: "I had the same problem when I was in your school. I know what its like. But, if we work together, maybe we can overcome it."

Receiver: "You know, I'm really bored in school, but I have a lot of pressure from my family to do well so that I can go to college. So I'll just do what I have to do to get into college."

_____4. LEADER: "Yeah, I understand. Math is one of those subjects that seems pretty unimportant. But you may have to do it well so that you can go to college and please your parents."

Receiver: "Yeah, I do feel that way, but it's more than just my parents. I feel like many areas of my life are controlled by others."

Conversation 2 (RECEIVER TO LEADER)

Receiver: "I sure am happy since we moved to this town. It's just great! I have met so many nice people and I go to parties now. I'm ten times happier than I've ever been!"

LEADER RESPONSES:

_____5. "I guess you're saying you have never been this happy in other towns."

_____6. "Don't be too sure all these parties are good for you. All the teachers have heard about what goes on at your parties! Things have changed for the worse since I was at your school."

_____7. "You feel that a lot of good things have happened to you since you moved here."

Page 4 - Model 4: Pre and Post-Training Peer Leader Competency Assessment (Index of Perception)

_____8. "Going to parties is something new for you."

Conversation 3 (LEADER TO TEACHER)

Leader: "I spoke to Jim today. We went over his work and he seems to be improving, now that he's putting forth an honest effort."

Teacher's Reply: "He doesn't really want to try hard. Maybe he's doing this so you'll like him."

LEADER RESPONSES:

_____9. "You seem to be at the point where you've given up hope on Jim. It must be frustrating for you. But maybe together we can do something to help him."

_____10. "All you really care about is your own reputation as a teacher. You're hung up about being a failure."

_____11. "Yes, I may want Jim to like me, but if it helps us to work together so so that he can do it better, then we'll all benefit from it in the long run."

_____12. "I understand that based on your past experience with Jim, things don't look too good. But, I don't see him in the same way. He does seem to be genuinely improving himself."

Conversation 4 (TEACHER TO LEADER)

Teacher: "I feel like one of my students is having trouble at home. He seems to be uncooperative in class. He does just the opposite of what he is supposed to do. If you think you can do something to help him, you better do it right now."

LEADER RESPONSES:

_____13. "This is a problem for many teachers since some students really can't focus on their work because of their home problems."

_____14. "What do you think I'm here for? If you could help the student, then I wouldn't have to!"

_____15. "It must make it hard to teach when the kid is so uncooperative. I wish I had the answer to this right now, but you know that's impossible. I'm in the same spot as you are. Maybe we can work together to help this student solve his problems."

_____16. "I'm sure you've had lots of kids who are uncooperative. You're more qualified than I am, so you handle it."

Modified from *Human Relations Development: A Manual for Educators* by G. Gazda, F. Asbury, and F. Balzar, Boston: Allyn and Bacon, Inc. (1973)

Page 5 - Model 4: Pre and Post-Training Peer Leader Competency Assessment (Index of Perception)

Conversation 5 (RECEIVER TO LEADER)

Receiver: "Look, leave me alone! I don't want to study history. It has no meaning to me. It's hard, and I don't see how it's ever going to help me earn a living."

LEADER RESPONSES:

_____17. "Ancient history can have a lot of meaning for you. Present events can be understood better when you know history."

_____18. "You don't want me to force you to study since you feel history is not important enough for you to study hard."

_____19. "There's more to life than just earning a living."

_____20. "You find ancient history unnecessary and difficult, and it doesn't seem to be related to any job you will ever have."

Modified from *Human Relations Development: A Manual for Educators* by G. Gazda, F. Asbury, and F. Balzar, Boston: Allyn and Bacon, Inc. (1973)

Gadza Perception Scale Answer Sheet

1. 2

2. 3

3. 4

4. 1.5

5. 2

6. 1.5

7. 2.5

8. 2.0

9. 2.5

10. 1.5

11. 3.0

12. 3.0

13. 2

14. 1

15. 3.0

16. 1.5

17. 2.0

18. 2.5

19. 1.5

20. 2.5

Modified from *Human Relations Development: A Manual for Educators* by G. Gazda, F. Asbury, and F. Balzar, Boston: Allyn and Bacon, Inc. (1973)

Model 5:
Peer Leader Parent Consent Form

Date _____

Dear Parent:

Your son/daughter has volunteered to participate in an ongoing student help program coordinated by_____. The program trains your son/daughter to work with younger students who are in need of academic help and social support. Your son/daughter becomes a part of a (program name), which is a group of high school tenth, eleventh, and twelfth graders who volunteer and are selected to perform several helping functions.

Your son/daughter will be active in Program #___. Please refer to attached Program Description for full details of his/her program involvement.

Your son/daughter will be learning human relations skills and study skills improvement techniques. This new learning will be applied to his/her work with other students. The arrangement is totally voluntary.

(Program name) includes training, alternate week advisory sessions, and approximately two periods per week at the target school for helping sessions. Group sessions are usually held for one period a week.

(Program name) operates on a yearly basis. When sessions are held during the student's regular school day, transportation between schools is provided at the school's expense.

Teachers of the classes from which peer leaders are released will be notified in writing. Students are requested to make up any missed assignments or other work and are expected to continue high academic levels of achievement.

Any questions you may have should be addressed to_____. Please sign the attached sheet to indicate your approval for your son/daughter to be involved in the (program name).

Sincerely,

_____
Program Coordinator(s)

Training Date _____

Training Time_____

Training Location _____

Page 2 - Model 5: Peer Leader Parent Consent Form

I,_____ parent/guardian of_____ approve of my

son/daughter's involvement in (name) Program and training for the school year _____.

_____
Parent/Guardian Consent

Date_____

Program Description

(Program name) is a peer helping program which operates out of the (organization name). Each year, teen volunteers are trained to provide a multiplicity of services designed to meet the needs of various student populations. The following descriptions represent a composite overview of the services:

1. SMOOTH TRANSITIONS. Trained peers serve as guides to incoming high school students in order to facilitate academic and personal adjustment. The partnerships begin with a one-day structured experience at the middle-school level where high school students and graduating middle school students collaborate on a project. Then, the high school students continue the relationships by offering assistance to their younger, entering students.

2. WELCOME. Juniors and seniors are trained to guide students who enter a school or community from another district. The focus of this program is on social, emotional, and academic adjustment to a novel educational setting. Particular attention is paid to the selection of cocurricular activities, social networking, and survival within the informal peer system.

3. ONE-TO-ONE. This program trains peer leaders to offer social and academic support to young students. These students meet once a week during lunch (or other designated periods) to focus on one subject area and then follow up with a general discussion of social issues. This program is designed to prevent school failure, substance abuse, truancy, and potential dropouts.

4. PEER INTERVENTION NETWORK (PIN). This program establishes an ongoing support group for middle school underachievers. Students form partnerships to identify problems, generate goals, and develop action plans. Groups meet weekly before, during, and/or after school as necessary. When members improve their academic functioning, their group status is elevated as they assume roles as "experts."

5. PLANNING LEISURE ACTIVITIES NOW (PLAN). High school students who have coped well with independent time assist groups of younger students in grades six through eight. The high school peer leaders help them to overcome loneliness, time management problems, and anxiety. Typically, a trained high school junior or senior leads eleven sessions of structured experiences which begin with icebreakers and then move into supportive activities and development of alternative uses of open-time.

Coping strategies are also generated throughout the sessions. During Session 11, the group elects to continue or disband. All sessions are voluntary and held during lunch.

6. HUMAN RELATIONS. Trained students provide structured experiences to middle school special education classes. These sessions are designed to promote self-awareness, self-esteem, positive social interaction, and coping skills. The students learn about the high school milieu from the high school students, who prepare them for their transitions to the new setting.

7. KIDS 'R SAFE. Trained peer leaders conduct workshops on child safety and tactics to avoid contact with harmful strangers. High school students lead workshops with kindergarten through second grade students which initiate discrimination skills necessary to distinguish friendly strangers from hostile strangers.

Page 2 - Program Description

Mini-dramas and puppet shows presented by leaders illustrate safety strategies to avoid being kidnapped or abused. The youngsters are also cautioned against accepting any food or other substance from strangers. The program is presented from a positive perspective.

8. CLOSE ENCOUNTERS. This program enlists trained peer role models to lead four structured experiential and informational sessions with the younger students in order to prevent chemical dependency. Peer partners present some of the facts and myths of substance abuse and then assist younger students in developing and using refusal skills to avoid the temptations of chemical use and abuse.

The sessions also elicit from the group members some of its own personal triumphs. Using symbols to represent earlier positive states, the peer leaders help receiving students to access these positive experiences in order to avoid the temptations of abusing drugs and alcohol.

9. PARTNERS AGAINST SCAPEGOATING (PAS). In this program two peer leaders enter middle school family life/health classes to lead four sessions of structured experiences designed to sensitize students to the adverse effects of verbal assaults, degradation, and stereotyping behavior.

High school partners begin the program with an intimidating posture and then shift the focus to assist the middle school students in developing ways to live in harmony. Coping skills to resist verbal abuse are also promoted. The PAS mission advocates cooperation as a pathway to the survival of humanity.

10. PEERS ASSISTANTS TO INTERPERSONAL RELATIONSHIPS (PAIRS). This program enlists the aid of four trained high school peer leaders (two boys and two girls) to hold six sessions on friendship and dating awareness for students in health or family life classes in grades eight and nine. The sessions are designed to be upbeat, active, and student-centered, using group experiences and role playing to illustrate the principles.

Participants are asked to define their existing relationships, explore how conflicts develop and can be avoided, and use refusal skills and conflict resolution techniques to develop more positive friendships. Assumptions and beliefs about the nature of friendship and cross-gender relationships are explored in impartial, nonthreatening formats.

11. HIV AWARENESS PROGRAM (HAP). This program enables peer leaders to conduct four sessions for health or family life classes to reinforce the school's HIV prevention curriculum. Recommended grade levels are eighth through tenth. Facts and myths about HIV, potential risks and consequences, and reactions to victims from their peers and family members are presented. Strategies to distinguish negative from positive responses to infected individuals and to support to others are also presented.

Page 3 - Program Description

Facts About (Program Name)

(Name) is derived from a field tested peer support model developed in 1973 and found to be effective in raising self-esteem and academic performance.

Training

(Name) perceives its training as an ongoing process which begins before student service, continues with regular supervision, and then recycles former peer leaders as trainers of new recruits. The training incorporates one-day collaborative experience to promote group cohesiveness, and a three-day training session to teach nondirective, active listening skills, and meta-communication skills such as unconscious and conscious communication, pacing, leading, and the use of metaphor.

Trainees are taught to discern behavioral warning signals and respond by making a referral to an appropriate professional. During the program, ongoing supervision sessions occur with the support of additional staff members who supervise one or two of the peer leaders. Supervisory sessions meet at alternate week intervals and more frequently as needed. They are supplemented by peer contact and staff contact facilitated by a phone network.

Implementation

(Name) operates under the auspices of the_____
and receives approximately _____ ($ amount) per year, most of which is used for transportation expenses. The mode of transportation from school to school is taxi. Written parental consent is secured before (name) participants enter the program. Once a month, high school peer leaders lunch together with their advisors to discuss mutual concerns and plan events.

Screening, Recruitment, and Evaluation

The assessment component of (name) includes a modified Gazda Perception Scale and a statement sheet to assess candidates' communication skills upon entering and leaving the program. Each target group (PAS), (PLAN), etc. receives an evaluation questionnaire, and its results are incorporated into the subsequent program cycles.

Teachers' evaluations of individual recipients' progress are received periodically through meetings with peer leaders staff. Through this on-going self-scrutiny, (name) is constantly evolving and generating new programs to meet emergent needs.

Model 6:
Program Announcement
(High School Staff)

Date: _____

To: All High School Staff Members

From: _____ (Program Coordinator(s))

Re: Peer Leader Program

This year, some upper grade students have volunteered to participate in a peer support pro-gram. This project is designed to enable older students to learn helping skills and work with younger pupils who are in need of academic assistance and social support.

The program intends to prevent at-risk youngsters from self-damaging behavior. Some ses-sions are held on a one-to-one basis with an older peer helping a younger peer in one academic area. Group sessions are conducted by peer leaders to promote positive behavior in younger peers. Training will be held on_____,_____, and_____.

We are asking your cooperation in allowing peer leaders to make up class and homework assignments for classes they miss. The sessions on these days will be held for the entire school day. The alternative would be to take students out of class for two periods a week, but this arrangement would reduce the impact of the training period. Students are requested to get their assignments one day in advance and are responsible to make up any work they miss in their classes. The names of the students to be excused on the above dates are:

_____   _____

_____   _____

When the program begins, some of the students will be conducting sessions at the _____School. Others will work in our school with younger stu-dents. The peer leaders will ask you to sign an Off-Campus Pass Form so they may be excused on these days.

In addition, each leader will be required to attend one supervision session every week. These sessions will be staggered to prevent leaders from missing the same class more than once each month. After five weeks, we shall be issuing a Student Classroom Performance Check Form for you to fill out. This will give you an opportunity to assess any changes in the leader's academic work in your class. If you feel that any of these leaders' grades are being adversely affected by their participation, please do not hesitate to notify_____, Program Coordinator. After training is completed, we will announce the dates of the program's com-mencement and sessions.

Model 7:
Receiving Student Referral Form
(One-to-One)

Date _____

Dear _____:

We would appreciate your help in recruiting receiving students for the student helping program. The subjects targeted for assistance are _____ _____ _____.

The selection criteria are as follows:

• Average ability (I.Q.) in your judgment.

• No more than two years below grade level in mathematics or reading.

• Students who look withdrawn or headed for failure.

• Students who began the year with some effort but are now beginning to "turn off."

• Students not already receiving supplementary assistance from teachers.

Please list on the next page any names of pupils in your classes who fit the above description. We will check standardized scores and select students who fit the criteria, express interest, and have schedules which coincide with those of the peer leaders.

Please place these recommendations in Mr./Mrs._____mailbox within _____days. We will inform you as to which pupils have been selected to be in the program. If your recommended student(s) enter(s) the program, we will arrange mutually convenient times and places for conferences between you and the peer leader.

Respectfully,

_____
Program Coordinator(s)

Page 2 - Model 7: Receiving Student Referral Form (One-to-One)

Student	Class	Grade Avg.	Homeroom
_____	_____	_____	_____
_____	_____	_____	_____
_____	_____	_____	_____
_____	_____	_____	_____
_____	_____	_____	_____
_____	_____	_____	_____
_____	_____	_____	_____
_____	_____	_____	_____
_____	_____	_____	_____
_____	_____	_____	_____
_____	_____	_____	_____
_____	_____	_____	_____
_____	_____	_____	_____
_____	_____	_____	_____
_____	_____	_____	_____

Teacher _____ Date_____

School _____ Subject _____

Model 8:
Receiving Student Application Form
(One-to-One)

Date _____

Dear Student:

In about_____weeks we will begin a student-helping program with high school students visiting your school each week to spend time with a limited number of students. If you need help with social problems, English, math or_____, you may sign up for help in one of these areas.

The peer leader will help you with any other school related problem. We cannot guarantee that you will receive help, but we will do our best to supply a leader. Please drop this form off in the main office, and we will get back to you with an answer in about_____weeks.

- -

Name_____   Date_____

School _____   Class _____

Subject(s) needing attention

_____   _____

_____   _____

My Schedule

Period	Subject	Teacher	Room
1.	_____	_____	_____
2.	_____	_____	_____
3.	_____	_____	_____
4.	_____	_____	_____
5.	_____	_____	_____
6.	_____	_____	_____
7.	_____	_____	_____

Model 9:
Memo to Referring Staff (One-to-One)

Date: _____

To: All Teachers Referring Pupils to Student Helping Program

From: _____, Program Coordinator

Re: Referral Information

We wish to thank you for recommending students in need of academic and social support as potential receivers of help from our program. We are selecting pupils in the following subject areas:

_____

_____

_____

Your involvement in the final step of the selection will help us to complete the process. Kindly fill out the enclosed Florida Key observation sheet which describes the student's behavior. We will use this information to screen the receivers and to match them up with appropriate helpers.

Once we receive these forms and make final decisions, we will inform you of our decisions and call a meeting with the consulting teachers who will be involved.

We are now in the process of training the leaders. We anticipate that the process of training will be completed by_____.

Thank you for your cooperation.

Model 10:
Receiving Student Evaluation
(One-to-One and Smooth Transitions)

Directions
Please enter whatever number applies on lines:

0 Cannot tell	**4** Occasionally
1 Never	**5** Fairly often
2 Very seldom	**6** Very often
3 Once in a while	

Compared with other students of the same age, does this student:

RELATING

_____1. Get along with other students?

_____2. Get along with the teacher?

_____3. Keep calm when things frustrate him/her?

_____4. Tell the truth about his/her school work?

ASSERTING

_____5. Speak up for his/her own ideas?

_____6. Offer to speak in front of class?

_____7. Offer to answer questions in class?

_____8. Ask meaningful questions in class?

_____9. Join in school activities?

Modified from:
Florida Key: Elementary Form
Dr. William Purkey
Dr. Bob Cage
Dr. William Graves
University of Florida January 1971

Page 2 - Model 10: Receiving Student Evaluation (One-to-One and Smooth Transition)

INVESTING

_____10. Act in a reliable and trustworthy fashion?

_____11. Seek out new things to do in school on his/her own?

_____12. Offer to do extra work?

_____13. Write independently?

COPING

_____14. Finish work in school?

_____15. Pay attention to class activities?

_____16. Work with care?

_____17. Accept responsibility?

_____18. Recognize his/her realistic limitations?

Teacher _____

Student _____

Sex_____Age _____Grade _____

Modified from:
Florida Key, Elementary Form
Dr. William Purkey
Dr. Bob Cage
Dr. William Graves
University of Florida January 1971

Model 11:
Receiving Student Parent Consent Form
(All Programs)

Date _____

Dear Parent:

Your son/daughter had consented to participate in (Program name), a student helping program at his/her school. This program enlists the assistance of trained high school peer helpers who work with younger students through a variety of approaches designed to enhance academic and social growth.

Please refer to attached service description sheets which will explain the various initiatives. Your child will be receiving services in Program # _____. The starting date is_____. The program number is_____

Your signature below will indicate that you grant approval for your son/daughter to receive the above described services rendered by a trained high school peer leader. Any questions may be addressed to_____ Tel_____.

Sincerely,

_____
Program Coordinator

_____
Parent/Guardian

_____
Date

Note: Attached is the Program Description and Fact Sheet.

Model 12:
Letter to Receiving Student Applicants
Placed on Waiting List
(One-to-One)

Date_____

Dear_____:

At last we have made the assignments for the student-helping program. We are sorry to let you know that at this time we are unable to schedule peer leaders to work with you in the subject that you requested.

However, your name has been put on the waiting list, in case we have some openings in the near future. If there are no openings in two months, we will meet with you and try to arrange a way to offer you assistance.

Model 13:
Assignment Memo
(One-to-One, Smooth Transition, Welcome)

Date: _____

To: All Teachers

From: Program Coordinator

Re: Peer Program Starting Date

The student helping-program will begin on_____. Below is a list of students with their schedules of helping sessions. Please file this for your information.

Thank you,

_____
Program Coordinator

Receiving Student	Peer Leader	Day	Time	Room
_____	_____	_____	_____	_____
_____	_____	_____	_____	_____
_____	_____	_____	_____	_____
_____	_____	_____	_____	_____
_____	_____	_____	_____	_____

Model 14:
Memo to Staff at the Sending School
(High School)

Date: _____

To: All High School Staff

From: Program Coordinator(s)

Re: Peer Program Starting Date

The student-helping program will begin on_____. This program enables trained, high school students to work with younger students in academic remediation and peer support in individual and group sessions.

The following students have received passes to leave the building each week to help younger students at the_____ school:

_____

_____

_____

_____

In addition, these students will be meeting with the coordinators for supervision on

_____.

If any of the students begin to decline in their academic progress, please let one of us know. Just drop a note in our mailbox. Once again, the coordinators appreciate your cooperation in making this project a success.

Model 15:
Peer Leader Pass

Name_____   Date_____

Grade _____   Homeroom_____

Directions
Fill out the information below, and have your teachers of the periods you will miss sign.

Length of Planned Program: From_____To_____

Projected Released Time to be Used

Date (Day of Week)	Period and Time	To Be Released From (Subject and Teacher)	To Report To (Area)
_____	_____	_____	_____
_____	_____	_____	_____
_____	_____	_____	_____
_____	_____	_____	_____
_____	_____	_____	_____

Required Signatures

Period	Classroom Teachers	Program Coordinator
1.	_____	_____
2.	_____	_____
3.	_____	_____
4.	_____	_____
5.	_____	_____
6.	_____	_____
7.	_____	_____
8.	_____	_____

Model 16:
Receiving Student Pass

Directions
Go to office and pick up a pass each week before your session. Show it to the teacher of the class you will miss during helping periods. Ask the teacher to sign it after he/she has given you the assignment. Be sure to complete your assignment.

Name_____   Date of session_____

Room_____   To_____

Period and time_____

Teacher's signature_____

Coordinator's signature_____

Model 17:
Peer Leader ID Card Prototype

Coordinator _____ Tel. # _____

Program Name

_____

Peer Leader

_____

Program and School

_____

Date and Time of Service

_____

Model 18:
Program Checklist

Date _____

Peer Leader _____

Receiving Student's Name _____

(or Group's Name)_____

Day of helping _____

Time (period) _____

Room _____

Teacher _____

Subject (or program purpose) _____

Transportation _____

Day and Period of Advisory Meeting _____

Day and Time of Referring Teacher's Meeting _____

Attendance Sheet

_____   _____

_____   _____

_____   _____

_____   _____

_____   _____

_____   _____

Model 19:
Peer Leader Classroom Performance Check

Date_____

Dear_____:

_____is a peer leader in the_____ program.
Accordingly, he/she is obliged to maintain a satisfactory performance record in his/her class-room subject areas. If he/she is performing satisfactorily in your class, please indicate this by placing your signature in the appropriate column below.

For example, if he/she is maintaining his/her usual grade, sign your name in the Satisfactory column, but if he/she is falling below her/his usual performance, sign your name in the Unsatisfactory column. If problems are developing or his/her work is becoming unsatisfactory, I will confer with you about the student's classwork. I can be reached in Room_____on_____.

Period	Subject	Teacher	Room Number	Satis-factory	Unsatis-factory
_____	_____	_____	_____	_____	_____
_____	_____	_____	_____	_____	_____
_____	_____	_____	_____	_____	_____
_____	_____	_____	_____	_____	_____
_____	_____	_____	_____	_____	_____
_____	_____	_____	_____	_____	_____
_____	_____	_____	_____	_____	_____
_____	_____	_____	_____	_____	_____

As a further check, would you please indicate below approximately how much released time this student has taken from your class since:

Date_____   Released Time_____

Thank you.

_____
Program Coordinator

Model 20:
Receiving Student Work Sample Rating Form

Date _____

Directions
Look at these two pieces of work in the order they appear. Compare the first with the second and check the statement you think applies.

Example: If the second piece of work shows marked improvement over the first, check Item 3.

_____0 Second paper shows deterioration or decline over first

_____1 No improvement or unknown

_____2 Slight improvement

_____3 Marked improvement

Model 21:
Receiving Student Follow-Up Interview Questions
(One-to-One and Smooth Transitions)

Name of Interviewee _____ Date_____

Directions
Use this interview format to assess the impact of the leaders on their students. Audiotape or write notes on the responses to each question.

1. How did you get involved in the program?

_____

_____

_____

2. What did you think you might get out of it?

_____

_____

_____

3. What were the sessions like?

_____

_____

_____

4. How did you feel when you were with your peer leader?

_____

_____

_____

Page 2 - Model 21: Receiving Student Follow-Up Interview Questions (One-to-One and Smooth Transitions)

5. What did you do with your peer leader?

_____

_____

_____

6. What did you think about your peer leader?

_____

_____

_____

7. What do you think your peer leader felt about you?

_____

_____

_____

8. Did anything that happened in the sessions change the way you acted in school?

_____

_____

_____

9. If a student was having trouble in school and asked you about this program, what would you say?

_____

_____

_____

Model 22:
Peer Leader Program Evaluation

Name (optional) _____   Date_____

Directions
Please assist us in improving the program by indicating with checks your reactions below.

1. How much of the time do you think you really helped the receiving student(s)?

____ Most of the time.   ____Never really helped.

____Some of the time.

2. Do you feel more tolerant of others after working with these students?

____A lot.   ____Not really.

____A little bit.

3. How much of the time do you feel your student(s) could relate to you?

____Most of the time.   ____Occasionally.

____Some of the time.   ____Never.

4. How much of the time do you feel your student(s) could trust you?

____Most of the time.   ____Occasionally.

____Some of the time.   ____Never.

5. How worthwhile were the advisory sessions?

____Very worthwhile.   ____Not very worthwhile.

____Somewhat worthwhile.   ____A waste of time.

6. How would you rate the outcomes of your group sessions?

____Complete.   ____Totally incomplete.

____Partly complete.

Page 2 - Model 22: Peer Leader Program Evaluation

7. How would you rate the reaction of your group participants?

____Receptive.   ____Indifferent.

____Turned off.

8. How much do you feel that you profited from this project?

____A great deal.   ____Not very much.

____Somewhat.   ____Not at all.

9. In your opinion, how supportive was the program coordinator?

____Very supportive.   ____Occasionally supportive.

____Somewhat supportive.   ____Not at all.

10. Do you feel that the coordinator placed realistic expectations upon you in your role as a peer leader?

____Expectations too high.   ____Not enough expectations.

____Adequate expectations.

11. Which of the following forms should be changed, shortened, or eliminated?

____Logs.

____Receiving Student Evaluation Sheets.

____Off-Campus Passes.

____Checklists.

____Personal Evaluations.

____Action Plans.

12. How effective was the communication between teachers and you?

____Adequate.

____Did not meet enough times.

____Meetings unnecessary because of lack of cooperation.

Page 3 - Model 22: Peer Leader Program Evaluation

_____Meetings unnecessary because they were nonessential to helping process.

13. Having been a peer leader, how do you think you and your receiving student should be matched?

_____Should be based on common student interests.

_____Should be based on leader's knowledge of subject.

_____Should be based on personality similarities.

_____Should be based on a mixture of two different cultures.

14. Having been a tutor, how do you now see your own teachers?

_____I am more sympathetic toward their struggles.

_____I think too many have given up hope.

_____They should be more caring.

_____No changes in my attitude.

15. How this experience changed your career plans?

_____Made me more interested in teaching field.

_____Made me turn off the idea of teaching.

_____Made me more interested in going into human services.

_____Made me turn off the human services.

_____Made little or no difference.

16. Please list below any suggestions you might have that would improve the program.

_____

_____

_____

_____

Model 23:
Teacher Referral Form

Teacher's Name _____   Date_____

We are assembling a group of students who might benefit from a Peer Intervention Network, a highly structured support group which will utilize peer pressure and peer status to create positive, goal directed behaviors in underachieving students.

We would appreciate your cooperation in supplying the name(s) of any students in grades six through nine who might benefit from this program. We are looking for the following characteristics:

• Withdrawn.

• Abdicates responsibility.

• Intelligent, but poorly motivated.

• Influenced by negative peer subculture.

• Poor homework.

• Poor classwork.

• Passive.

• Directionless.

Name _____   Homeroom _____

Name _____   Homeroom _____

Name _____   Homeroom _____

Please place this in my mailbox.

Sincerely,

_____
Program Coordinator(s)

Model 24:
Kids 'R Safe Sample Announcement

Date _____

Dear Parent:

The (program name),_____School's peer leadership program, has initiated a project to help your child become aware of how to differentiate between harmful and helpful strangers. This program is part of the Family Life Curriculum.

The three sessions are described below:

SESSION 1: PICTURE DRAWING. Peer leaders enter a classroom, introduce themselves, and distribute paper and crayons to the class. Then they request students to draw pictures of their favorite place to go, their methods of transportation, with whom they go, the time of day, and the activities that take place at the particular location.

After the students have completed their drawings, the peer leaders ask for volunteers from the class to talk about the artwork.

Leaders then collect the papers to review and discuss them with the program coordinator after the session is completed. The drawings usually portray universal locations such as public places, restaurants, park scenes, baseball fields, urban centers, and friends' houses.

SESSION 2: PUPPET SHOWS. Leaders select two three possible story lines from the following:

1. The Public Place
This is a story of a boy who gets lost in a toy store and is reunited with his father.

2. The Park
This is a story about a young child who is accosted by a stranger and seeks help to return home safely.

3. The Zoo
In this story, two children have a close encounter with Bad Man Bob at the zoo. They are rescued by their mother.

SESSION 3: KIDS 'R SAFE GAME. This session reinforces and reviews some of the concepts which have unfolded throughout the first two sessions. The format includes a game called "The Kids 'R Safe Game," which is a board game set up in a step by step format. The students must help Ann, the main character in the game, arrive home safely from a park through a pathway with several steps along the way.

The sessions will be led by two senior peer leaders on_____.

Page 2 - Model 24: Kids 'R Safe Sample Announcement

Please sign below to indicate your consent.

I grant permission for my son/daughter _____ to participate in the KIDS 'R SAFE Program.

_____
Parent or Guardian

_____
Date

APPENDIX B —
PEER SUPPORT: A REVIEW OF THE HISTORY

Any indepth peer training and program guide would be incomplete without a section on the early efforts and evolution of the field. Most administrators require substantive research support before validating aninnovative approach and offering their support.

This section presents a brief sample of the early programs and contemporary research about state-of-the-art programs. It is intended to help you gain knowledge and support for initiating programs.

Research Approaches to Peer Programs

PRE TO POST-TEST MODELS. Several of the studies reporting the effects on peer support programs use the longitudinal approach. This approach sets up a program goal, establishes a baseline level of competence in the participants, and then measures changes and growth as a result of the peer interventions.

COMPARISON GROUP MODELS. In this approach, the target population of a given program is compared with another population who did not receive the intervention. Often self-concept, academic achievement, peer helping skills, attendance, leadership ability, and other behavioral dimensions are compared. Other studies research the different types of intervention and their effects on training methods, behavioral change, and attitudes of target populations.

SELF-REPORT MODELS. Researchers often use rank order or incremental scales to determine attitudes of peer leaders or recipients of their services. These attitudes toward the peer helping experience generate important data about the qualitative aspects of any program and often result in innovative change and future developments based on expressed needs of the participants.

Foundations of Peer Support

References in the literature to the practice of students helping students date as far back as the First Century. The Roman teacher Quintillian wrote in *Institutio Oratoria* that younger students learn from older children in an educational setting (Wright, 1960, p. 353.)

During the latter part of the eighteenth century, the Industrial Revolution generated widespread interest in education as a means to meet the demand of an increasingly technical society. Peer and cross-age support grew rapidly because there were not enough teachers to instruct the increasing student population.

In the 1790's Joseph Lancaster, an English Quaker, opened a private school for disadvantaged children. Because he lacked funds to hire enough teachers, he developed a "monitorial system" which encouraged students to assist each other in their learning (Gartner, Kohler, and Riessman, 1971, p. 15). By the end of the Eighteenth Century, peer support advocates had oversold their programs and drew adverse reactions from discontent, poverty stricken populations who often received a "second rate" education.

In 1927, the monitorial system was revived by William Bently Fowle, an educator who criticized public schools for their rigidity and artificial atmospheres. He championed the pupil centered approach and believed in incorporating the natural "give and take" processes between children into educational programs (Fowle, 1866 p. 190).

Peer support programs proliferated in the 20th century both in the United States and Europe. Horst (1931) was the first to describe a student helping program at the secondary level in the United States. He dispatched students to one-to-one tutorial sessions held in a tutoring room during students' open periods. Other programs at the elementary and secondary level also sprang up in the early 20th century.

During the 1950's, educational research focused upon ways in which students were used as "substitute teachers" (Gordon, 1956) in high schools. Nelson (1958) and Achtenhagen (1952) described the types of personal growth experienced by peer leaders in their helping activities. Up until this time, most of the literature on peer support programs was sketchy and incomplete, lacking formal research components.

The advent of the 1960's, with renewed interest in educational innovation, spawned a series of more sophisticated program designs, training models, and research components. The pioneer programs, implemented in Detroit by Ronald and Peggy Lippitt and their colleagues, enlisted secondary students to help elementary school pupils in what they termed "cross-age learning" (Lippitt, Eiseman, and Lippitt, 1969).

These researchers focused on learning which occurred in both peer leaders and receiving students through their social interaction. Cloward (1967) reported on an inner city program, Mobilization for Youth, which established cross-age tutorial centers in New York City public schools. The project promoted reading improvement for minority students in ghetto areas. Their studies found that both tutors and tutees improved dramatically in their reading scores.

The 1960's saw other tutoring projects spring up in the high school and elementary school settings where tutoring efforts focused on older students helping younger pupils (Thelan, 1967). College level cross-age peer support programs also developed during the 1960's, the most innovative approaches initiated by Robert Carkhuff (1967, 1968, 1969a, 1969b, 1972).

He sharpened counselors' natural communication skills emphasizing empathy, warmth, positive regard, genuineness, and openness. Carkhuff developed extensive training models which are used today. He pointed out that nonprofessionals can be trained quickly to function at levels which facilitate constructive change in clients (Carkhuff, 1968).

The history of peer support programs shows that the movement's origin was precipitated by lack of educational resources and that its decline was due to an emergence of professional education, supplemented by increased resources and new technology. The greatest proliferation of programs occurred in the 1960's which spawned a systemic differentiation of approaches, training methods, research designs, and varied applications. Unfortunately, most of the early reports were descriptively written, lacking rigorous empirical validation and hard data. This weakness endures even in contemporary research.

Contemporary Developments

By far the greatest number of peer initiatives occur at the middle and high school levels. Included is a sample of some of the more effective programs described in the literature. Their impact on both peer leaders and receiving students is considered.

ACADEMIC. In the area of peer tutoring, Lobitz (1970) reported on a project at Del Mar High School, Del Mar, California, which trained senior volunteers to tutor sixth grade students failing English. In a comparison group research design, 80% of the experimental group passed English while only 50% of the control group (receiving no peer tutoring) attained passing grades.

Several studies investigated the impact of peer tutors on the recipients' reading skills. Hassinger and Via (1969) and Willis and Crowder (1976) compared reading gains of low achieving peer leaders and their target population. Using a pre to post-test model, the results showed significantly higher reading scores in both peer tutors and recipients.

McClenathan (1975), described an interesting project in Fairfax, Virginia, where fifth grade students created high interest reading materials by interviewing first grade students and writing articles about their lives.

The author reported benefits to both older and younger students, with the peer helpers improving their social skills and creative writing techniques. The benefits to the first graders included reading and writing skills improvements.

Carlton, Gretna, Litton, and Zinkgraf (1985) studied effects of a peer tutoring program using mildly mentally retarded middle school students. Participants formed tutor-tutee partnerships based on their sight word recognition skills. Using a pre to post-test model measuring change scores on vocabulary and reading subtests of the Gates MacGinitie Reading Tests, the study concluded that both tutors and tutees gained at about the same rate as a result of the six week program. Thus, the mutual helping effect appears to accrue positive results in this special education population.

By contrast, Willis and Crowder (1976) used a comparison group model to study the effects of tutoring on the improvement of inner city eighth grade peer tutors in Birmingham, Alabama. Using standardized tests, the study found no significant differences between control and experimental group reading scores.

SOCIAL INTERACTION. There have been several studies of the effectiveness of peer leaders in reducing negative, destructive behaviors in their receiving populations and of peer support sessions upon the behavior of the receiving students. One study conducted in Dade County, Florida in 1975 concluded that the implementation of a peer support program resulted in decreased disruptive incidents as well as improved student self-concept in the receiving population (Samuels and Samuels, 1975).

Hoover (1984) reported on a program implemented in three Chicago Public High Schools which used peer influence in group meetings to alter the peer culture. An evaluation study showed reductions in destructive and detrimental behaviors in the target population.

Maher and Barack (1983) trained professional counselors and twelfth grade peer leaders to provide ten weeks of individual behavioral counseling to emotionally disturbed and mentally retarded adolescents. These students had been mainstreamed into regular classes and exhibited behavioral problems.

Research results indicated that students counseled by twelfth grade peer leaders showed the higher levels of goal attainment than those counseled by adults.

In another study comparing professional and peer group leaders, Maher and Christopher (1982) investigated a program which trained twelfth grade students to run groups with ninth graders to prevent and reduce maladaptive

behaviors. Using a comparison group research model, the study compared the effects of professional counseling services with peer led counseling services on school attendance, grade point averages, referral to special services, and disciplinary referrals.

Research results showed that peer led and professionally led interventions had equally positive impact on all four variables. The study suggests that peer-mediated groups may be as successful as those professionally led in promoting behavior change.

A study by Asper (1973) tested the assumptions of early researchers that receiving students attain social growth from cross-age tutoring. At St. Agnes' Elementary School in Wall, South Dakota, Asper designed a project to measure the frequency of social contacts initiated with peers and teachers. He observed social interactions of first and fourth grade pupils tutored by sixth and eighth grade peer leaders.

Asper set up two experimental groups and one control group. Trained observers recorded frequencies of social contacts during weekly observations. Results showed that after the tutoring, the students' contacts with their teachers increased significantly. Furthermore, a slight increase in peer contacts within the experimental groups also suggested that the bonding with older positive role models may have improved social interaction.

Buck (1977) reported on an urban peer support program which helped to facilitate the social growth and development of other students. In general, the report suggested gains in receiving students' communication skills, interpersonal relationships with students and adults, and problem-solving abilities.

At the middle school level, Shorey (1981) used a comparison group method to study the effects of peer group counseling sessions and achievement motivation counseling on academic performance and social behavior. The results showed no differences in achievement or acting out but did show significant increases in attendance for both groups.

Cooper and Phillips (1983) reported on an inner city program which provided multiservice fieldwork experience to referred youngsters with disciplinary problems, academic deficits, and traumatic experiences. Results after two years, based on faculty reports, revealed improved attendance, few disciplinary problems, and improved academic functioning in a target population. Of the 200 students served over a two year period, no repeat referrals were made.

The above review of the literature suggests that peer leaders are quite effective role models who promote positive behavior in their receiving students.

SELF-ESTEEM. Other studies followed up on Lippitt's (1965) premise that peer tutors improve socially as a result of their tutoring activities. Thus, self-concept has become a recent area of focus in the peer leadership literature.

One study by Schmitt and Furniss (1974) investigated the impact of peer leader, one-to-one helping sessions on younger receiving students. At Mt. Gilead Village School, in Mt. Gilead, Ohio, twenty peer leaders were trained and assigned elementary students with low self-esteem. Using the Myklebust Pupil Rating Scale (1971), this study measured the operationally defined behavior indicators of self-esteem throughout eight months of helping sessions, two days per week. Schmitt and Furniss reported that their post-tests showed improvements in self-concepts in eleven of the fifteen students.

Tindall and Gray (1974) used comparison group models to show that trained peer leaders improve in their helping skills significantly more than untrained control group students. They also found that both peer leaders and their receiving students improved in their academic behaviors and that teachers perceived peer leaders as more interpersonally sophisticated as a result of their participation.

Arkell (1975) compared the self-concept changes of high school peer leaders with changes in other similar students. He used the Coopersmith Self-Esteem Inventory (1963) to reveal no significant changes in self-esteem or attitudes towards school as compared with control group subjects.

Another study (Houser, 1974) investigating both reading and self-concept in the peer leader population showed that peer leaders made significantly higher gains in reading scores and

self-concept scores than control group subjects who did not offer help. Thus, this study used standardized instruments and empirical methods to reach conclusions which contradicted previously mentioned findings.

Hannaway and Senior (1989) studied the effects of a peer leader program on ninth grade students who received peer helping services from upper grade, trained peer leaders. The study, based on control group comparison, concluded that both peer leaders and receiving students improved in their grades, behavior, and attendance as a result of the program.

When looking at the above studies, it becomes apparent that the results are equivocal and even contradictory. Thus, the positive impact on self-esteem for peer leaders and their receiving students remains unproven.

CHEMICAL DEPENDENCY PREVENTION. Winters and Malione (1975) described a project using students as preventive agents, involved in group teaching as well as individual helping sessions. This project, run at Everett High School, Everett, Massachusetts, trained fifty high school volunteers to run a referral hotline and to lead discussion groups on the effects of drugs, alcohol, and tobacco.

This seven week program was targeted toward elementary students. The peer leaders taught a portion of the younger students' health education, frequently using audiovisual materials in their presentations. Although the project was enthusiastically supported by teachers, students, and parents, no empirical research was incorporated into the format, and therefore any behavioral benefits were inconclusively reported.

Carpenter (1985) reported on a program which trained peer leaders to assist American Indian adolescents in developing limited alcohol consumption self-contracts. Measurements of frequency of drinking and peak blood alcohol levels showed significant decreases in subjects who received peer assisted self-control training. The results suggest that peers can be effective agents in implementing specific treatment modalities in this area of chemical dependency.

Hudson and Sparks (1984) described how a team of eleventh grade peer counselors were trained in group skills and how a program model was targeted to ninth grade students within the school setting. The group sessions focused on health related issues such as stress management and nutrition. While the article did not describe formal evaluation procedures or "hard" data, concepts and practices of the model were outlined.

Perry, Cleep, Halper, and Hawkins (1986) trained 207 seventh grade peer leaders to conduct a drug abuse and smoking prevention program for other seventh grade students.

The peer leaders conducted groups using a structured, experiential, preventive approach. They experienced difficulty keeping the group quiet, capturing the participants' attention, promoting participation from group members, and managing social interaction.

Despite group management difficulties, 50% of the recipients perceived the program as effective in promoting abstinence. The peer leaders were surveyed to determine their attitudes about the program. It was found that 82% of the participants perceived the experience as positive, although males were more critical than females. Females were more likely to recommend peer leader involvement to other students and to report support from peers and parents.

Tobler's (1986) comprehensive analysis of 143 adolescent drug prevention programs concludes that peer programs had significantly higher impact ($p < .0005$) than professionally led programs in reducing alcohol, soft and hard drug, and cigarette use in recipient students.

The above literature makes a convincing case that peer leaders can communicate effectively the need to resist peer pressure and abuse chemicals.

College Level Programs

The most extensive early research efforts to concentrate specifically on personal counseling were carried out by Carkhuff and his associates in the 1960's (Carkhuff, Kratchovil and Friel, 1963; Carkhuff, 1968, 1969A; Carkhuff, Piaget, and Pierce, 1968).

Carkhuff established several facilitative skills which were positively correlated with receiving students' personal growth. His studies com-

pared the effectiveness of professional and student counseling training. He offered evidence that nonprofessionals were better trained to perform competently than some professionals. He also developed a peer counselor training model that is widely used today in helping programs (Carkhuff, 1969b).

Ware and Gold (1971) trained students as peer counselors in the Los Angeles City College. These trained role models assisted other students who were experiencing academic difficulty during their college adjustment. The study compared counseled students with a control group experiencing academic adjustment difficulties. The research indicated that the peer counselors were effective in preventing students from dropping out of school because of their poor academic adjustment. Ample evidence also pointed to the usefulness of peer leaders in improving receiving students' academic performance throughout their college careers.

There are now several college peer support programs which involve one-to-one tutoring and advisory approaches and assist freshman students in their academic transition to college life. These programs often help new students to formulate an academic direction and choose a major (Lukufahr, 1986; Puig, 1982; Kramer and Hardy, 1985).

Other reports describe the efficacy of using peer assisted career counseling programs to provide students with educational guidance in career exploration and vocational orientation (Ash and Mandelbaum, 1982; France, 1984; Kenzler, 1983; and Thompson, 1983).

There has been a proliferation of college advisement programs which use advanced students as trained peer advisors. Most of these advisors must meet grade point average criteria before entering such programs. Their training usually includes team building, basic counseling skills, tutoring skills, and educational programs in college services. Such programs often free the faculty from routine counseling tasks in undergraduate programs (Daniels, 1981; Barman, 1981; Goldberg, 1981; Devlin-Scheren, 1985).

Gaber, E. (1986) described a program which trained college students to become liaisons for professors and disseminate career and occupational information to freshman students. These trained students also operated a computerized information center for career awareness. They conducted a research project on career planning effectiveness.

Most of the college programs reported that receiving students were satisfied with the quality of rapport achieved in their helping interactions with older peer role models. Several studies showed that student counselors promoted grade improvement, study skills application, and improved potential to complete college.

Although many studies require methodological improvements, it appears that college oriented programs have used more sophisticated designs in their assessment and evaluation procedures. They have also studied more advanced concepts such as counseling skills, methods in achieving rapport, and comparisons between professional and student counselor effectiveness.

By and large, the results show that peer assisted counseling and advisement programs have proven to be valuable resources in college and university settings.

Training

TRAINING PROGRAMS. No literature review would be complete without focusing upon the area of training. Below you will look at some of the activities, results, and training design formats surveyed in the literature. A listing of additional resources on training and program models is presented at the completion of this chapter. For convenience, we have divided the training into two basic types: academic and interpersonal.

In the academic areas, some of the training materials and procedures used to train peer tutors include: assessment of study habits, test taking skills, study skills, questioning techniques, test preparation, and test taking procedures (Brown, 1964a, 1964b, 1965b, 1977; Lippitt and Lohman, 1965; and Anderson, 1979). An extensive program design has been written by Brown (1977) and is listed in the bibliography of this section as a resource.

A variety of interpersonal training programs and procedures prepare peer and cross-age assistants. Some of these activities include: role

playing and modeling (Tindall and Gray, 1985; McAnaney, 1973; Mosher and Sprinthall, 1971; Cooker and Cherichia, 1976; Evans and Livneh, 1982; and Summers, 1987); practice interviews (Samuels and Samuels, 1983; Tindall and Gray, 1985; Myrick and Erney, 1977); communication skills exercises (Cooker and Cherichia, 1976; Samuels and Samuels, 1983; Tindall and Gray, 1985; Myrick and Bowman, 1981; Cooper and Phillips, 1983; Summers, 1987; and Evans and Livneh, 1982); trust building and self-disclosure (Mosher and Sprinthall, 1971); problem-solving and decision-making (Summers, 1987; Tindall and Gray, 1985); group counseling (Roucin, 1982; Barrow and Heterington, 1981); and referral skills (Myrick and Erney, 1978; Tindall and Gray, 1985; Hamburg and Varenhorst, 1972; and Pertizky, 1981).

Summers, (1987) described a training program used at Eastwake High School in Wendell, North Carolina. He used a weekend retreat training model to train fifty selected positive role models as high school peer leaders.

The students attended this weekend retreat training program and were taught nondirective responding skills, communication skills, and self-disclosure experiences. Reports showed that the students found the experience to be valuable both from a personal and educational perspective. Several other training programs used a weekend residential format.

Cooper and Phillips (1983) reported on an extensive peer facilitated program at Warren Central High School, Indianapolis, Indiana. One credit per semester was offered to carefully selected junior and senior peer leaders who were trained extensively in listening skills, helping behaviors, interpersonal communication, human interaction, feedback, positive statements vs. killer statements, and decision-making.

Elaborate training models were developed by Hamburg and Varenhorst (1972); Tindall and Gray (1985); Myrick and Bowman (1981); Mosher and Sprinthall (1972); and Samuels and Samuels (1983).

TRAINING OUTCOMES. Although the literature is replete with descriptive summaries of training approaches, activities, and models, few studies measure impact upon the trainees. Those studies that measure changes in the skill levels of facilitative behaviors (Truax and Carkhuff, 1967; Gray and Tindall, 1974; Albee, 1976; and Saunders, 1982) support the notion that carefully trained peer leaders can and do improve their communication skills, abilities to empathize, accuracy of responses, and interpersonal behaviors.

Clearly one of the most comprehensive training studies was performed by Mosher and Sprinthall (1971). It is considered a classic hallmark of training and research. Using the Carkhuff Human Relations Training Model in a one semester course offered to high school students, their research used a pre to post-test method to measure improvements in trainees' moral development, ego development, and counselor effectiveness (facilitator skills).

Using standardized instruments and observational techniques, their study showed that the training model generated significant improvements on all three dimensions.

Using a similar human relations model of role playing and simulation to practice communication skills, Leibowitz and Rhoades (1974) also used standardized instruments to measure a pre to post-test change score in trainees' levels of empathic understanding. The results showed significant increases in these empathic discrimination skills after a nine session training program.

A follow-up study, using a comparison group model, was conducted by Cooker and Cherichia (1976) to measure the effects of short term training on communication abilities and peer group facilitation.

This study used judges to rate the peer leaders on standardized group management skills. It reported that the trained students functioned at higher levels of communication and facilitation than untrained students, supporting the evidence of Mosher and Sprinthall which attests to the effectiveness of training as a teaching process.

As a result of the above mentioned pioneer research efforts and increased outspokenness from experienced program coordinators, there has been a proliferation of recommended trainee program formats that have been found to be highly effective.

Zwibelman (1977) advocates a model consisting of three distinct elements:

• A therapeutic contact with a high functioning trainer.

• A distinctly well-defined program of experiential techniques.

• A group experience to facilitate processing and integration of personal beliefs by trainees.

Gilmore (1973) posits four general procedures to foster development of effective communication skills:

• Practice interviews.

• Oral and written feedback.

• Group interviews.

• Modeling or role playing.

Summers (1987) strongly advocates the retreat experience, which allows students to remove themselves from their usual milieu, enabling them to step back for two or three days and focus totally on their own communication skills, goal-setting, and decision-making activities.

The literature clearly suggests that effective training needs to be well-planned and experiential, endowed with constant, objective feedback, and focused on facilitative skills as well as personal beliefs. Additional activities should include problem-solving, rapport techniques, positive resource sharing, and group building activities. The trainer's empathy, leadership skills, and commitment are essential to the success of any training program.

Program Design Guidelines

Recent literature on peer-mediated programs has used previous research results as well as practical experience to advocate specific program guidelines and formats which appear to be useful and effective. Tindall (1978) and Albee (1976) recommend well-differentiated training models as a prerequisite to successful programs.

Myrick and Bowman (1981) advise program planners to take care in program preparation and development of program tasks. They suggest carefully selected program procedures based on the tasks they need to accomplish.

Most of the literature and research studies formulating program models for the training and implementation of peer outreach activities advocate a sequential process including:

• Planning.

• Identifying needs.

• Selecting and recruiting peer leaders.

• Training.

• Implementing.

• Monitoring.

• Supervising.

• Evaluating the program (Allan, 1978).

Erney (1984) suggests that all program formats should include a needs assessment, clearly stated goals, and personal contracts from student participants. He also suggests that the program completion be highlighted by some type of celebration.

The success of any peer-mediated program depends upon its leadership, its design, and its flexibility. A subjective look from personal experience as well as data based results supports the following conditions to promote positive outcomes:

• Careful needs assessment.

• Involvement from all staff and participants.

• Commitment from its volunteers.

• Carefully delineated goals and objectives.

• Training formats which include human relations skills.

• Rapport building.

• Group building exercises.

It is this author's impression that program formats should be written to include careful super-

vision by trained adults as well as constant, ongoing evaluation throughout the program process. The activities carried out by nonprofessional peer leaders should be carefully chosen to match their skills. Particular attention should be paid to the needs of the target population, which should aspire to attain realistic goals rather than grandiose expectations.

In an early article, Fox, Lippitt, and Lohman (1969) listed the types of children most apt to improve from peer led interventions:

• Pupils who find it difficult to be successful with peers.

• Younger siblings needing opportunities to develop interpersonal skills.

• Older siblings who never had another sibling to model.

• Children who never had an opportunity to be in an educational environment as equals with their peers.

• Young children who never had a chance to observe or have companionship with older children of the same gender.

Gender matching appears to be an important guideline to follow when using cross-age peer leader interventions. It makes sense to avoid cultivating idealized relationships between younger students and older role models of the opposite sex. Such idealized conceptions often lead to great disappointment. Same gender role models can promote positive attributes for younger students to introject.

The literature clearly suggests that "wounded healers" serving as peer leaders in service delivery functions incur more program liabilities than benefits.

Therefore, it is essential to be cautious and careful to apply stringent selection criteria for peer leaders. They should be strong, versatile, able to relate to others, and committed. Their tasks should be worthy of their abilities, and their participation should be well-connected into the program structure with responsibilities for growth, evaluation, and program input.

Parents should be aware and supportive of any

peer-mediated program. It is essential to include their input into the preparation of a peer support initiative. Program coordinators and trainers should also be exemplary role models who possess adequate professional credentials, training, warmth, and commitment. They need to have patience and inexhaustive energy.

There are a variety of sources, which in this author's opinion, exemplify high level program models, training models, and positive activities. Please refer to the Bibliography for resources providing a broadened perspective on this growing field.

BIBLIOGRAPHY

Allan, J. (1978). "Peer helpers: a model for establishing and supervising children helping children program." *Journal of Special Education*, 2, (4), 301-309.

Allbee, R. (1976). *A comparison of the effects of two variations of microcounseling paradigms on the development of human relations skills of students in community college setting.* Unpublished doctoral dissertation. St. Louis University, St. Louis, Mo. Anderson, M.B. (ed.)

Arkell, R. (1975). "Are student helpers helped?" *Psychology in the Schools*, 12, 113-115.

Ash, K., and Mandelbaum, D. (1982). "Using peer counselors in career development." *Journal of College Placement*, 42, (3), 47-51.

Asper, A. (1974). *The effects of cross-age tutoring on the frequency of social contacts initiated by withdrawn elementary school students.* (Doctoral dissertation, University of South Dakota, 1973). Dissertation Abstracts International, 34, 2A. (University Microfilms No. 74-18, 215)

Barman, C. and Benson, P. (1981). "Peer advising: a working model." *NACDA Journal*, 1, (2), 33-40.

Barrow, J. and Heterington J. (1981). "Training paraprofessionals to lead social anxiety management groups." *Journal of College Student Personnel*, 22, 269-233.

Benard, B. (1991). "The case for peers." *Peer Facilitator Quarterly*, 8, (4). 20-27.

Borba, M. (1989). *Esteem builders.* Rolling Hills Estates, CA.: Jalmar Press.

Brown, W., and Holtzman, W. (1964). *Survey of study habits and attitudes (grades 12-14).* New York: Psychological Corporation.

Brown, W. (1964a). *Counseling evaluation questionnaire (college edition).* San Marcos, TX.: Effective Study Materials.

Brown, W. (1964b). *Effective study test.* San Marcos, TX.: Effective Study Materials.

Brown, W. (1965a). "Student-to-student counseling for academic adjustment." *Personnel and Guidance Journal*, 43, 811-817.

Brown, W. (1965b). *Study skills survey.* San Marcos, TX.: Effective Study Materials.

Brown, W. and Holtzman, W. (1961). *Effective study guide (college edition).* San Marcos, TX.: Effective Study Materials.

Brown, W. (1977). *Student to student counseling.* Austin TX.: University of Texas Press.

Buck, M. (1977). "Peer counseling in an urban high school setting." *Journal of School Psychology*, 15, (4), 362-369.

Candler, A. and Goodman, G. (1979). "SPACE for students to manage behaviors: student participation and counseling effort." *Academic Therapy*, 15, 87-90.

Carkhuff, R. (1984). *The art of helping.* Amherst, MA.: Human Resource Development Press.

Carkhuff, R. (1968). "Differential functioning of lay and professional counselors." *Journal of Counseling Psychology*, 15, 117-126.

Carkhuff, R. (1969a). "Helper communication as a function of helper affect and content." *Journal of Counseling Psychology*, 16, 126-131.

Carkhuff, R. (1969b). *Helping and human relations (Vols. I and II).* New York: Holt, Rinehart and Winston.

Carkhuff, R. (1967). "Towards a comprehensive model of facilitative interpersonal processes." *Journal of Psychology* 14, 67-72.

Carkhuff, R., Kratochil, D., and Friel, T. (1963). "The effects of professional training and discrimination of facilitative conditions." *Journal of Counseling Psychology*, 15, 68-74.

Carkhuff, R. Piaget, G. and Pierce, R. (1968). "The development of skills in interpersonal functioning." *Counselor Education and Supervision*, 7, 102-106.

Carpenter, R. (1985). (Florida Mental Health Institute, Tampa, FL.) Lyons, C. and Miller, W. "Peer-managed self-control program of alcohol abuse in American Indian High School Students. A pilot evaluation study." *International Journal of the Addictions*, 20, 299-310.

Carlton, M. (1985). (Jefferson Parish Public Schools, 8 Gretan LA.) Litton, F. and Zinkgraf, S. "The effects of interclass peer tutoring program on the sight-word recognition ability of students who are mildly mentally retarded." *Mental Retardation*, 23, 74-78.

Cloward, R. (1967). "Studies in tutoring." *The Journal of Experimental Education*, 36, 14-25.

Cooker, P., and Cherichia C. (1976). "Effects of communication skills training on high school students' ability to function as peer group facilitators." *Journal of Counseling Psychology*, 23, 464-467.

Cooper, M. and Phillips, G. (1983). "Peer facilitators as participants in program development." *Peer Facilitator Quarterly*, 1, (1), 5.

Daniels, J. (1981). "Undergraduates as academic advisors: a model." *Engineering Education*, 71, (5), 350-352.

Devlin-Scherer, R. (1985). "Peer advising in a school of business." *NACADA Journal*, 5, (1), 17-26.

Erney, T. (1984). "Peering ahead." *Peer Facilitator Quarterly*, 2, (2), 4.

Evans, J. and Livnch, H. (1982). "Peer counseling—a training program." *Journal of Rehabilitation*, 48, (1), 52-59.

Fort Lee Board of Education AIDS Prevention Curriculum. (1989). Developed by the AIDS prevention committee: Nancy Bowden, Carol Burghardt, Ginger Collichio, James Devorak, Lucille DiGiovanni, John Findura, Harold France, Carol Hellinger, Elaine Licata, Alan Reich, Linda Straffi. Fort Lee, N.J.

Fowle, W. (1966). *The teacher's institute*. New York: H.J. Barnes.

Fox, C. L. (1990). *Unlocking doors to friendship*. Rolling Hills Estates, CA.: Jalmar Press.

Fox, C. L. (1992). *Self-esteem: the affiliation building block*. Rolling Estates, CA.: Jalmar Press.

Fox, R., Lippitt, R. and Lohman, J. (1969). *Teaching of social science in the elementary school. (Final Report, Cooperative Research Project, E-oil. U.S. Office of Education)*. Washington, D.C.: U.S. Government Printing Office.

France, K. (1984). "Peer trainers in an interviewing techniques course." *Teaching Psychology*, 11, (3), 171-173.

Gaber, E. (1966). "Peer counseling in the career planning services." *Peer Facilitator Quarterly*, 4, (2), 12-13.

Gartner, A., Kohler, M., and Reissman, F. (1971). *Children teach children: Learning by teaching*. New York: Harper and Row.

Gazda, G. (1973). *Index of perception. In G. Gazda F. Asbury, and F. Balzer, Human relations development: a manual for educators*. Boston: Allyn and Bacon, Inc.

Gidden, N., Roszczika, G., and Robertson, A. (Eds.). (1983). *Bibliography of self-help, peer counseling and paraprofessionals in the human services*. OH: Author. (ERIC Document Reproduction Services No. ED 230 853)

Gilmore, S. (1973). *Counselors in training*. New York: Appleton, Century and Crofts.

Goldberg, L. (1981). "Peer advising: a supplement to but not a substitute for faculty advising." *ACADA Journal*, 1 (2), 41-43.

Gordon, L. (1956). "Operation salvage: future teachers of america tutors," *Clearing House*, 31, 171-173.

Hamburg, D., and Varenhorst, B. (1974). "Peer

counseling in the secondary school: a community mental health project for youth." *American Journal of Orthopsychiatry*, 42, 566-581.

Hannaway, J. and Senior, A. (1989). *An evaluation of a peer leadership program: an examination of students' attitudes, behavior, and performance*. Executive Summary: Educational Testing Service. Princeton, N.J.

Hassinger, J., and Via, M. (1969). "How much does a tutor learn through teaching reading?" *Journal of Secondary Education*, 44, 42-44.

Hoover, T. (1984, November). "Peer culture development: a focus on the behavioral problem student." *Small Group Behavior*, 15, (4), 511-525.

Horst, H. (1931). "History of student tutoring at west high school, Akron, OH." *Clearing House*, 6, 245-249.

Houser, V. (1974). "Effects of student experiences on tutors' self-concept and reading skills." (Doctoral dissertation, Brigham Young University, Provo, Utah, 1973). *Dissertation Abstracts International*, 35, 6A. (University Microfilms No. 74-27, 252.)

Hudson, G., and Sparks, R. (1984). "Health advocates: the use of trained peer counselors." *Health Education*, 22, (3), 2-5.

Kehayan, V. (1990). *Self awareness growth experiences* (SAGE). Rolling Hills Estates, CA.: B. L. Winch and Associates.

Kelley, E. (1980). *Peer group facilitation with secondary students in an alternative high school*. Denton, Texas: North Texas State University.

Kenzler, B. (1983). "A model for paraprofessionals in career planning." *Journal of College Placement*, 44, (1), 55-61.

Kramer, G. and Hardy, H. (1985). "Facilitating freshman experience." *College and University*, 60, (3), 242-252.

Leibowitz, Z. and Rhoads, D. (1974). "Adolescent peer counseling." *School Counselor*, 21, 280-283.

Lippitt, P., Eiseman, J. and Lippitt, R. (1969). *Cross-age helping program: orientation, training and*

related materials. Ann Arbor: University of Michigan, Center for Research on Utilization of Scientific Knowledge, Institute for Social Research.

Lippitt, P., and Lohman, J. (1965). "Cross-age relationships: an educational resource." *Children*, 12, 113-117.

Lukefahr, R. (1986). "Peer advisors - academic planning services." *Peer Facilitator Quarterly*, 4, (2), 13.

Maher, C. and Christopher S. (1982). "Preventing high school maladjustment: effectiveness of professional and cross-age behavioral group counseling." *Behavior Therapy*, 13, 259-270.

Marisco, J. and Nelson, J. (1983). *"A do it yourself kit" for implementing a high school peer counseling program in three easy steps*. Lakewood, CO.: Jefferson County School District R-1 (ERIC Document Reproduction Service N. ED 232-123).

Marnarchev, H. (1981). *Peer counseling. In Searchlight plus: relevant resources in high interest areas. No 52t. contract No. 400-78-0005*. Ann Arbor, MN: ERIC Clearing House on Counseling and Personnel Services (ERIC Document Reproduction Services No. ED 211904).

McAnaney, A. (1973). *Peer counseling training manual*. Unpublished manual. Miami, FL.: Dade County Public Schools.

McCarthy, B., and Michaud, P. (1971). "Companions: an adjunct to counseling." *Personnel and Guidance Journal*, 49, 830-841.

McClenathan, D. (1975). "Fifth graders as authors." In J. J. Watts (Ed.), When big kids work with little kids, everyone learns: symposium. *Instructor*, 88, 101.

Mooney, R. (1978). *Mooney problem checklist, middle school form*. New York: Psychological Corporation.

Mosher, R. and Sprinthall M. (1971). "Psychological education: a means to promote personal development during adolescence." *Counseling Psychologist*, 2, 3.

Myrick, R. and Bowman, R. (1981). *Children help-*

ing children. Minneapolis, MN.: Educational Media Corporation.

Myrick, R. and Erney, T. (1978). *Youth helping youth: a handbook for training peer facilitators.* Minneapolis, MN.: Educational Media Corporation.

Myrick, R. and Erney, T. (1978). *Caring and sharing.* Minneapolis, MN.: Educational Media Corporation.

Myrick, R. and Sorenson, D. (1988). *Peer helping: A practical guide.* Minneapolis, MN.: Educational Media Corporation.

National Institute on Drug Abuse (1985). *Use of licit and illicit drugs by America's high school students 1975-1984. Johnson, C.; O'Malley, P. and Buchman, J. DHHS Publication No. (ADM) 85-1394.* Washington, D.C.: Superintendent of Documents, U.S. Government Printing Office.

National Self Help Clearing House 33 West 42nd St., Room 1222, New York, N.Y. 10036

Paritzky, R. (1981). "Training peer counselors: the art of referral." *Journal of College Student Personnel,* 22, (6), 528-532.

Peer Facilitator Quarterly, the official Journal of the National Peer Helpers Association. Edited by Robert Bowman, Ph. D. 2370 Market Street, San Francisco, CA.

P.E.E.R.S: Providing effective empathic resources and strategies: A peer counselor training manual. St. Louis, Mo.: Special Student Concerns. (ERIC Document Reproduction Service No. ED 225 092)

Perry, C. (1986) (University of Minnesota, Minneapolis, MN.), Klepp H., Halper A, Hawkins, K., and Murray, D. "A process evaluation study of peers in health education." *Journal of School Health,* 56, 62-67.

Puig, A. (1982). "Use of paraprofessional student counselors in orientating the parents of college freshmen." *Journal of College Student Personnel,* 23, (4), 351-356.

Purkey, W., Cage, B., and Graves, W. (1971). *Florida key.* Gainesville, FL: University of Florida.

Rouson, W. (1982). *A training guide for peer group counselors, revised.* Riverside, CA: Riverside County Superintendent of Schools. (ERIC Document Reproduction Service No. ED 220 763).

Samples, B. *Metaphoric mind.* (1991) Rolling Hills Estates, CA.: Jalmar Press.

Samuels, M. and Samuels, D. (1983). *The complete handbook of peer counseling.* Miami, FL.: Fiesta Publishing Corporation.

Sanders, B. (1983). *The wrong kind of laughter.* Unpublished poem. 8495 Valleywood Lane, Kalamazoo, MI. 49002

Saunders, G. (1982). *The development, implementation and evaluation of a peer counselor training programme for secondary schools.* Unpublished Masters thesis, University of Victoria, Victoria, British Columbia.

Schmitt, L., and Furniss, L. (1975). "An elementary adjunct: high school helpers." *Personnel and Guidance Journal,* 53, 778-781.

Shorey, A. (1981). *Peer counseling and achievement motivation: a comparison of two counseling approaches to an urban middle school.* Chicago: Northwestern University.

Schriner, C. (1990) *Feel better now.* Rolling Hills Estates, CA.: Jalmar Press.

Simon, S. (1972). *I am loveable and capable: an allegory.* Niles, IL.: Argus Communications.

Summers, T. (1987). "The leadership retreat peer facilitator training program." *Peer Facilitator Quarterly,* 4, (4), 5.

Thompson, S. (1983). "The career education information connection through peer facilitation." *Journal of Career Education,* 9, (3), 240-244.

Tindall, J., and Gray, H. (1974). "Communications training study: a model for training junior high school peer counselors." *The School Counselor,* 22, 107-112.

Tindall, J. and Gray, H. (1989). *Peer counseling: an in-depth look at training peer helpers.* Muncie, IN.: Accelerated Development.

Tindall, J. and Gray, H. (1973). *Procedures for training peer counselors.* Edwardsville, IL.: Southern Illinois University Press.

Tobler, N. (1986). "Meta-analysis of 143 adolescent drug prevention programs: quantitative outcome results of program participants compared to a control or comparison group." *The Journal of Drug Issues*, 16, (4), 537-567.

Todres, R. (1983). *Self-help groups: an annotated bibliography 1970 through 1982*, New York: National Self Help Clearing House.

Truax, C. and Carkhuff, R. (1967). *Toward effective counseling and psychotherapy: training and practice.* Chicago: Aidine.

U.S. Department of Health and Human Services. (1983). *Fifth special report to the U.S. Congress on alcohol and health. DHHS publication No. (ADM) 84-1291.* Washington, D.C.: Superintendent of Documents. U.S. Government Printing Office.

U.S. Department of Education. (1988). *Aids and the education of our children.* Washington, D.C.: U.S. Office of Education Printing Office.

Varenhorst, B. (1983). *Real friends.* New York: Harper and Row.

Varenhorst, B. (1980) *Curriculum guide for student peer counselor training.* Palo Alto, CA.: Palo Alto Peer Counseling Program.

Ware, C. and Gold, B. (1971). *The los angeles city college peer counseling program.* Washington, D.C.: American Association of Junior Colleges.

Willis, J. and Crowder, J. (1976). *Does tutoring enhance the tutor's academic learning?* Unpublished manuscript. Department of Psychology, University of Guelph, Ontario, Canada.

Winters, R. and Malione, A. (1975). "High school students as mental health workers, the everett experience." *The School Counselor*, 23, 43-44.

Wright, E. (1965). "Upper graders learn by teaching." *Instructor*, 75, 102-103.

Wright, E. (1989). *Good morning class, I live you.* Rolling Hills Estates, CA.: Jalmar Press.

Yeager, J. (1990). *The goal strategy book.* Linguis-Techs. Newtown, PA.: Comm-Tech Group Inc.

Youngs, B. (1991). *The six vital ingredients of self-esteem and how to develop them in your students (K-12).* Rolling Hills Estates, CA.: Jalmar Press.

Youngs, B. (1991). *Enhancing self-esteem: a guide for professional educators.* Rolling Hills Estates, CA.: Jalmar Press.

Youngs, B. (1991). *Stress management for educators: a guide to managing our response to stress.* Rolling Hills Estates, CA.: Jalmar Press.

Youngs, B. (1991). *You and self-esteem: the key to happiness and success (Grades 5-12).* Rolling Hills Estates, CA.: Jalmar Press.

Zwibelman, F. (1977). "Effects of training." *Journal of Counseling Psychology*, 23 (4), 359-364.

About the Author

V. Alex Kehayan is an educator, psychologist, and author. He and his wife, Carolyn, direct Edu-Psych Inc., a comprehensive network of practitioners who provide training, workshops, and personal improvement programs for children, adults, and professionals. He coordinates Peer Outreach Service Team (Post), an award-winning peer support network in the Fort Lee (New Jersey) Public Schools. He continues to develop new peer approaches, offering training and consulting to a variety of programs throughout the nation.

The author is currently the president of the New Jersey Peer Helping Association, a professional organization of peer helping professionals founded to unite the peer programs and promote standards of excellence.

Dr. Kehayan has authored two books (*SAGE*, and *Partners for Change*), and numerous articles on adolescent critical issues and effective responses to them. As a therapist specializing in adolescent development, he has pioneered innovative personal support initiatives. Having served on the National Peer Helpers Association Board of Directors, Dr. Kehayan continues as chair of the publications committee and assitant editor of the *Peer Facilitator Quarterly*.

A former professor at Montclair State College and public school teacher in New York City, Dr. Kehayan has extensive classroom experience and understanding of the formidable challenges facing our nation's educators.

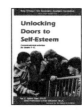

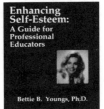

20 YEARS
AWARD WINNING
PUBLISHER
JP

DISCOVER materials for positive self-esteem.
CREATE a positive environment in your classroom or home by opening a world of understanding.

Esther Wright, M.A.

Good Morning Class - I Love You (Staff)

Contains thought provoking quotes and questions about *teaching from the heart.* Helps love become an integral part of the learning that goes on in every classroom. Great for new teachers and for experienced teachers who sometimes become frustrated by the system. Use this book to begin and end your day. Greet your students every day with: *"Good morning class - I love you."*

0-915190-58-3, 80 pages, **JP-9058-3 $7.95**
5½ x 8½, paperback, illus./**Button $1.50**

Enhancing Educator's Self-Esteem: It's Criterion #1 (Staff)

For the educator, a *healthy self-esteem* is job criterion No. 1! When high, it empowers us and adds to the vitality of our lives; when low it saps energy, erodes our confidence, lowers productivity and blocks our initiative to care about self and others. Follow the *plan of action* in this great resource to develop your self-esteem.

0-915190-79-6, 144 pages, **JP-9079-6 $16.95**
8½ x 11, paperback

NEW

Bettie B. Youngs, Ph.D.

NOT JUST AUTHORS BUT RESEARCHERS AND PRACTITIONERS.

Elaine Young, M.A. with R. Frelow, Ph.D.

I Am a Blade of Grass (Staff)

Create a school where all — students, teachers, administrators, and parents — see themselves as both learners and leaders *in partnership.* Develop a new *compact for learning* that focuses on results, that promotes *local initiative* and that *empowers* people at all levels of the system. How to in this *collaborative curriculum.* Great for self-esteem.

0-915190-54-0, 176 pages, **JP-9054-0 $14.95**
6 x 9, paperback, illustrations

Stress Management for Educators: A Guide to Manage Our Response to Stress (Staff)

Answers these significant questions for educators: *What is stress? What causes it? How do I cope with it? What can be done to manage stress to moderate its negative effects? Can stress be used to advantage? How can educators be stress-proofed to help them remain at peak performance? How do I keep going in spite of it?*

0-915190-77-X, 112 pages, **JP-9077-X $12.95**
8½ x 11, paperback, illus., charts

NEW

Bettie B. Youngs, Ph.D.

NOT JUST WRITTEN BUT PROVEN EFFECTIVE.

REVISED

Eva D. Fugitt, M.A.

He Hit Me Back First: Self-Esteem Through Self-Discipline (Gr. K-8)

By whose authority does a child choose right from wrong? Here are *activities* directed toward *developing* within the child an *awareness* of his own *inner authority* and ability to choose (will power) and the resulting sense of *responsibility,* freedom and *self-esteem.* 29 seperate activities.

0-915190-64-8, 120 pages, **JP-9064-8 $12.95**
8½ x 11, paperback, appendix, biblio.

Self-Esteem: The "Affiliation" Building Block (Gr. K-6)

Making friends is easy with the activities in this thoroughly researched book. Students are paired, get to know about each other, produce a book about their new *friend,* and present it in class. Exciting activities help discover commonalities. Great *self-esteem booster.* Revised after 10 years of field testing. Over 150 activities in 18 lessons.

0-915190-75-3, 192 pages, **JP-9075-3 $19.95**
8½ x 11, paperback, illustrations, activities

NEW

Self-Esteem:
THE "AFFILIATION"
BUILDING BLOCK

C. Lynn Fox, Ph.D.

100% TESTED — 100% PRACTICAL — 100% GUARANTEED.

Chris Schriner, Rel.D.

Feel Better Now: 30 Ways to Handle Frustration in Three Minutes or Less (Staff/Personal)

Teaches people to *handle stress as it happens* rapidly and directly. This basic requirement for *emotional survival* and *physical health* can be learned with the methods in this book. Find your own recipe for relief. Foreword: Ken Keyes, Jr. *"A mine of practical help"* — says Rev. Robert Schuller.

0-915190-66-4, 180 pages, **JP-9066-4 $9.95**
6 x 9, paperback, appendix, bibliography

Peace in 100 Languages: A One-Word Multilingual Dictionary (Staff/Personal)

A candidate for the Guinness Book of World Records, it is the *largest/smallest dictionary ever published.* Envisioned, researched and developed by *Russian peace activists.* Ancient, national, local and special languages covered. A portion of purchase price will be donated to joint U.S./Russian peace project. **Peace Button $1.50**

0-915190-74-5, 48 pages, **JP-9074-5 $9.95**
5 x 10, glossy paperback, full color

NEW

IN 100 LANGUAGES

By:
M. Kabattchenko,
V. Kochurov,
L. Koshanova,
E. Kononenko,
D. Kuznetsov,
A. Lapitsky,
V. Monakov,
L. Stoupin, and
A. Zagorsky

Shalom • Paz
IPEACEI
Paix • Vrede

ORDER NOW FOR 10% DISCOUNT ON 3 OR MORE TITLES.

Joanne Haynes-Klassen

Learning to Live, Learning to Love (Staff/Personal)

Important things are often quite simple. But simple things are not necessarily easy. If you are finding that learning to live and learning to love are at times difficult, you are in good company. People everywhere are finding it a tough challenge. This simple book will help. *Shows how to separate "treasure" from "trash" in our lives.*

0-915190-38-9, 160 pages, **JP-9038-9 $7.95**
6 x 9, paperback, illustrations

Reading, Writing and Rage (Staff)

An autopsy of one profound *school failure,* disclosing the complex processes behind it and the *secret rage* that grew out of it. Developed from educational therapist's viewpoint. A must reading for anyone working with the *learning disabled, functional illiterates* or *juvenile delinquents.* Reads like fiction. Foreword by Bruce Jenner.

0-915190-42-7, 240 pages, **JP-9042-7 $16.95**
5½ x 8½, paperback, biblio., resources

D. Ungerleider, M.A.

ORDER FROM: B.L. Winch & Associates/Jalmar Press, 45 Hitching Post Drive, Bldg. 2, Rolling Hills Estates, CA 90274-5169
CALL TOLL FREE — (800) 662-9662. • (310) 547-1240. • FAX (310) 547-1644 • Add 10% shipping; $3 minimum

4/92

DISCOVER books on self-esteem for kids.
ENJOY great reading with Warm Fuzzies and Squib, the adventurous owl.

Larry Shles, M.A.

Moths & Mothers/Feathers & Fathers: The Story of Squib, The Owl, Begins (Ages 5-105)

Heartwarming story of a tiny owl who cannot fly or hoot as he learns to put words with his feelings. He faces frustration, grief, fear, guilt and loneliness in his life, just as we do. Struggling with these *feelings*, he searches, at least, for *understanding*. *Delightfully illustrated.* Ageless.

0-915190-57-5, 72 pages, **JP-9057-5 $7.95**
8¹/₂ x 11, paperback, illustrations

Hoots & Toots & Hairy Brutes: The Continuing Adventures of Squib, The Owl (Ages 5-105)

Squib, who can only toot, sets out to learn how to give a mighty hoot. Even the *owl-odontist* can't help and he fails completely. Every reader who has struggled with *life's limitations* will recognize his own struggles and triumphs in the microcosm of Squib's forest world. A parable for all ages.

0-915190-56-7, 72 pages, **JP-9056-7 $7.95**
8¹/₂ x 11, paperback, illustrations

Larry Shles, M.A.

NOT JUST AUTHORS BUT RESEARCHERS AND PRACTITIONERS.

Larry Shles, M.A.

Hugs & Shrugs: The Continuing Saga of Squib, The Owl (Ages 5-105)

Squib feels lonely, depressed and incomplete. His reflection in the pond shows that he has lost a piece of himself. He thinks his missing piece fell out and he searches in vain outside of himself to find it. Only when he discovers that it fell in and not out does he find *inner-peace* and become whole. Delightfully illustrated. Ageless.

0-915190-47-8, 72 pages, **JP-9047-8 $7.95**
8¹/₂ x 11, paperback, illustrations

Aliens in my Nest: Squib Meets the Teen Creature (Ages 5-105)

What does it feel like to face a snarly, surly, defiant and non-communicative older brother turned *adolescent*? Friends, dress code, temperament, entertainment, room decor, eating habits, authority, music, isolation, *internal and external conflict* and many other areas of change are dealt with. Explores how to handle every situation.

0-915190-49-4, 80 pages, **JP-9049-4 $7.95**
8¹/₂ x 11, paperback, illustrations

Larry Shles, M.A.

NOT JUST WRITTEN BUT PROVEN EFFECTIVE.

NEW

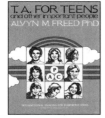

Larry Shles, M.A.

Do I Have to Go to School Today? Squib Measures Up! (Ages 5-105)

Squib dreads going to school. He day-dreams about all the reasons he has not to go: the school bus will swallow him, the older kids will be mean to him, numbers and letters confuse him, he is too small for sports, etc. But, in the end, he goes because his *teacher accepts him "just as he is."* Very esteeming. Great metaphor for all ages.

0-915190-62-1, 64 pages, **JP-9062-1 $7.95**
8¹/₂ x 11, paperback, illustrations

Scooter's Tail of Terror A Fable of Addiction and Hope (Ages 5-105)

Well-known author and illustrator, Larry Shles, introduces a new forest character — a squirrel named Scooter. He faces the challenge of addiction, but is offered a way to overcome it. As with the Squib books, the story is *simple*, yet the message is *dramatic*. The story touches the child within each reader and *presents the realities of addiction*.

0-915190-89-3, 80 pages, **JP-9089-3 $9.95**
8¹/₂ x 11, paperback, illustrations

Larry Shles, M.A.

100% TESTED — 100% PRACTICAL — 100% GUARANTEED.

REVISED

Alvyn Freed, Ph.D.

TA for Tots (and other prinzes) Revised (Gr. PreK-3)

Over 500,000 sold. New upright format. Book has helped thousands of young children and their parents to better understand and relate to each other. Helps youngsters realize their *intrinsic worth* as human beings; builds and strengthens their *self-esteem. Simple* to understand.
Coloring Book $1.95 / I'm OK Poster $3

0-915190-73-7, 144 pages, **JP-9073-7 $14.95**
8¹/₂ x 11, paperback, delightful illustrations

TA for Kids (and grown-ups too) (Gr. 4-9)

Over 250,000 sold. An ideal book to help youngsters develop *self-esteem*, esteem of others, *personal and social responsibility*, critical thinking and independent judgment. Book recognizes that each person is a unique human being with the capacity to learn, grow and develop. Hurray for TA! Great for parents and other care givers.

0-915190-09-5, 112 pages, **JP-9009-5 $9.95**
8¹/₂ x 11, paperback, illustrations

Alvyn Freed, Ph.D. & Margaret Freed

ORDER NOW FOR 10% DISCOUNT ON 3 OR MORE TITLES!

Alvyn Freed, Ph.D.

TA for Teens (and other important people) (Gr. 8-12)

Over 100,000 sold. The book that tells teenagers they're OK! Provides help in growing into adulthood in a mixed-up world. Contrasts freedom and irresponsibility with knowing that youth need the skill, determination and *inner strength* to reach *fulfillment* and *self-esteem*. No talking down to kids.

0-915190-03-6, 258 pages, **JP-9003-6 $18.95**
8¹/₂ x 11, paperback, illustrations

The Original Warm Fuzzy Tale (Gr. Pre K-12)

Over 100,000 sold. The concept of Warm Fuzzies and Cold Pricklies originated in this delightful story. A *fairy tale* in every sense, *with* adventure, fantasy, heroes, villians and a *moral*. Children (and adults, too) will enjoy this beautifully illustrated book. Great for parents and other care givers. **Songs of Warm Fuzzy Cass. $12.95**

0-915190-08-7, 48 pages, **JP-9008-7 $7.95**
6 x 9, paperback, full color illustrations

Claude Steiner, Ph.D

ORDER FROM: B.L. Winch & Associates/Jalmar Press, 45 Hitching Post Drive, Bldg. 2, Rolling Hills Estates, CA 90274-5169
CALL TOLL FREE — (800) 662-9662. • (310) 547-1240. • FAX (310) 547-1644 • Add 10% shipping; $3 minimum

4/92

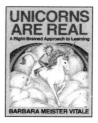